W9-CGV-389

RESEARCH IN THE HISTORY OF ECONOMIC THOUGHT AND METHODOLOGY

A Research Annual

RESEARCH IN THE HISTORY OF ECONOMIC THOUGHT AND METHODOLOGY

Series Editors: Warren J. Samuels, Jeff E. Biddle and Ross B. Emmett

RESEARCH IN THE HISTORY OF ECONOMIC THOUGHT AND METHODOLOGY

A Research Annual

EDITED BY

WARREN J. SAMUELS

Department of Economics, Michigan State University,
East Lansing, MI 48824, USA

JEFF E. BIDDLE

Department of Economics, Michigan State University,
East Lansing, MI 48824, USA

ROSS B. EMMETT

James Madison College, Michigan State University,
East Lansing, MI 48824, USA

2005

ELSEVIER
JAI

Amsterdam – Boston – Heidelberg – London – New York – Oxford
Paris – San Diego – San Francisco – Singapore – Sydney – Tokyo

ELSEVIER B.V.	ELSEVIER Inc.	**ELSEVIER Ltd**	ELSEVIER Ltd
Radarweg 29	525 B Street, Suite 1900	**The Boulevard, Langford**	84 Theobalds Road
P.O. Box 211	San Diego	**Lane, Kidlington**	London
1000 AE Amsterdam	CA 92101-4495	**Oxford OX5 1GB**	WC1X 8RR
The Netherlands	USA	**UK**	UK

First edition 2005

Library of Congress Cataloging in Publication Data
A catalog record is available from the Library of Congress.

British Library Cataloguing in Publication Data
A catalogue record is available from the British Library.

ISBN: 0-7623-1164-9
ISSN: 0743-4154 (Series)

♾ The paper used in this publication meets the requirements of ANSI/NISO Z39.48-1992 (Permanence of Paper). Printed in The Netherlands.

CONTENTS

vi

LIST OF CONTRIBUTORS

William J. Barber	Department of Economics, Wesleyan University, USA
Bradley W. Bateman	Department of Economics, Grinnell College, USA
Daniel W. Bromley	Department of Agricultural Economics, University of Wisconsin, USA
Andy Denis	Department of Economics, City University, London, UK
Robert W. Dimand	Department of Economics, Brock University, Canada
Robert S. Goldfarb	Department of Economics, George Washington University, USA
Willie Henderson	School for Professional and Continuing Education, University of Birmingham, UK
Glenn L. Johnson[†]	Department of Agricultural Economics, Michigan State University, USA
Marianne Johnson	Department of Economics, University of Wisconsin-Oshkosh, USA
J. E. King	Department of Economics and Finance, La Trobe University, Australia
Thomas C. Leonard	Department of Economics, Princeton University, USA
Julian Reiss	Center for Philosophy of Natural and Social Science, London School of Economics, UK

[†] Deceased.

Warren J. Samuels   Department of Economics, Michigan State University, USA

Eric Schliesser   Department of Philosophy, Washington University, USA and Research Associate, Amsterdam Research Group in History and Methodology of Economics, Department of Economics, University of Amsterdam

William Waller   Department of Economics, Hobart and William Smith Colleges, USA

EDITORIAL BOARD

ACKNOWLEDGMENTS

The editors wish to express their gratitude for assistance in the review process and other consultation to the members of the editorial board and to the following persons:

Roger Backhouse

David Colander

Jerry Evensky

Leon Montes

Spencer Pack

Malcolm Rutherford

Malcolm Sawyer

Eric Schliesser

Anthony Waterman

Jeffrey Young

THE INVISIBLE HAND OF GOD
IN ADAM SMITH[☆]

Andy Denis

ABSTRACT

Adam Smith is revered as the father of modern economics. Analysis of his writings, however, reveals a profoundly medieval outlook. Smith is preoccupied with the need to preserve order in society. His scientific methodology emphasises reconciliation with the world we live in rather than investigation of it. He invokes a version of natural law in which the universe is a harmonious machine administered by a providential deity. Nobody is uncared for and, in real happiness, we are all substantially equal. No action is without its appropriate reward – in this life or the next. The social desirability of individual self-seeking activity is ensured by the "invisible hand," that is, the hand of a god who has moulded us so to behave, that the quantity of happiness in the world is always maximised.

1. INTRODUCTION

Karl Marx classed political economists into a "classical" or scientific group, on the one hand, with Adam Smith and Ricardo representing the pinnacle of this

☆This paper is based on Chapter 4 of my PhD thesis (Denis, 2001). Material derived from the chapter has appeared as Denis (1999), and I am grateful to the publishers, SAGE Publications, London, for permission to republish material contained therein.

A Research Annual
Research in the History of Economic Thought and Methodology, Volume 23-A, 1–32
ISSN: 0743-4154/doi:10.1016/S0743-4154(05)23001-8

group, and a "vulgar" or apologetic group, on the other, comprising, roughly, all the mainstream economists after Ricardo (Marx, 1972, p. 501). I want to argue here, however, that there is a very significant apologetic aspect to Smith, and that this apologetic aspect is intimately concerned with Smith's conception of the articulation between micro and macro levels, between individual actions and social consequences.

The purpose of this paper is to examine Adam Smith's view that the hand of God would invisibly, "by that eternal art which educes good from ill" (*TMS* I.ii.3.4), ensure that uncoordinated individual actions would always lead to desirable social consequences, "the greatest possible quantity of happiness" (*TMS* VI.ii.3.1), and to show how this is related to his philosophy as a whole. The starting point of the paper is that the "invisible hand" concept in Smith is an unambiguously theological category. It is by no means a matter of making a case for a new and radical reading of Smith: the theological interpretation is the first and most obvious meaning to strike the reader of what Smith actually wrote. It is the non-theological interpretation, the interpretation which says that, in spite of what Smith wrote, he actually meant something different, which requires demonstration. There is a huge literature on the interpretation of the invisible hand in Adam Smith, to review which would require another and much longer article, which would not change the verdict reached here.

It is of course easy to point to specific passages in Smith and throw up one's hands at the ease with which he satisfies himself that we are living in the best of all possible worlds – and just as easy to dismiss such passages as *obiter dicta* unrelated to his basic theme. Here, for example, is a famous passage, the second, in fact, of the three occasions on which Smith makes explicit use of the notion of an "invisible hand":

> The rich . . . are led by an invisible hand to make nearly the same distribution of the necessaries of life, which would have been made, had the earth been divided into equal portions among all its inhabitants, and thus without intending it, without knowing it, advance the interest of the society, and afford means to the multiplication of the species. When providence divided the earth among a few lordly masters, it neither forgot nor abandoned those who seemed to have been left out in the partition. These last too enjoy their share of all that it produces. In what constitutes the real happiness of human life, they are in no respect inferior to those who would seem so much above them. In ease of body and peace of mind, all the different ranks of life are nearly upon a level, and the beggar, who suns himself by the side of the highway, possesses that security which kings are fighting for (*TMS* IV.1.10).

So the poor should be content with their lot – they are just as well off as the rich in the things that really matter. Perhaps the typical reaction on reading this is to dismiss it as a vulgar aside, a mere personal prejudice, having no bearing on Smith's scientific researches. This, however, would be profoundly mistaken. The thesis of this paper is that Smith's whole system of thought can be best understood, not as a scientific project aiming at discovery of the world, but as a rhetorical one aiming at reconciliation with it – indeed, he plainly says as much – and the notion of the 'invisible hand' lies at the heart of this rhetorical project.

The next section, on *The History of Astronomy*, argues that in his major methodological work, Smith presents a view of science as an activity aimed, in the first instance, at reconciling us with the world, rather than at theoretically apprehending it. Section 3 presents Smith's conception of the world as a harmonious machine operated by a providential deity. This conception first arises and is presented with great clarity in *The Theory of Moral Sentiments*; and subsequently underlies the social world in *The Wealth of Nations*. Section 4 sets out Smith's notion of the "invisible hand" as an expression of the activity on our behalf of an omniscient, omnipotent and benevolent deity. The following section establishes the links between Smith and his contemporaries, showing how profoundly in tune he was with the *Zeitgeist* of the second half of the eighteenth century. The penultimate section discusses Smith's failure to deal with some critical contradictions in his system. The conclusion notes two possible responses to Smith: that an evolutionary mechanism can replace a providential deity as a mechanism ensuring that macro optimality corresponds to micro rationality; and, alternatively, the recognition that there is no such automatic mechanism behoves us to construct one ourselves.

2. SMITH'S METHODOLOGICAL STANCE

Denis (1999) argued that Smith's policy prescription was one of freedom for capital, freedom for the individual, that is, in so far as he is the bearer of property. The present paper argues that Smith adopts a providentialist rhetorical strategy to underpin that policy prescription. However, not only does Smith attempt to sustain a policy recommendation of *laissez-faire* by invoking a providential invisible hand mechanism, but he announces clearly, though in general terms beforehand, that this is what he will be doing. For Smith, scientific activity has a clear purpose and tendency, namely reconciliation to what is. The purpose of this section is to establish Smith's general programme and his conception of science as a rhetorical enterprise.

The fragment commonly known as Smith's "History of Astronomy" is more properly called, in full, *The Principles which Lead and Direct Philosophical Enquiries; Illustrated by the History of Astronomy; by the History of the Ancient Physics; and by the History of the Ancient Logics and Metaphysics*. The full title makes clear that Smith's intention is to set out his conception of scientific method. For Smith, in his discussion of successive schools of thought in these *Histories*, the purpose of a system of thought is not to disclose the truth of how the world is, but to soothe the imagination, previously agitated by wonder at the marvels of the world.

At the level of appearances, Smith says, the world throws up phenomena which appear incoherent and therefore disagreeably inflame the imagination with a sense of wonder. The job of a science is allay wonder and to soothe the imagination by suggesting connections between things, and by tracing the unknown back to the familiar, so that the observer may regain his tranquillity:

> Philosophy is the science of the connecting principles of nature. Nature . . . seems to abound with events which appear solitary and incoherent . . . which therefore disturb the easy movement of the imagination. . . . Philosophy, by representing the invisible chains which bind together all these disjointed objects, endeavours to introduce order into this chaos of jarring and discordant appearances, to allay this tumult of the imagination, and to restore it . . . to [its former] tone of tranquillity and composure . . . Philosophy, therefore, may be regarded as one of those arts which address themselves to the imagination (*Astronomy* II.12).

Again, "the repose and tranquillity of the imagination is the ultimate end of philosophy" (*Astronomy* IV.13); "it is the end of Philosophy, to allay that wonder, which either the unusual or seemingly disjointed appearances of nature excite" (*Astronomy* IV.33).

Smith, therefore, is not concerned with the truth or otherwise of the findings of a science – what matters is its success or otherwise in "smoothing the passage of the imagination betwixt . . . seemingly disjointed objects" (*Astronomy* II.12). It is this criterion alone, he says, which we should bear in mind when considering the sequence of schools of thought in a science such as astronomy:

> Let us examine, therefore, all the different systems of nature, which . . . have successively been adopted by the learned and ingenious; and, without regarding their absurdity or probability, their agreement or inconsistency with truth and reality, let us consider them only in that particular point of view which belongs to our subject; and content ourselves with inquiring how far each of them was fitted to sooth the imagination, and to render the theatre of nature a more coherent . . . spectacle (*Astronomy* II.12).

It is striking that Smith concludes his discussion of Newton's system of astronomy by confessing that it is so compelling that he had, despite himself, been seduced into speaking of the latter's system as if it embodied real knowledge of the world:

> even we, while we have been endeavouring to represent all philosophical systems as mere inventions of the imagination, to connect together the otherwise disjointed and discordant phenomena of nature, have insensibly been drawn in, to make use of language expressing the connecting principles of [Newton's philosophical system], as if they were the real chains which Nature makes use of to bind together her several operations (*Astronomy* IV.76).

And this is a measure of the success of Newton's system. The implication is, as Raphael and Skinner (1980, pp. 19–21) point out, that it would be mistaken, or at best off the point, to regard Newton's connecting principles as "the real chains" of Nature.

"It may well be said of the Cartesian philosophy," Smith says, "that in the simplicity, precision and perspicuity of its principles and conclusions, it had the same superiority over the Peripatetic system, which the Newtonian philosophy has over it" (*EPS*, p. 244).

> We need not be surprised . . . that the Cartesian philosophy . . . though it does not perhaps contain a word of truth . . . should nevertheless have been so universally received by all the learned in Europe at that time. The great superiority of [Descartes'] method . . . made them greedily receive a work which we justly esteem one of the most entertaining romances that have ever been wrote (cited in *EPS*, p. 244 editorial Note 3).

Although completely untrue, a romance, the principles and conclusions of Descartes' narrative are to be regarded as constituting an improvement over previous approaches equal to Newton's, because it provides simple, precise and perspicuous . . . entertainment. Descartes' vortices successfully soothe our imagination, and reconcile us to our world, even though "these pretended causes of those wonderful effects, not only do not actually exist, but are utterly impossible, and if they did exist, could produce no such effects as are ascribed to them" (*TMS* VII.ii.4.14).

For Smith, science starts off, as indeed all science must, with the level of appearances: but then, instead of penetrating those appearances to reality, the truth, to the essence of the thing, science *remains* at the level of appearances, merely contrasting one set of appearances with another. In place of a congeries of apparently incoherent, isolated phenomena, Smithian science gives us a coherent and interconnected vision of the world. But, for Smith, that vision is no more real, no less apparent than either the raw appearances or the connecting principles proposed by rival explanations. The criterion for choosing between these appearances is not their greater or lesser degree of truth, but a purely *aesthetic* consideration: which is the more pleasing? Thus a scientific explanation of a phenomenon is to be preferred to none, and a later system is preferred to an earlier one, because and to the extent to which they are able to provoke greater admiration (*Astronomy* II.12). For example: though much to be preferred to the earlier systems, there is no suggestion that the Newtonian system is more *profound*, indeed, it may well be replaced when an even more pleasing system is proposed. "Philosophy" is to be traced, he says, "from its origin, up to that summit of perfection to which it is at present supposed to have arrived [with Newton], and to which, indeed, it has equally been supposed to have arrived in almost all former times"

(*Astronomy* II.12). In every period, Smith says, science is believed to have reached "the summit of perfection," since the science of that period is just the scientific explanation the period finds most pleasing. Whether there is any *progress* in this is left entirely moot.

So is there an objective truth standing behind these appearances, these entertaining romances? For Smith, there is indeed objective truth, but human, finite minds cannot grasp, or even approach it: only the infinite mind of God can grasp all the ultimate "connexions and dependencies of things." Smith adopts the Thomist view of an unbridgeable gulf between the finite and the infinite, between the human and the divine. This contrast forms the basis for the very restricted role of reason and philosophy (the sphere of finitude), relative to that of sentiment and religion (the sphere of infinity), in Smith's system.

This section has set out the main lines of Smith's methodological stance and suggested links between his methodology and his underlying intellectual goals. Smith's writings on methodology set out a research programme which Smith then followed in his psychological (*TMS*) and economic (*WN*) investigations. He says in advance that the task of science is to allay the discomfort we experience from observing the world. In *TMS* and *WN* he sets out his entertaining romance designed to underpin his political stance.

3. SMITH'S *WELTANSCHAUUNG*

This section sets out the elements of the "entertaining romance" that Smith tells to reconcile us to our world. The universe in this story is a machine administered by a deity, with the sole purpose of maximising happiness. All parts of that machine, including individual people, play their allotted roles. We do what we do because it is what we are led to do by the feelings implanted in our nature by the deity. Even human folly and weakness are part of God's plan. Everyone has nearly the same level of happiness and we should therefore be content with our lot. The failure to realise this, mistaking wealth for happiness, leads people to be industrious: the economy depends on their being so deceived. Appearances, too, are part of the divine plan. People mistake wealth and good fortune for wisdom and virtue. This allows them to be reconciled to class distinctions and oppressive rulers. We like morality and dislike immorality only because we only see their proximate effects on human welfare. This weakness, too, is desirable as morality, particularly justice, is a prerequisite for society. This underpins an interpretation of the "invisible hand" which is set out in the next section.

For Smith the universe is a machine supervised by an omnipotent, omniscient and beneficent, deity. The sole aim of the machine is the maximisation of happiness: "That divine Being['s] . . . benevolence and wisdom have, from all eternity, contrived and conducted the immense machine of the universe, so as at all times to produce the greatest possible quantity of happiness" (*TMS* VI.ii.3.5. See also *TMS* VI.ii.3.1). So the world is perfect: we *do* live in the "best of all possible worlds" – Smith is a true Panglossian. Since the world is really perfect, our apparent troubles stem from our finite, partial view of the world, our failure to see "all the connexions and dependencies of things":

> [Since the] benevolent and all-wise Being can admit into the system of his government, no partial evil which is not necessary for the universal good, [the wise and virtuous man] must consider all the misfortunes which may befal himself, his friends, his society, or his country, as necessary for the prosperity of the universe, and therefore as what he ought, not only to submit to with resignation, but as what he himself, if he had known all the connexions and dependencies of things, ought sincerely and devoutly to have wished for (*TMS* VI.ii.3.3).

For Smith, therefore, what is good is good, and what is bad is good as well: everything is for the best, so – whatever happens – rejoice, and accept. Though similar ideas can be found in the earlier editions, the passages above are taken from Part VI, a new section written by Smith, in the last year of his life, for the 1790 edition. Hence it cannot be the case that they represent a juvenile stage in Smith's thought long passed by the time he came to write *WN*.

When Smith argues that what appears bad is actually good, but we don't see it because we are only finite minds, "good" refers only to "the good of the whole" (*TMS* VI.ii.3.4) and says nothing about the good of the individual. For the system to seem attractive, Smith must show that, not only the total quantity of happiness is maximised, but its allocation to individuals is in some sense "fair." Recognising this, Smith says explicitly that all our virtue and vice will be appropriately rewarded, if not here, then hereafter.

Firstly, if we look at the lives of individuals as a whole and in the long run, then we can in general expect everyone will get their just deserts.

> notwithstanding the disorder in which all things appear to be in this world, yet even here [i.e., in this world rather than the next one] every virtue naturally meets with its proper reward, with the recompense which is most fit to encourage and promote it; and this too so surely, that it requires a very extraordinary concurrence of circumstances entirely to disappoint it (*TMS* III.5.8).

And if such an "extraordinary concurrence of circumstances" should occur, as to frustrate the "natural" process of rewarding every virtue in this life, then we may hope for a settling of accounts in the next one: "Our happiness in this life is . . . upon many occasions, dependent on the humble hope and expectation of a life to come: a hope and expectation deeply rooted in human nature . . . a world to come, where exact justice will be done to every man" (*TMS* III.2.33; see also *TMS* II.ii.3.12).

Smith combines the idea of justice in the hereafter with that of the limits to reason and the scope for religion and sentiment. To those such as the wrongly condemned man, Smith says,

> humble philosophy which confines its views to this life, can afford, perhaps, but little consolation. . . . Religion can alone afford them any effectual comfort. She alone can tell them, that it is of little importance what man may think of their conduct, while the all-seeing Judge of the world approves of it. She alone can present to them the view of another world . . . where their innocence is in due time to be declared, and their virtue to be finally rewarded (*TMS* III.2.12).

So reason is incompetent to tell us about the really important things, such as the afterlife and our "final reward." Instead we must trust religion. Smith's rhetoric weaves together elements of reason and belief, philosophy and religion, to present a seductive world-view within which he can then embed his policy proposals.

The world is a machine for the production of happiness. But this includes not just nature but also human nature. In Smith's view the deity chooses the mental composition of individual persons, and hence leads them to desirable behaviours: "[God's] wisdom . . . contrived the system of human affections, as well as that of every other part of nature" (*TMS* VI.ii.2.4). Smith's argument here further illustrates his Panglossian view, firstly, that everything is predetermined by the deity, predestined to turn out for the best, and, secondly, that if we are misled by appearances, then this deception, too, is part of the plan and hence a Good Thing.

A major instance of the former concerns the predisposition to benevolence and the very much stronger one, not just to obey, but to enforce, the "sacred laws of justice" (*TMS* II.ii.2.3), which God has placed in our personal make-up, what Smith calls "this constitution of Nature" (*TMS* II.ii.3 title). Man, he says, "who can only subsist in society, was fitted by nature to that situation for which he was made" (*TMS* II.ii.3.1). While it would be nice if everyone could cooperate from sheer love of one's fellows, we can still live without society-wide benevolence; but not without justice: "Society may subsist, among different men, as among different merchants, from a sense of its utility, without any mutual love or affection . . . but the prevalence of injustice must utterly destroy it" (*TMS* II.ii.3.2–3).

Nature has therefore endowed men with consciences in order that they may behave justly:

> Though Nature, therefore, exhorts mankind to acts of beneficence, by the pleasing consciousness of deserved reward, she has not thought it necessary to guard and enforce the practice of it by the terrors of merited punishment in case it should be neglected. It is the ornament which embellishes, not the foundation which supports the building, and which it was, therefore, sufficient to recommend, but by no means necessary to impose. Justice, on the contrary, is the main pillar that upholds the whole edifice. If it is removed, the great, the immense fabric of human society, that fabric which to raise and support seems in this world . . . to have been the peculiar and darling care of Nature, must in a moment crumble into atoms. In order to enforce the

> observation of justice, therefore, Nature has implanted in the human breast that consciousness of ill-desert, those terrors of merited punishment which attend upon its violation, as the great safe-guards of the association of mankind, to protect the weak, to curb the violent, and to chastise the guilty (*TMS* II.ii.3.4).

It is clear that Smith is saying here that Nature, in order to preserve society, has placed in our personalities a desire for justice, even if it is unclear whether this is based on a love of justice for its own sake, or a fear of retribution. A sense of justice is an endowment of nature, but nature seen as an active force in the world, conscious and intentional.

Despite Smith's claim that justice is fundamental for society, *order* is in reality of more basic importance to him. If there is any tension between the two, it is order which comes first. Speaking of the tendency for members of the different "orders and societies" in the state to resist any diminution in their "powers, privileges and immunities," he argues that:

> This partiality, though it may sometimes be unjust, may not, upon that account be useless. It checks the spirit of innovation. It tends to preserve whatever is the established balance among the different orders and societies into which the state is divided; and while it sometimes appears to obstruct some alterations in government which may be fashionable and popular at the time, it contributes in reality to the stability and permanency of the whole system (*TMS* VI.ii.2.10).

The assumption is that what is, is likely to be best, and should in general be preserved, even at the expense of justice. Having said that, however, we should note that, for Smith, just as there can be no profound antagonism between investigation and reconciliation, there cannot be any serious conflict between order and justice. Indeed, as we saw above, everyone always gets their just deserts in the end, either later in this life or, should that fail, in the next one. It is precisely this concept of an automatic mechanism rationally allocating welfare to individual persons that allows Smith to defend principles, such as the partiality of the orders of society in defence of their own interests, and the contempt "unjustly" bestowed upon poverty and weakness instead of on vice and folly (*TMS* II.ii.3.4), when they conflict with the claims of justice.

So when Smith speaks of justice he is actually thinking of social order – but when he talks of order he is thinking of property. This is nowhere more clear than in his discussion about theft by the poor from the rich:

> The poor man must neither defraud nor steal from the rich, though the acquisition might be much more beneficial to the one than the loss could be hurtful to the other . . . by [doing so] he renders himself the proper object of the contempt and indignation of mankind; as well as of the punishment which that contempt and indignation must naturally dispose them to inflict, for having thus violated one of those sacred rules, upon the tolerable observation of which depend the whole security and peace of human society. There is no commonly honest man who does not more dread the inward disgrace of such an action, the indelible stain which it would for

ever stamp upon his own mind, than the greatest external calamity which, without any fault of his own, could possibly befal him; and who does not inwardly feel [that such an action] is more contrary to nature, than death, than poverty, than pain, than all the misfortunes which can affect him (*TMS* III.3.6).

Thus theft by the poor from the rich — even when, as he concedes, it would augment social welfare — calls down more Smithian abuse upon their heads than any other crime. In one passage a murderer or parricide, by contrast, is dismissed as merely "ungrateful" (*TMS* II.ii.3.11), while in another, murder, though stigmatised as "this most dreadful of all crimes" (*TMS* II.i.2.5), is dealt with matter-of-factly without any of the excitement shown in his discussion of theft from the rich. Again, it is well known that Smith regarded the state as an institution guarding the rich from the poor:

Till there be property there can be no government, the very end of which is to secure wealth, and to defend the rich from the poor (Smith *Lectures on Jurisprudence*, cited in *WN* V.i.b.12 n21). Civil government, so far as it is instituted for the security of property, is in reality instituted for the defence of the rich against the poor, or of those who have some property against those who have none at all (*WN* V.i.b.12).

This fact, however, has been subjected to the almost comical misinterpretation that somehow this represented a *complaint*, a plea on behalf of the underdog. Viner (1958, p. 233), for example, cites these passages as evidence for Smith's desire to limit government activity, and Raphael (1985, p. 8) says that the *WN* passage strikes a "radical note." Nothing could be further from the truth. The context of these passages shows unambiguously that Smith was simply, and, in his view, uncontroversially, setting out how things were and how they should be:

The affluence of the rich excites the indignation of the poor, who are . . . prompted by envy to invade his possessions . . . which [are] acquired by the labour of many years, or perhaps of many successive generations . . . He is at all times surrounded by unknown enemies, whom, though he never provoked, he can never appease, and from whose injustice he can be protected only by the powerful arm of the civil magistrate continually held up to chastise [the injustice of those enemies]. The acquisition of valuable and extensive property, therefore, necessarily requires the establishment of civil government (*WN*: V.i.b.2).

What these passages reveal is that at the heart of Smith's system is the privacy of property. He is concerned above all to preserve private property — whether from the disorganised action of the poor, or the organised intervention of the state. In all these cases, our social behaviour is sustained by features of our personalities inculcated by a deity, by "Nature."

Our strengths are thus implanted in us by divine providence. Not only our strengths but our weaknesses, too, however, are endowed by nature. A particularly striking example concerns the tendency of a fickle public to admire people merely for being lucky:

> Fortune has . . . great influence over the moral sentiments of mankind, and, according as she is
> either favourable or adverse, can render the same character the object, either of general love and
> admiration, or of universal hatred and contempt. This great disorder in our moral sentiments
> is by no means, however, without its utility; and we may on this as well as on many other
> occasions, admire the wisdom of God even in the weakness and folly of man. Our admiration
> of success is founded upon the same principle with our respect for wealth and greatness, and
> is equally necessary for establishing the distinction of ranks and the order of society. By this
> admiration of success we are taught to submit more easily to those superiors, whom the course
> of human affairs may assign to us; to regard with reverence, and sometimes even with a sort
> of respectful affection, that fortunate violence which we are no longer capable of resisting;
> not only the violence of such splendid characters as those of a Caesar or an Alexander, but
> often that of the most brutal and savage barbarians, of an Attila, a Gengis, or a Tamerlane
> (*TMS* VI.iii.30).

This is a remarkable passage. Admiration for the merely lucky is, admittedly, a
"great disorder" in our morals. But even our folly reflects God's wisdom, and this
particular folly, like everything else, has been given us by God for a reason. The
good thing about this weakness is that it reconciles us with our rulers, even those
who only achieved this status by means of "fortunate violence," inspiring us even
to a kind of affection for brutal tyrants such as Tamerlane, who reputedly made
mountains of his enemies' skulls.

As Smith reminds us, this view of the role of fortune in moral sentiments parallels
that of public admiration of the great in preference to the good:

> This disposition to admire, and almost to worship, the rich and the powerful, and to despise,
> or, at least, to neglect persons of poor and mean condition . . . is . . . the great and most universal
> cause of the corruption of our moral sentiments. That wealth and greatness are often regarded
> with the respect and admiration which are due only to wisdom and virtue; and that the contempt,
> of which vice and folly are the only proper objects, is often most unjustly bestowed upon poverty
> and weakness, has been the complaint of moralists in all ages (*TMS* I.iii.3.1).

And the moralists were wrong – in Smith's view – since, as we have seen,
even injustice can be part of a higher Good. Even this "universal cause of
moral corruption," however, is god-given and has its purpose: it is "necessary
both to establish and maintain the distinction of ranks and the order of society"
(*TMS* I.iii.3.1):

> The distinction of ranks, the peace and order of society, are, in a great measure, founded
> upon the respect which we naturally conceive for [the greatly fortunate . . . the rich and
> powerful]. . . . The peace and order of society is of more importance than even the relief of
> the miserable. . . . Moralists . . . warn us against the fascination of greatness. This fascination,
> indeed, is so powerful, that the rich and the great are too often preferred to the wise and the
> virtuous. Nature has wisely judged that the distinction of ranks, the peace and order of society
> would rest more securely upon the plain and palpable difference of birth and fortune, than upon
> the invisible and often uncertain difference of wisdom and virtue. The undistinguishing eyes of
> the great mob of mankind can well enough perceive the former: it is with difficulty that the nice

discernment of the wise and the virtuous can sometimes distinguish the latter. In the order of all
those recommendations, the benevolent wisdom of nature is equally evident (*TMS* VI.ii.1.20).

So even this particular weakness, which Smith has earlier damned in the most
severe terms, is evidence of the "benevolent wisdom of nature," and it is so because
there has to be a ruling stratum, and Nature has judged it best to have an obvious
one to which the masses can easily be led to give their loyalty.

This leads us to a very important point concerning the admiration of wealth,
and the "deception of nature" which, again, illustrates Smith's view that deceptive
appearances can still be desirable. For Smith, the outward appearance of great
disparity in wealth between the rich and the poor conceals a very large measure of
real equality in welfare. In *TMS*, he says of the poor that:

> These last too enjoy their share of all that it produces. In what constitutes the real happiness of
> human life, they are in no respect inferior to those who would seem so much above them. In
> ease of body and peace of mind, all the different ranks of life are nearly upon a level, and the
> beggar, who suns himself by the side of the highway, possesses that security which kings are
> fighting for (*TMS* IV.1.10).

So the poor should be content with their lot – they are just as well off as the rich in
the things that really matter. The sources of real happiness were divided by divine
providence – or by the rich who are, in turn, led by divine providence – so that
we all get an equal share. This theme is repeated throughout Smith's works, often
combined with the notion that great happiness and grief are occasioned not by a
state or condition but by a change in condition. Smith draws the conclusion that
much of the evil in life can be attributed to failure to understand that all permanent
conditions are alike, and that it is only changes which matter:

> The great source of both the misery and disorders of human life, seems to arise from over-rating
> the difference between one permanent situation and another. Avarice over-rates the difference
> between poverty and riches. . . . The person under the influence of [avarice], is not only miserable
> in his actual situation, but is often disposed to disturb the peace of society, in order to arrive at that
> which he so foolishly admires . . . [although] in all the ordinary situations of human life, a well-
> disposed mind may be equally . . . contented. . . . In all the most glittering and exalted situation
> that our idle fancy can hold out to us, the pleasures from which we derive our happiness, are
> almost the same with those which, in our actual, though humble station, we have at all times at
> hand, and in our power (*TMS* III.3.31).

But in even *this* cloud there is a silver lining! To be deceived by appearances is
often desirable:

> The poor man's son, whom heaven in its anger has visited with ambition . . . admires the
> condition of the rich. . . . He is enchanted with the distant idea of this felicity . . . and, in order
> to arrive at it, he devotes himself for ever to the pursuit of wealth and greatness. . . . Through
> the whole of his life he pursues the idea of a certain artificial and elegant repose which he
> may never arrive at, for which he sacrifices a real tranquillity, that is at all times in his power,

and which, if in the extremity of old age he should at last attain to it, he will find to be in no
respect preferable to that humble security and contentment which he had abandoned for it. It
is then . . . that he begins at last to find that wealth and greatness are mere trinkets of frivolous
utility. . . . And it is well that nature imposes upon us in this manner. It is this deception which
rouses and keeps in motion the industry of mankind (*TMS* IV.1.8–10).

This "deception by nature" (Raphael & Macfie, 1976, p. 8), which leads people to
fulfil what they think are their own purposes, only to find they were fulfilling the
purposes of a superior force or interest, is the counterpart in Smith of the "cunning
of reason" in Hegel,[1] and the "divine tactic" of history in Burke (Sabine, 1951,
p. 519), both whom are known to have read and admired Smith.[2]

The deception of nature is not ancillary but fundamental to Smith's principal
doctrine. This becomes clear in the first few pages of *TMS* (I.i.1.1–13), where we
find that, according to Smith, the whole structure of moral sentiments is built on
illusion. The basis for morality is *sympathy*, that is, our ability to a limited extent
to enter into the emotions of other people. But this participation in the pains and
pleasures of others is achieved solely by an act of the imagination, divorced from
the material causes of those pains and pleasures in the person we sympathise with.
This sympathy even extends to fictional characters and the dead — people, that is,
who are themselves incapable of feeling pain and pleasure. This shows sympathy
to be a "very illusion of the imagination" (*TMS* I.i.1.13), the imagination of "what
perhaps is impossible" (*TMS* I.i.1.11). We place ourselves, in the imagination, in
the position of the other person, without in fact being in that position, and often
without it being possible that we ever could be in such a position. We cannot help
it: it is a god-given compulsion from which even the most hardened criminal is not
exempt (*TMS* I.i.1.1).

Smith's God treats individual humans in an extremely cavalier manner,
subjecting them to all sorts of illusions and deceptions, and other weaknesses
and indignities, and in general treating them like puppets, often with quite
deleterious consequences to the individual in question, supposedly in the interest
of maximising human welfare. A classic case of this occurs at the end of the first
chapter of *TMS*, where he applauds even the fear of death as bad at the individual
but good at the social level: "one of the most important principles in human nature
[is] the dread of death, the great poison to the happiness, but the great restraint
upon the injustice of mankind, which, while it afflicts and mortifies the individual,
guards and protects the society" (*TMS* I.i.1.13).

In connection with this we should perhaps recall the value which Smith really
placed on the individual in the context of the overall system of which he is part.
Before his God, says Smith, man appears as a "vile insect" (*TMS* II.ii.3.12).[3]
Again, in *The History of the Ancient Physics* he describes "a God of all . . . who
governs the whole by general laws, directed to the conservation and prosperity

of the whole, without regard to [the conservation and prosperity] of any private individual" (*Astronomy*: Physics 9).

So Smith's God teaches us that it is permissible to "poison the happiness," to "afflict and mortify the individual," to disregard "the conservation and prosperity ... of any private individual" – in the interest of society, of "the whole"; and if we are to consider the individual a "vile insect" relative to the totality of which he is part, we will certainly be unrestrained by respect for individual lives and individual suffering in pursuit of what we take to be the interest of that totality. Smith's love of "the ennobling hardships and hazards of war" (*TMS* III.2.35) is germane here: "War is the great school for acquiring and exercising ... magnanimity." It teaches a "habitual contempt of danger and death" which "ennobles the profession of a soldier, and bestows upon it ... a rank and dignity superior to that of any other profession" (*TMS* VI.iii.7). Indeed, a "great warlike exploit" attracts a measure of "esteem" just because it is military, even "though undertaken contrary to every principle of justice" and by "very worthless characters" (*TMS* VI.iii.8). Passages showing a quite militaristic outlook on society (*TMS* VI.ii.3–4), passages introduced in the 6th edition of *TMS* at the end of Smith's life, have already been cited above. When twentieth and twenty-first century individualists and "libertarians" claim intellectual descent from Smith, one wonders whether they have read him.

The message of this section is thus that, according to Smith, people do things for apparent reasons – the real reasons being often hidden from them, and it is desirable that they should do so. They act justly from a sense of justice, but the reason why a desire for justice has been given us in this way is so that society may subsist; we admire the rich, the fortunate and the powerful, instead of the wise and virtuous, because it is in our nature to do so, but those feelings have been implanted in us to reconcile us to our lot; we mistake wealth for happiness, and are led to do so, so that trade and industry may flourish; we investigate the world thinking to discover its truth, so that by means of ever more pleasing stories about the world we may be reconciled to it.

In the next section we will see how these ideas relate to Smith's notion of an "invisible hand."

4. THE INVISIBLE HAND

Smith uses the term "the invisible hand" on three occasions. On the first occasion, in Astronomy, he refers to "the invisible hand of Jupiter." There is a contrast between the role of the invisible hand here, on the one hand, and in *TMS* and *WN*, on the other: the action of the former is seen only in "the irregular events of nature" rather than the "ordinary course of things" (*Astronomy* III.2). In polytheism and "early heathen antiquity," Smith says,

> it is the irregular events of nature only that are ascribed to the agency and power of their gods. Fire burns, and water refreshes . . . by the necessity of their own nature; nor was the invisible hand of Jupiter ever apprehended to be employed in those matters. But . . . irregular events were ascribed to his favour or his anger. . . . Those . . . intelligent beings, whom they imagined, but knew not, were naturally supposed . . . not to employ themselves in supporting the ordinary course of things, which went on of its own accord, but to stop, to thwart, and to disturb it (*Astronomy* III.2).

Smith says that this was because humans acted in this way to change the course of events which would have occurred without human intervention and so primitive peoples supposed that their gods acted likewise. This, says Smith, is "the lowest and most pusillanimous superstition" (*Astronomy* III.2). Smith contrasts this view of gods, like men, as responsible for only the exceptional, with his own view of the whole world, including societies and individuals within it, as a great machine designed and managed for the best interest of all by a divine administrator:

> In the first ages of the world, the seeming incoherence of the appearances of nature, so confounded mankind, that they despaired of discovering in her operations any regular system. Their ignorance, and confusion of thought, necessarily gave birth to that pusillanimous superstition, which ascribes almost every unexpected event, to the arbitrary will of some designing, though invisible beings, who produced it for some private and particular purpose. The idea of an universal mind, of a God of all, who originally formed the whole, and who governs the whole by general laws, directed to the conservation and prosperity of the whole, without regard to that of any private individual, was a notion to which they were utterly strangers (*Astronomy*: Physics 9).

So, firstly, not only the irregular, but, and much more importantly, the most regular occurrences are the work of the deity; and, secondly, human actions, too, far from being contrary to nature, are profoundly in harmony with it. Natural events and human actions alike and without exception are part of the divine plan: "Instead of acting capriciously, [the invisible hand] becomes [the hand of] the 'all-wise Architect and Conductor,' the 'author of nature,' who governs and animates 'the whole machine of the world' " (Macfie, 1971, p. 598).

In contrast to that in the Astronomy, Smith's use of the expression in *TMS* and *WN* is in a context where Smith is presenting his own views, not criticising someone else's. The second instance of Smith's use of the term "invisible hand," in *TMS*, has already been given at the beginning of this paper. In *WN* he says:

> By preferring the support of domestick to that of foreign industry, [every individual][4] intends only his own security; and by directing that industry in such a manner as its produce may be of the greatest value, he intends only his own gain, and he is in this, as in many other cases, led by an invisible hand to promote an end which was no part of his intention. Nor

is it always the worse for society that it was no part of it. By pursuing his own interest he
frequently promotes that of the society more effectually than when he really intends to promote it
(*WN* IV.ii.9).

In both cases he claims that the invisible hand will ensure that the unintended
outcome of self-seeking behaviour will be socially desirable. Without it, in the
TMS case, individuals would be subject to large differences in welfare; and
in the *WN* case, the total wealth available to society would be smaller than it
actually is.

It should by now be clear that the use of the phrase "an invisible hand" is
just another expression of Smith's deist philosophy. The machine of the universe
is managed by a deity determined on the maximisation of happiness, and our
emotions and motives are predetermined by that deity to lead us to behave in a
manner consonant with the divine plan. The administration of the plan is carried
out by God – but, of course, we cannot see anything: his hands are invisible[5].
Hence the concept of the invisible hand requires no separate treatment. We have
already seen how agents are "deceived by nature" to act in socially desirable ways,
how the unintended consequences of our desire for justice, or riches, make society
possible. The notion of an invisible hand is of a piece with this philosophy.

The fallacious view that the "invisible hand" is not to be taken literally, but was
a metaphor (or even simile), for competition, is extremely widespread. Arguments
that Smith's invisible hand is "the hand of competition" are not to the point. Of
course this is true: Smith's whole argument is that God's wisdom works itself out
through spontaneous processes, such as competition, through the "simple system
of natural liberty," as well as in other ways, such as our desire for the approbation
of the "impartial spectator." But the notion of competition by no means exhausts
the notion of the invisible hand, to which it is wholly subordinate.

A much earlier version of this paper followed conventional usage in referring
to a *metaphor* of "the invisible hand." I now think this mistaken. Smith was very
consistent in flagging any such comparison by the use of simile instead of metaphor.
In my opinion, Smith intended us to read his statements in *WN* and *TMS* of agents
being "led by an invisible hand" quite literally: the invisible hand leading them is
just the hand of God. Had he desired another interpretation he would have written
"led *as*" or "*as if*," or "*as though* by an invisible hand." It is interesting that Smith
is frequently misquoted, with the words "as" or "as if" inserted into the passage in
WN in question in an unconscious misrepresentation as simile of what Smith saw
only as literal truth. I have found extraordinary resistance to the idea that he did
not say that.

The central claim of this paper, therefore, is that the invisible hand concept in
Smith was entirely and unambiguously theological. There is no question of setting
out a case for a new and radical reinterpretation of Smith's meaning: the theological

interpretation is the first and most obvious meaning to strike the reader of what Smith actually wrote. It is the non-theological interpretation, the interpretation which says that, in spite of what Smith wrote, he actually meant something different, which requires demonstration. What is remarkable is the regularity with which those writers who wish to separate the invisible hand from the universal mind which guides it simply resort to assertion without setting out the case for the their alternative interpretation.

The other tactic frequently employed is to counterpose divine intervention with spontaneous process such as the market forces of supply and demand. But that is not the question. There is no debate over whether these supposedly socially desirable outcomes are achieved by these spontaneous forces in Smith. God, in Smith, does not intervene *directly*, unmediatedly, in human affairs. We do not know what Smith did or did not privately believe – very likely he shared his friend, David Hume's, well known rejection of miracles. If there are miracles then any intellectual project is at an end since the world is irregular and arbitrary. Certainly the public Smith of the Astronomy, *TMS* and *WN* shows no evidence whatsoever of belief in such miraculous direct intervention. What he does very clearly show is a belief that human happiness is the distal, not proximal, consequence of God's will, mediated by the totality of natural and social phenomena. The latter, including the "simple system of natural liberty," competition, supply and demand, and so on, are the indirect manifestations of God's will, and instruments for the working out of God's purposes. Competition is able to act as an equilibrating mechanism in Adam Smith, solely because the individual interests which it has to balance have already been pre-reconciled by a kindly Great Administrator of the system of the universe.

It is the case that the expression "an invisible hand" only appears once in *WN*, and the deistic explanation of it does not appear at all. A great deal of empirical material, however, does appear, and, while the overwhelming bulk of that material is directed towards showing the superiority of the *laissez faire* system, he does indicate exceptions to its desirability. It is easy to see how modern, nineteenth and twentieth century readers of *WN* in isolation from Smith's other works and from those of his contemporaries, should assume that this was a predominantly empirical study drawing the conclusion that in general, free competition was a good thing. It is easy to overlook the fact that the empirical material only plays the role of illustrating a preconceived order. Smith does not in fact anywhere make the inductive judgement that, as a generalisation, individual self-seeking behaviour leads automatically to socially desirable outcomes — on the contrary, this is assumed beforehand and illustrated by details of many empirical circumstances where it is *asserted*, over and over again, that this has occurred, or would occur if only enterprise were free. It is only by exploring the totality of Smith's thought, not only in the *WN* but in *TMS* and Astronomy as well, that we can clearly see the *a priori* and deductive nature of Smith's procedure, the assumption that the spontaneous system of free enterprise will lead to desirable outcomes because, in general, agents' interests are pre-reconciled by the invisible hand of a providential deity. Whatever the stylistic and presentational differences between *TMS* and *WN*, this invocation of *faith* remains the starting point of Smith's account of the invisible hand throughout.

Adam Smith's starting point was a belief in a benign, omniscient and omnipotent deity. It is hard, perhaps, for us to see it now, but that was the standard view in Smith's time, that was the default, that was part of what Becker (see below) calls the medieval "climate of opinion" which characterised eighteenth century thought. To have argued anything else would have been both more remarkable, and more difficult. It is not that Smith *chose* a theological approach, but that he accepted one as the common coin of the time – why should he not, since it was perfectly consistent with his rhetorical strategy and it meant he was speaking the same language as his audience.

The phrase "an invisible hand" occurs throughout nineteenth century literature – in Mary Shelley (1818) *Frankenstein* Ch. XII, Thomas Hardy (1874) *Far From the Madding Crowd* Ch. 42, and in H. G. Wells (1898) *The War of the Worlds* Ch. 6, to give just three examples – in each case in utterly pedestrian contexts. Raphael (1985, p. 67) gives an instance of its use in the early eighteenth century, when a captain wrote in his log that the ship had been saved from sinking by "the invisible hand of Providence." That the idea of the guiding hand of an unseen god, ensuring the desirable social consequences of self-seeking behaviour – without the phrase of the "invisible hand" itself, however – was a commonplace of late eighteenth century social commentary is shown by Hayek by reference to Smith, Tucker, Ferguson and Edmund Burke (Hayek, 1948, p. 7). Taking the latter, writing in 1795, as an example: "The benign and wise disposer of all things . . . obliges men, whether they will it or not, in pursuing their own selfish interests, to connect the general good with their own individual success" (Burke cited in Hayek, 1948, p. 7).

Smith's biographer, Dugald Stewart, emphatically shares this standpoint, consciously echoing Smith's pronouncements by referring explicitly to the invisible hand. The motivations of each individual, he writes,

act in subserviency to [nature's] designs, and . . . conduct him . . . to certain beneficial arrangements . . . he is led by an invisible hand, and contributes his share to the execution of a plan, of the nature and advantages of which he has no conception (cited in Poovey, p. 274). A firm conviction that the general laws of the moral, as well as of the material world, are wisely and beneficently ordered for the welfare of our species, inspires the pleasing and animating persuasion, that by studying these laws, and accommodating to them our political institutions, we may . . . [consider] ourselves . . . as *fellow-workers with God* in forwarding the gracious purposes of his government. It represents to us the order of society as much more the result of Divine than of human wisdom (cited in Poovey, p. 277).

Let Stewart's words stand as a conclusion to this section. The next section looks in more detail at the relationship between Smith and his contemporaries.

5. SMITH'S INTELLECTUAL ENVIRONMENT[6]

5.1. The "Heavenly City" of the 18th Century Philosophes

All are but parts of one stupendous whole,
Whose body nature is, and God the soul;
. . .
All discord, harmony not understood;
All partial evil, universal good:
And, in spite of pride, in erring reason's spite,
One truth is clear, *Whatever is, is right.*
(Alexander Pope, cited in Becker, 1932, p. 66).[7]

Adam Smith was very much a man of his time. Smith's "modified Stoicism typical of Cicero" was "almost conventional in the Enlightenment" (Macfie, 1959, p. 210). This is a theme which is taken up at length in Carl Becker's *The Heavenly City of the Eighteenth-Century Philosophers* (Becker, 1932), in which, especially in Ch II "The Laws of Nature and of Nature's God" (Becker, 1932, pp. 33–70), he makes a powerful case that the intellectuals of this period[8] were not in any meaningful sense "modern," but that, on the contrary, they were living in a medieval world and "demolished the Heavenly City of St Augustine only to rebuild it with more up-to-date materials" (Becker, 1932, p. 31):

We are accustomed to think of the eighteenth century as essentially modern in its temper. . . . And yet I think the *Philosophes* were nearer the Middle Ages, less emancipated from the preconceptions of medieval Christian thought, than they quite realized or we have commonly supposed. . . . [T]hey speak a familiar language. . . . But I think our appreciation is of the surface more than of the fundamentals. . . . [I]f we examine the foundations of their faith, we find that at every turn the *Philosophes* betray their debt to medieval thought without being aware of it. . . . They had put off the fear of God, but maintained a respectful attitude towards the Deity. They ridiculed the idea that the universe had been created in six days, but still believed it to be a beautifully articulated machine designed by the Supreme Being according to a rational plan as an abiding place for mankind . . . they renounced the authority of church and Bible, but exhibited a naïve faith in the authority of nature and reason. . . . [T]he underlying preconceptions of eighteenth century thought were still . . . essentially the same as those of the thirteenth century (Becker, 1932, pp. 29–31).

On the overall aim of the philosophers, he cites Hume – with whom Smith shared a mutual admiration and close friendship – as an example, "Hume is representative of his century" (Becker, 1932, p. 39). Like Smith, Hume was sufficiently concerned with preservation of the social order to be willing to lay down his pen in its service. In his own words:

> I am at present castrating my work . . . that is, endeavouring it shall give as little offence as possible (cited in Becker, 1932, p. 38). A man has but a bad grace who delivers a theory, however true, which leads to a practice dangerous and pernicious. Why rake into those corners of nature, which spread a nuisance all around? . . . Truths which are *pernicious* to society . . . will yield to errors, which are salutary and *advantageous* . . . (ibid).

Here, as in Smith, we find the idea that error can be "advantageous." Following through the programme just mentioned,

> in mid career Hume abandoned philosophical speculations for other subjects, such as history and ethics, which could be treated honestly without giving 'offense' (Becker, 1932, pp. 38–39). These are, no doubt, the reasons why Hume locked his *Dialogues* away in his desk . . . his contemporaries, could they have looked into that locked desk, would have found . . . the brilliant argument that demolished the foundations of natural religion. . . . Hume . . . refused to publish his Dialogues, and never, in public at least, failed to exhibit a punctiliously correct attitude toward the Author of the Universe (Becker, 1932, p. 78).

It is well known that Adam Smith was a close friend of Hume's and admired his work enormously. He described Hume as the nearest possible to "a perfectly wise and virtuous man" (*TMS*: Appendix II, p. 383). Hume's words are in perfect agreement with Smith's project of prioritising reconciliation over investigation.

In Becker's view, the *Philosophes* faced

> the ugly dilemma, emerging from the beautiful premises of the new philosophy: if nature is good, then there is no evil in the world; if there is evil in the world, then nature is so far not good. . . . Will they, closing their eyes to the brute facts, maintain that there is no evil in the world? In that case there is nothing for them to set right. Or will they, keeping their eyes open, admit that there is evil in the world? (Becker, 1932, p. 69).

The philosophers were at a crossroads: reason pointed forwards, to atheism and to the project of rebuilding a haphazard, spontaneous and irrational society in the image of the order they had previously ascribed to nature; the alternative was the denial of reason and a return to medieval Christian faith. Open-eyed, they could adopt an empirical, materialist standpoint, recognising the need to take control of, and responsibility for, spontaneous human institutions; or with eyes closed they could take an *a priori* stance, imposing on the world a scheme derived from religious belief. "Well, we know what the Philosophers did in this emergency. They found . . . that reason is amenable to treatment. They therefore tempered reason with sentiment . . ." (Becker, 1932, p. 69). "Sometime about 1750, men of sense became men of sentiment . . ." (Becker, 1932, p. 41).

None of this was written with Smith specifically to the forefront of Becker's mind – but the description fits like a glove. Smith is the epitome of this intellectual retreat of the enlightenment in the late eighteenth century, the retreat from rationalism to romanticism. In every respect, reason is belittled and sentiment and religion brought to the fore. At best, for Smith, reason only confirms what we know anyway by means of sentiment and religion:

> This reverence [for general rules] is still further enhanced by an opinion which is first impressed by nature, and afterwards confirmed by reasoning and philosophy, that those important rules of morality are the commands and laws of the Deity, who will finally reward the obedient, and punish the transgressors of their duty.... [R]eligion ... gave a sanction to the rules of morality, long before the age of artificial reasoning and philosophy. That the terrors of religion should thus enforce the natural sense of duty, was of too much importance to the happiness of mankind, for nature to leave it dependent on the slowness and uncertainty of philosophical researches. These researches, however, when they came to take place, confirmed those original anticipations of nature. (*TMS* II.5.3).

Reasoning, for Smith, is artificial, and only sentiment is natural:

> That the Deity loves virtue and hates vice ... for the effects which they tend to produce ... is not the doctrine of nature, but of an artificial, though ingenious, refinement of philosophy. All our natural sentiments prompt us to believe [the opposite] ... (*TMS*: 91 note, editions 1 and 2).

For Smith reason is "the abstruse syllogisms of a quibbling dialectic," and sentiment, "the great discipline which Nature has established" (*TMS* III.3.21).

The medieval view of the world, and the role of reason within it – the view of the world to which Smith and his contemporaries turned – is well summarised by Becker:

> Existence was ... regarded by the medieval man as a cosmic drama, composed by the master dramatist according to a central theme and on a rational plan. Finished in idea before it was enacted in fact ... the drama was unalterable either for good or evil ... the duty of man was to accept the drama as written, since he could not alter it; his function, to play the role assigned.... Intelligence was essential, since God had endowed men with it. But the function of intelligence was strictly limited.... The function of intelligence was therefore to demonstrate the truth of revealed knowledge, to reconcile diverse and pragmatic experience with the rational pattern of the world as given in faith (Becker, 1932, p. 7).

Smith, therefore, was in many ways typical of the philosophers of the period, on Becker's interpretation of the eighteenth century. Like Hume, who was a major influence on his philosophy, Smith regarded the preservation of the social order as of primary importance. Like his contemporary, Kant, who was also, though in a different direction, influenced by Hume,[9] Smith wanted to place limits on the legitimate field of action of reason, to find a space for instinct and religious belief. Perhaps the greatest overlap between Smith and his contemporaries lay in their application of the doctrine of natural law. This is the topic of the next subsection.

5.2. *"Nature" and the Natural in Smith*

> With Adam Smith and his disciples . . . nature means the totality of impulses and instincts by
> which the individual members of society are animated; and their contention is that the best
> arrangements result from giving free play to those forces in the confidence that partial failure
> will be more than compensated by success elsewhere, and that the pursuit of his own interest
> by each will work out in the greatest happiness of all (A. W. Benn cited in Hayek, 1949, p. 12
> note 15).

The reader may have noticed the number of times, in the passages cited above, Smith uses the term "Nature" interchangeably with that of the Deity. Far from being the passive background or substrate of our activities, nature is seen as a direct manifestation of the deity, as an active principle intervening in our lives. These citations illustrate Smith's adoption and adaptation of the archaic conception of natural law so popular amongst eighteenth century philosophers (Becker, 1932: Ch. II; Sabine, 1951: Ch. XXVIIff).

The late eighteenth century French philosopher, Comte de Volney, defined natural law in eminently Smithian terms:

> What is natural law? It is the regular and constant order of facts by which God rules the universe;
> the order which his wisdom presents to the sense and reason of men, to serve them as an equal
> and common rule of conduct, and to guide them . . . towards perfection and happiness (cited in
> Becker, 1932, pp. 33, 45).

Here again we see the universe as an orderly system administered by a god. The order implicit in it, which is presented to both the senses and the reason of humans, issues in both factual statements about the way the world is, and normative statements as to how people are to behave, so as to correspond with the divine will. Again the god is a utilitarian, maximising the happiness of mankind.

Becker cites this definition as typical of the eighteenth century philosophers, among whom he explicitly includes Adam Smith (Becker, 1932, p. 33). His commentary certainly applies well to Smith:

> The language is familiar, but the idea, once we examine it critically, is as remote as that of
> Thomas Aquinas. Important if true, we say; but how comes it, we ask, that you are so well
> acquainted with God and his purposes? Who told you . . . that there is a regular and constant
> order of nature? . . . Indeed it is all too simple. It assumes everything that most needs to be
> proved and begs every question we could think of asking (Becker, 1932, p. 45).

I keep stressing the primacy of *order* in Smith, and the same is true of the *philosophes*: they wanted to be able to point to an ordered *natural* world in order to justify the conceptions of *social* order to which they variously subscribed:

> Most eighteenth-century minds were too accustomed to a stable society with fixed ranks, too
> habituated to an orderly code . . . to be at all happy in a disordered universe. It seemed safer,

therefore, . . . to retain God . . . as a . . . guaranty that all was well in the most comfortable of common-sense worlds (Becker, 1932, pp. 49–50).

And if a god did not exist, it would be necessary, as Voltaire (in)famously declared, to invent one. But a god in isolation, separate from the world, was not to the point. Their programme demanded that God directly reveal himself in nature:

> God had revealed his purpose to men in a . . . simple and natural . . . way, through his works. To be enlightened was to understand . . . that it was . . . in the great book of nature . . . that the laws of God had been recorded. This is the new revelation . . . This open book of nature was what Jean Jacques Rousseau and his philosophical colleagues went in search of when they wished to know what God had said to them. Nature and natural law – what magic these words held for the philosophical century! . . . Hume, Voltaire, Rousseau, Volney: in each of them nature takes without question the position customarily reserved for the guest of honor. . . . Search the writings of the new economists and you will find them demanding the abolition of artificial restrictions on trade and industry in order that men may be free to follow the natural law of self-interest . . . controversialists of every party unite in calling upon nature as the sovereign arbiter of all their quarrels (Becker, 1932, pp. 51–52).

Perhaps we can best see the importance of this view of nature in the popular and scholarly response to a figure towering over the eighteenth century, that of Newton. During the course of the century, a large number of popular guides to Newton's philosophy were published. The point of interest was not the technical detail but the overall philosophy, in particular Newton's approach to the most fundamental of human problems – the relations between humanity, nature and God. Colin Maclaurin, Professor of Mathematics in the University of Edinburgh, set out the nature of these relationships in his own guidebook, *An Account of Sir Isaac Newton's Philosophical Discoveries*, published in 1748:

> To describe the *phenomena* of nature, to explain their causes . . . and to enquire into the whole constitution of the universe, is the business of natural philosophy. . . . But natural philosophy is subservient to purposes of a higher kind, and it is chiefly to be valued as it lays a sure foundation for natural religion and moral philosophy; by leading us, in a satisfactory manner, to the knowledge of the Author and Governor of the universe . . . .

> We are from his works, to seek to know God, and not to pretend to mark out the scheme of his conduct, in nature, from the very deficient ideas we are able to form of that great mysterious Being. . . .

> Our views of Nature, however imperfect, serve to represent to us, in the most sensible manner, that mighty power which prevails throughout . . . and that wisdom which we see displayed in the exquisite structure and just motions of the greatest and subtilest parts. These, with perfect goodness, by which they are evidently directed, constitute the supreme object of the speculations of a philosopher; who, while he contemplates and admires so excellent a system, cannot but be himself *excited and animated to correspond with the general harmony of nature* (Maclaurin, 1748, cited in Becker, 1932, pp. 62–63).

After citing this passage, Becker immediately adds: "The closing words of this passage may well be taken as a just expression of the prevailing state of mind about the middle of the eighteenth century. Obviously the disciples of the Newtonian philosophy had . . . deified nature" (Becker, 1932, p. 63).

The deification of nature led, as it was supposed to lead, to the sanctification of the particular model of human behaviour the philosophers wished to hold up as "natural." The Declaration of Independence, for example, invokes "the laws of nature and of nature's God" (cited in Becker, 1932, p. 52) to sanction its particular programme. Macfie, speaking of the "Scottish Tradition in Economic Thought," says that "The main faith which the Law of Nature and Stoicism inspired in Scotland was a faith in natural liberty in a natural society" (Macfie, 1967, p. 26). In Smith we see frequent references to the "sacred laws of justice" (*TMS* II.ii.2.3), a "sacred regard to general rules" of morality (*TMS* III.5.2); "by the wisdom of Nature, the happiness of every innocent man is . . . rendered holy, consecrated, and hedged round against the approach of every other man" (*TMS* II.iii.3.4). And in *WN*, we read that Britain's trade policy with America, though in fact "not very hurtful to the colonies" was, in diverting trade from its spontaneous course, "a manifest violation of the most sacred rights of mankind" (*WN* IV.vii.b.44).

For Smith, therefore, as was commonly the case in natural law theorists, what is natural is god-given and therefore implicitly good. When Smith describes certain institutional arrangements in *WN* as "natural," and others, on the contrary, as "artificial" (as, for example, in *WN* IV.ii.3), he is saying that the former are not just spontaneous, but spontaneous *and therefore* an expression of the will of God, whereas the latter must at the very least lie under the suspicion of sacrilege. There are many occasions where Smith invokes nature in this way in *WN*. For example: "All systems of preference or of restraint [of trade by the government] . . . being . . . completely taken away, the obvious and simple system of natural liberty establishes itself of its own accord" (*WN* IV.ix.5). "[V]iolations of natural liberty [are] . . . unjust" (*WN* IV.v.b.16).

In his lectures as early as 1749 Smith was linking the ideas of an active, beneficent and rational nature – in short, a *teleological* nature – to the policy prescription of *laissez-faire*: "Projectors disturb nature in the course of her operations in human affairs, and it requires no more than to let her alone, and give her fair play in the pursuit of her ends that she may establish her own designs" (Smith, cited in Gay, 1969, p. 354). "To let alone" is, almost certainly, a conscious translation of the phrase "*laisser faire*," which had been in use in France since the end of the previous century to denote freedom from government interference.

But Smith extends the idea of what is natural to include human nature. What is instinct in us was implanted there by Nature, for a purpose – and this includes our weaknesses as well as our strengths. Thus, speaking of resentment and its issue in revenge, "the most detestable of all the passions," he remarks that even here "Nature . . . does not seem to have dealt so unkindly with us, as to have endowed us with any principle which is wholly and in every respect evil, or which, in no degree and in no direction, can be the proper object of praise and approbation" (*TMS* II.i.5.8). Thus resentment, like every other emotion, is divinely appointed, an endowment of "Nature," but can become vicious when taken to an excess. This tactic, however logical in itself, involves Smith in inescapable contradictions once he attempts to derive his *laissez-faire* policy prescription from it, as we shall see below.

So Smith has a similar approach to nature and the natural as his contemporaries. If anything, however, Smith is even more archaic than his contemporaries. Prior to the eighteenth century, according to Becker,

> philosophers . . . argued that, since God is goodness and reason, his creation must somehow be, even if not evidently so to finite minds, good and reasonable. Design in nature was thus derived *a priori* from the character which the Creator was assumed to have; and natural law, so far from being associated with the observed behaviour of physical phenomena, was no more than a conceptual universe above and outside the real one, a logical construction dwelling in the mind of God and dimly reflected in the minds of philosophers (Becker, 1932, p. 55).

In the eighteenth century, however, – he cites Hume, in the person of Cleanthes in his *Dialogues*, as epitome – the logical process is reversed:

> Cleanthes does not conclude that nature *must* be rational because God *is* eternal reason; he concludes that God *must* be an engineer because nature *is* a machine (Becker, 1932, p. 56). [T]he very foundation of the new philosophy was that the existence of God, if there was one, and his goodness, if goodness he could claim, must be inferred from the observable behaviour of the world. Following Newton, the Philosophers had all insisted on this to the point of pedantry (ibid, p. 67).

Smith in this particular respect is out of step with his contemporaries. He clearly *starts* by deducing the nature of the world from a prior consideration of the "necessary" qualities of the deity, and only afterwards claims to be able to support his conclusions by reference to observations of nature itself:

> The happiness of mankind, as well as of all other rational creatures, seems to have been the original purpose intended by the Author of nature, when he brought them into existence. No other end seems worthy of that supreme wisdom and divine benignity which we necessarily ascribe to him; and this opinion, which we are led to by the abstract consideration of his infinite perfections, is still more confirmed by the examination of the works of nature, which seem all intended to promote happiness, and to guard against misery (*TMS* III.5.7).

There is no reason to believe that Smith would have seen any opposition between these two approaches – deductive vs. inductive, *a priori* vs. empirical – to the relation between God and nature. But he would certainly have rejected the latter as sole, or even major, support for his philosophy. Reason is "artificial" and fallible, and our finite minds do not perceive the remote ramifications of things. Things, as he stresses in *Astronomy*, often appear to us to be discordant and unconnected. This is precisely why we need a "soothing" scientific explanation of things, and God's will, manifested in natural law, is the most pleasing general explanation available. So it would be a mistake to deduce God's attributes from a finite and partial examination of nature: on the contrary, it is the assumption of God's omnipotence, omniscience and benevolence which makes the discordant world of appearances at once comprehensible and safe. Smith in this respect is thus conservative even with respect to his contemporaries.

Smith explicitly links the superiority of our natural feelings over the artificiality of reason, to the preservation of social order:

> That kings are the servants of the people, to be obeyed, resisted, deposed, or punished, as the public conveniency may require, is the doctrine of reason and philosophy; but it is not the doctrine of Nature. Nature would teach us to submit to them for their own sake, to tremble and bow down before their exalted station . . . (*TMS*: I.iii.2.3).

The message is clear: the natural sentiments placed in us by a providential deity, expressed in established traditions, for example, of granting legitimacy to monarchs, are to be heeded in preference to whatever reason may tell us, so that social order may be preserved.

6. SMITH'S CONTRADICTIONS

There are many logical inconsistencies in Smith's theory, and I have noted some of them in passing. However, at base, there is one particular contradiction which confronts Smith, in various guises, at every turn. In his *Weltanschauung*, everything is predetermined for the maximisation of the "quantity of happiness" in the world at every instant. In empirical reality, there is obvious suffering and injustice. How is the latter to be reconciled with the administration of the machine of the universe by a beneficent, omniscient and omnipotent god? To quote Hume: "Epicurus's old questions are yet unanswered. Is [God] willing to prevent evil, but not able? Then he is impotent. Is he able, but not willing? Then he is malevolent. Is he both able and willing? Whence then is evil?" (cited in Becker, 1932, p. 68).

Presumably even the most pious would concede that there must be *logical* restrictions on what a god can do. Can the deity create a weight so heavy that he cannot lift it? No: he is necessarily restricted to what is logically possible in what he can simultaneously achieve. It is far less obvious, however, that suffering in general, let alone any specific instance of suffering, is a logical necessity for the achievement of God's presumed aims, and, indeed, Smith makes no attempt to put the case. Instead, its necessity for the good of the "greater system" is simply asserted and assumed. This is not a subtle point and neither is it new: it was certainly as well known in Smith's time as in ours that it was a problem for theories of this kind. He never addressed the issue, however, and failed to present any explicit theodicy going beyond these assumptions.

Theodicy generally involves at some point an invocation of free will: God had to permit evil if he was to allow man free will and hence moral responsibility. Here again, Smith is on shaky ground, because he has made everything, including human nature, a part of nature; all behaviour, including human behaviour, is natural, and hence god-given. Our behaviour is prompted by the sentiments placed in our breast by "a wise providence." Since we do what we are led to do, what we are predestined to do, choice is presumably an illusion. When we act, our hand is held and guided with parental concern by the deity. Our judgement of the moral quality of an action, as we have seen, is for Smith essentially a sentimental and aesthetic judgement without rational content. Arguably, it was open to Smith to adopt the compatibilist position of Chrysippus. But Smith carefully avoids addressing this issue, too, and the logic of his position, that we may admire "the wisdom of God even in the folly of man," is surely that of determinism.

The problem for Smith is this: if God is maximising happiness, he cannot at the same time permit either evil and suffering or free will. If he allows suffering, then the quantity of happiness is presumably not at its logically possible maximum; if he allows free will, then he is again not maximising happiness, as he is leaving that to the outcome of the considerations of errant finite minds.

Finally, the further consequence of the view that everything in the world is part of the great machine, playing its part in God's plan to maximise happiness, and that human nature and the behaviour to which man is led is a part of nature, is that regulation and state planning are just as natural and god-inspired as free trade and *laissez-faire*. Viner (1958, p. 233) asks, "was not government itself a part of the order of nature, and its activities as 'natural' as those of the individuals whom it governed?" As Becker says,

if nature be the work of God, and man the product of nature, then all that man does and thinks, all that he has ever done or thought, must be natural, too, and in accord with the laws of nature and of nature's god. Pascal had long since asked the fundamental question: 'Why is custom not natural?' Why, indeed! But if all is natural, then how could man and his customs ever be *out of harmony* with nature? (Becker, 1932, p. 66).

The concept of the natural only means anything – other than fatalistic acquiescence to anything and everything – if it is contrasted with something *else*, something unnatural. This Smith attempts to do by referring to liberty as "natural" and regulation as "artificial" in *WN*, sentiment as "natural" and reason as "artificial" in *TMS*. But he cannot sustain this contrast on the basis of his theory. The category of the artificial has no meaning in a theory where the natural is already all-encompassing. This is clearly a critical contradiction for Smith's espousal of *laissez-faire*, but again, he makes no attempt to address the issue.

The contradiction can be seen particularly clearly in a paradoxical passage in *TMS* where he attempts, unsuccessfully, to reconcile his Panglossian view of the outcome of natural processes with the human attempt to remedy nature's faults. But if natural outcomes are the best which are logically possible, then such faults are inconceivable. Smith says that "the general rules by which prosperity and adversity are distributed . . . appear to be perfectly suited to the situation of mankind in this life, yet they are by no means suited to some of our moral sentiments" (*TMS* III.5.9). In other words, God allocates prosperity by general rules which are designed to maximise human happiness, but the allocations which result, because of the finitude of human minds, do not always satisfy the moral sentiments which he has placed in us.

> Thus man is by Nature directed to correct, in some measure, that distribution of things which she herself would otherwise have made. The rules which for this purpose she prompts him to follow, are different from those which she herself follows . . . The rules which she follows are fit for her; those which he follows for him: but both are calculated to promote the same great end, the order of the world, and the perfection and happiness of human nature (*TMS* III.5.9).

So nature follows rules designed to maximise human happiness, and man, "correcting" this, does the same. The inconsistency could not be clearer. If nature's rules lead to optimising, happiness-maximising outcomes, then man's correction of nature must interfere with this and lead to a suboptimal outcome; if, on the contrary, man's correction of nature is happiness-maximising then nature's rules must themselves have been suboptimal. Smith cannot have it both ways. Or, rather, there is *one* interpretation which would allow him to have it both ways. If he were to say that nature *including* humanity were designed to optimise, but that nature *without* man were incomplete, imperfect, suboptimal, which is more or less what Hegel says, then he could reconcile both accounts. Then human action to correct spontaneous market outcomes and redistribute prosperity according to merit would be optimising as it would be the result of *both* the rules of nature *and* the rules of man.

To draw out the point, we may say that, while Smith's version of natural law formed a foundation for the invisible hand mechanism, it by no means follows that it undermines the case for a *visible* hand of state intervention. On the contrary, his *Weltanschauung* forms just as good a foundation for the latter as the former, and it is only Smith's prejudices, and not his theoretical system, which lead him to prefer one to the other. State intervention is a product of all the human strengths and frailties of those involved in the political process. On Adam Smith's account, those strengths and frailties are god-given and designed to lead individuals to act so as to maximise human happiness. There is nothing in the system of thought which Smith presents to say that the invisible hand active in the economic process will be inactive in the political process.

Smith cannot have been unaware of these inconsistencies in his standpoint. Yet there is a sense in which he, himself, is not inconsistent in neglecting them. Someone who kept faith with the Enlightenment ideal of following Reason wherever it may lead – a Ricardo, for example, a Marx, a Darwin, or an Einstein – would have concentrated attention on these contradictions and drawn the logical consequences. But we have already seen that Smith was not in this mould. The late eighteenth century philosophers turned their back on reason and, instead, promoted sentiment. It was not Smith's goal to present an intellectually unified, logically coherent system of thought, but to paint as pleasing as possible a picture of the world, such that the viewer would be "animated to correspond with the general harmony of nature."

7. CONCLUSION

The question we started with was, how Smith saw the articulation between individual behaviour at the micro level and social outcomes at the macro level. The answer I have given in this paper is that the articulating mechanism consists in the agency of a deity. Our behaviours at the micro level are always just what is required for the optimal macro outcome because the deity's invisible hands always lead us, through the pursuit of our own interests, our own illusions and fears, and our own fellow feeling for others, to perform just those actions required to fulfil the divine plan. This is what Smith meant by the "invisible hand." The implication is that invisible hand theorists of more recent times, such as Hayek, to the extent that, as representatives of a secular age, they cannot rely on an interventionist god, need an alternative mode of articulation between levels. The most frequently invoked alternative – to the extent that the problem is addressed at all – is some kind of evolutionary mechanism, but that lies beyond the scope of the present paper.

I have also argued in this paper that Smith's "invisible hand" mechanism is closely linked to the apologetic aspect in his political economy. While his confidence in a harmonious universe allowed him to make real scientific progress in political economy, without fear that it would destabilise the social order, Smith's principal objective was, nevertheless, to reconcile humanity with the spontaneous social order and the status quo. He invoked the idea of a divine teleological plan, of the universe as a machine administered by a god, in order to explain away suffering and evil as only the proximate manifestations of chains of connection whose distant ramifications would include more than compensatory benefits. The idea is to convince us that we need do nothing at the macro level. All we should do is pursue our own individual interests at the micro level, and display appropriate levels of patriotism and respect for our leaders. The rich, the powerful and the fortunate all ensure that the big decisions of society are for the best – because they are taken by the hand and led by God to do so. All is for the best, then, in this, the best of all possible worlds.

But does Smith not "protest too much?" Sometimes Smith's protestations seem to invite the speculation that the truth is just the opposite of what he says. Smith claims that the universe is a coherent and harmonic whole administered by a single intelligence. But we know that this is not the case. The world is a jungle, an arena of clashing interests: "It is as though cheetahs had been designed by one deity and antelopes by a rival deity" (Dawkins, 1995, p. 123). Smith claims that human nature and human society are a part of this organic unity, "all discord, harmony not understood." But, of course, society was as riven by sectional interest then as it is now. His claim is to be understood, not as a positive statement of what is the case but as a normative statement of what is to be desired. He claims that spontaneous human institutions, "the result of human action but not human design," such as the market, and the law, order and defence functions of the state, make an optimal contribution to human welfare because guided by the invisible hand of a beneficent, omnipotent and omniscient god. Again, we know of no reason even to suspect that any supernal agency exists, such that we can rely on its intervention to maximise social welfare.[10] Again, perhaps, Smith's claim is to be understood in a normative sense: what is required is a higher level *human* agency which will reconcile our differences and lead us through the pursuit of our own interests to the maximum achievable level of welfare:

> the invisible hand is only one of the many names given in the *Moral Sentiments* to the Deity – great Author of Nature, Engineer, Great Architect, and so on. . . . Adam Smith did believe (as a matter of faith) in this final reconciler. . . . Now, there is little doubt that we today do not accept this kind of argument. . . . The inevitable reaction is that, if the supernatural control is abandoned, human societies must supply their own. . . . [T]he state . . . must take the place of the invisible hand (Macfie, 1967, p. 111).

NOTES

1. See Hegel (1952, paras 344, 348) for the best expression of the "cunning of reason" in Hegel, even though the term itself is not employed there.

2. For Hegel, see the favourable comments on the political economy of Smith, Say and Ricardo in *The Philosophy of Right* (Hegel, 1952, para 189 and Addition); for Burke, see the long extracts from his review of *TMS* and letter to Smith of 1759 in Raphael and Macfie (1976, pp. 27–28).

3. Eds 1–5 only.

4. i.e., every capitalist. Smith naively adopts the standpoint of the individual capitalist and momentarily forgets that there exist other agents, who have *no* role in "directing . . . industry." It seems very ironic that the first of the two arguments for individual liberty which Smith gives here, is essentially a *mercantilist* argument: we do not need government intervention in foreign trade to give preference to domestic industry, because individual capitalists will be led by the invisible hand to prefer domestic industry without intervention.

5. Smith even furnishes us with an account of why God is invisible (*TMS* III.2.31, Eds 3–5 only). If we could see him, Smith says, we would be so dazzled that we would be unable to go about our normal business.

6. Much of this section relies on Becker (1932). Becker has been heavily criticised, notably in Peter Gay ("Carl Becker's Heavenly City" (1957) reprinted in Gay, 1964, pp. 188–210). The points made in this section remain substantially untouched by Gay's criticism, which boils down to little more than the complaint that Becker exaggerates. The same point could be made about Gay. Unfortunately, this is not the place for a thorough analysis of the problems raised by Gay's very interesting discussion of Becker, of Smith (Gay, 1969, passim), or of the *Philosophes'* "Revolt Against Rationalism" (Gay, 1969, pp. 187–207).

7. The italicised concluding statement is the exact counterpart of Hegel's assertion that "the real is the rational" (Knox in Hegel, 1952, p. 10), and has exactly the same purpose, namely, to "reconcile us to the actual" (ibid, p. 12). See also Hegel (1975, para 6).

8. He includes in the term *philosophes*, amongst others, from France: Montesquieu, Voltaire, Volney, Diderot, Savigny and Rousseau; from Germany: Leibniz, Lessing, Herder and Goethe; from Britain: Locke, Hume, Ferguson and Adam Smith; and from America: Jefferson and Franklin (Becker, 1932, p. 33).

9. See Kant (1950, 5 ff; or Academy edition, Vol IV, 258 ff).

10. And, even if there were such a power, some might argue, passing up all responsibility to it for our own actions and their consequences in this fashion, might scarcely be the best method of gaining its approval.

ACKNOWLEDGMENTS

I should like to record my gratitude, for support and valuable comments on earlier versions, to the late William Barber, Tony Brewer, Vivienne Brown, Pete Clarke, Mary Denis, William Dixon, Sheila Dow, the late Peter Holl, Geoffrey Kay, Steve Miller, Warren Samuels, Adrian Seville, Ron Smith, Richard Sturn, Anthony Waterman, two anonymous referees for this Journal, and participants at the City University, London, Economics Department research seminar, and the European Economics Association conference, Berlin, September 1998.

REFERENCES

Becker, C. L. (1932). *The heavenly city of the eighteenth-century philosophers*. London: Yale University Press.

Dawkins, R. (1995). *River out of Eden – A Darwinian view of life*. London: Phoenix/Orion.

Denis, A. (1999). Was Adam Smith an individualist? *History of the Human Sciences, 12*(3, August), 71–86.

Denis, A. M. P. (2001). *Collective and individual rationality: Some episodes in the history of economic thought*. PhD thesis. London: City University.

Gay, P. (1964). *The party of humanity. Studies in the French enlightenment*. London: Weidenfeld & Nicolson.

Gay, P. (1969). *The enlightenment: An interpretation* (Vol. II). *The Science of Freedom*. London: Weidenfeld & Nicolson.

Hayek, F. (1948). *Individualism and economic order*. Chicago: University of Chicago Press (reprinted, 1949; London: Routledge).

Hegel, G. W. F. (1952 [1820]). *Hegel's philosophy of right* (ed, trans T. M. Knox). Oxford: Clarendon Press/OUP.

Hegel, G. W. F. (1975 [1830]). *Logic* (Part One of the *Encyclopaedia of the Philosophical Sciences*) (trans William Wallace, forward by F. N. Findlay). Oxford: Clarendon Press/OUP.

Kant, I. (1950 [1783]). *Prolegomena to any future metaphysics which will be able to come forth as science* (trans L. White Beck). New York: Bobbs-Merrill.

Macfie, A. (1971). The invisible hand of Jupiter. *Journal of the History of Ideas, 32*, 595–599.

Macfie, A. L. (1959). 'Adam Smith's *Moral Sentiments* as Foundation for his *Wealth of Nations*' *Oxford Economic Papers* 2 (new series), October, 209–228.

Macfie, A. L. (1967). *The individual in society. Papers on Adam Smith*. London: George Allen & Unwin (series title: *University of Glasgow Social and Economic Studies* (new series) ed. D. J. Robertson, Vol. 11).

Marx, K. (1972). *Theories of surplus value* (Vol. III). Moscow: Progress Publishers.

Raphael, D. D. (1985). 'Smith'. In: K. Thomas (Ed.) (1997) *Three Great Economists*. Oxford: Oxford University Press (series title: *Past Masters*, K. Thomas (Ed.)).

Raphael, D. D., & Macfie, A. L. (1976). 'Introduction' in A. Smith (1976–1980, Volume I); In: D. D. Raphael & A. L. Macfie (Eds), *The Theory of Moral Sentiments*.

Raphael, D. D., & Skinner, A. S. (1980). 'General Introduction' in A. Smith (1976–1980, Volume III); In: W. P. D. Wightman & J. C. Bryce (Eds), *Essays on Philosophical Subjects*.

Sabine, G. H. (1951: 3e:). *A history of political theory*. London: Harrap.

Smith, A. (1976–1980). *The Glasgow edition of the works and correspondence of Adam Smith*. Oxford: Clarendon Press/OUP (reprinted (1981–1982) Indianapolis: Liberty Fund).
    Volume I (1976 [1759]). In: D. D. Raphael & A. L. Macfie (Eds), *The Theory of Moral Sentiments*. Abbreviated *TMS* in this paper.
    Volume II (1976 [1776]). In: R. H. Campbell, A. S. Skinner & W. B. Todd (Eds), *An Inquiry into the Nature and Causes of the Wealth of Nations* (in two volumes). Abbreviated *WN* in this paper.
    Volume III (1980). In: W. P. D. Wightman & J. C. Bryce (Eds), *Essays on Philosophical Subjects*. Abbreviated Astronomy in this paper, where it refers to the *History of Astronomy*, and EPS otherwise.

Viner, J. (1958). *The long view and the short*. Glencoe, IL: Free Press.

In Memoriam: I. Bernard Cohen

SOME PRINCIPLES OF ADAM SMITH'S NEWTONIAN METHODS IN THE *WEALTH OF NATIONS*

Eric Schliesser

1. SUMMARY AND INTRODUCTORY REMARKS

This paper gives an account of important aspects of Smith's methods in *An Inquiry Concerning the Nature and Causes of the Wealth of Nations* (WN). I reinterpret Smith's distinction between natural and market prices, by focusing on Smith's account of the causes of the discrepancies of market prices from natural prices. I argue that Smith postulates a "natural course" of events in order to stimulate research into institutions that cause actual events to deviate from it. Smith's employment of the fiction of a natural price should, thus, not be seen merely as an instance of general or partial equilibrium analysis, but, instead, as part of a theoretical framework that will enable observed deviations from expected regularities to improve his theory. For Smith theory is a research tool that allows for a potentially open-ended process of successive approximation. These are the Newtonian elements in Smith. I provide evidence from Smith's posthumously published *Essays on Philosophical Subjects* (EPS, 1795), especially "The History of Astronomy" ("Astronomy"), that this accords with Smith's views on methodology.[1] By way of illumination, Smith's explanation of the introduction of commerce in Europe is contrasted with that of Hume as

A Research Annual
Research in the History of Economic Thought and Methodology, Volume 23-A, 33–74
ISSN: 0743-4154/doi:10.1016/S0743-4154(05)23002-X

33

presented in "Of Commerce." I argue that Smith's treatment is methodologically superior.

It has been maintained that Smith was at most a grand synthesizer of economic ideas that were being discussed widely at the time.[2] This paper is relatively agnostic about the novelty or soundness of any of Smith's economic claims. However, a focus on the *content* of Smith's doctrines obscures the fascinating *evidential strategies* in Smith's work. An unintended benefit of my approach to the history and philosophy of economics is that it avoids a self-congratulatory presentism.

At the start of WN, Adam Smith observes, "Those theories [of political economy] have a considerable influence, not only upon the opinions of men of learning, but upon the public conduct of princes and sovereign states" ("Introduction and Plan of the Work," 8, 11).[3] That is, theories not only attempt to explain and predict economic behavior, but through the actions of rulers also deliberately or unintentionally influence it. Thus, they run the risk, for example, of becoming self-fulfilling prophecies. Smith's remark reveals considerable methodological self-awareness and sophistication. Smith may also be signaling a contrast between the opinions of the "men of learning" and the public conduct of "princes." This paper is mostly concerned with a topic of interest only to a narrow segment of these "men of learning."

WN is a very long treatise – about a thousand pages. Despite the remark just quoted, there are, nevertheless, very few methodological comments in the book, especially when we compare it to other 17th and 18th century treatises that often contain important statements on method or rules of reasoning. Instead we find many elaborate descriptions and homely examples. Even though Smith calls his book "a speculative work" (V.iii.68, 934), he clearly does not want to limit the appeal of his book to "men of learning." (For speculation on his readership, see II.ii.66, 309.) Sometimes Smith is even apologetic for being "obscure" and "extremely abstracted" (e.g. WN I.iv.43, 46). Smith leaves it to the careful reader to figure out his methods.[4] In what follows, I give an account of an overlooked, albeit important, strain of Smith's methodology in WN. I am not offering a complete account of all of Smith's methods in WN. Yet, my approach allows many parts of WN to be unified.

The argument of this paper has three major components. In the first and most lengthy one (presented in part II), I look at Smith's distinction between natural and market prices. I focus on Smith's account of the causes of the deviations of market prices from natural prices. By offering a detailed case-study, I argue that Smith postulates a "natural course" of events in order to stimulate research into *institutions* that cause real events to deviate from it. In order to forestall misinterpretation: my claim entails that Smith is committed to two, mutually reinforcing, elements of one evidential strategy: (i) to use deviations from expected regularities to uncover the causes at work in political economy (very broadly conceived), and (ii) to enable discovery of these causes to generate successive improvements in the theoretical idealization (or model) that was used to generate predictions. This method I attribute to Newton.[5] I provide some evidence that Smith was aware of the method; I focus on a very insightful passage in the "Astronomy" in which Smith takes Descartes to task for trying to explain away deviations from general rules instead of explaining them. Along the way, I discuss Smith's treatment of labor markets and his long "digression" on silver.

In part III, I provide further, albeit much more schematic, evidence from WN for my reading of Smith. I focus on Book III of WN, where Smith postulates a "natural" development of societies from hunting, to pasturage, to agriculture, to commerce. I show that Smith's employment of a *counterfactual* 4-stage theory is also designed to allow deviations from the natural course to provide a refined, *realistic* causal explanation of historical events. By way of illumination, I contrast Smith's explanation of the introduction of commerce in Europe with that of his friend and forerunner David Hume. I indicate why Smith's treatment is methodologically more sophisticated. I suggest, however, that Hume's essay (1750–1751), "Of the Populousness of Ancient Nations" (Ancient Nations),[6] may have inspired Smith to develop his method.

In part IV, I show that my reading of the method of WN is in accord with Smith's methodological views on science as revealed by the "Astronomy." I explain Smith's views on the nature of scientific theories – or "machines." It turns out that for Smith theories are tools for further research. This may seem an obvious use for a theory, but if one takes this idea seriously, it creates a shift in perspective; it makes one ask: how does this theory allow one to find and analyze data that can be turned into evidence? What kind of research can one do to improve the theory? (By contrast, the philosophic questions, "how well does this theory explain?" and "what does this theory explain?" become, while not ruled out, a bit less important.) I suggest that Smith is committed to something akin to a process of successive approximation.

2. NATURAL AND MARKET PRICES

In this part, I propose a novel explanation for the contrast that Smith draws between natural and market prices. I provide a rather detailed case study on behalf of my general methodological theses. The detail is necessary not only because of the intricacy and subtlety of Smith's thought, but also because it is widely agreed that Smith's account of natural price is one of the crucial elements of the analytic/theoretical core of WN. Hence, this is quite rightly seen as a crucial test-case of any account that is offered as an interpretation of substantive parts of the methodology or theory of WN.

2.1. The Natural Price

At the start of chapter vii of Book I, Smith writes,

> When the price of any commodity is neither more nor less than what is sufficient to pay the rent of the land, the wages of the labour, and the profits of the stock employed in raising, preparing, and bringing it to market, according to their natural rates, the commodity is then sold for what may be called its natural price.[7] The commodity is then sold precisely for what it is worth, or for what it really costs the person who brings it to market; for though in common language what is called the prime cost of any commodity does not comprehend the profit of the person who is to sell it again, yet if he sells it at a price which does not allow him the ordinary rate of profit in his neighbourhood, he is evidently a loser by the trade; since by employing his stock in some other way he might have made that profit. His profit, besides, is his revenue, the proper fund of his subsistence ... Though the price, therefore, which leaves him this profit is not always the lowest at which a dealer may sometimes sell his goods, it is the lowest at which he is likely to sell them for any considerable time; at least where there is perfect liberty, or where he may change his trade as often as he pleases. The actual price at which any commodity is commonly sold is called its market price. It may either be above, or below, or exactly the same with its natural price (WN I.vii.4–7, 72–73).

There is a lot to unpack here. I focus on the *purpose* of the distinction between natural and market prices, and how one would go about measuring the natural price. First I need to explain a few things about Smith's framework. For Smith, the price of a commodity is a composite of rents, wages, and profits.[8] What is true for a single commodity is also true for the "whole annual produce of a society, or what comes to the same thing, the whole price of that annual produce." Thus, these three components correspond to the three great classes in society: landowners, workers, and merchants (I.vi.17–19, 69–70 and I.xi.p.7, 265).[9] Now Smith assumes that in "every society or neighbourhood" there will be "an ordinary or average" rate of wages, profits, and rents. These average rates will be called the natural rates (for wages and so on) "at the time and place in which they commonly prevail" (I.vii.1–3, 72). If one knows these average rates one can then estimate the natural price. For simplicity's sake, assume that Smith's concept of a "society or neighbourhood" is not problematic.

It is worth stressing that the price is only said to be "natural" in a situation of what Smith calls "perfect liberty," that is, when the labor and commodity markets, especially, are competitive and free (I.vii.27, 78). Although capital markets were also not free (in many countries the exportation of gold was forbidden and interest rates were regulated), Smith often seems to assume, following Hume, that the regulations against the movement of capital are much more ineffective than other economic statutes (II.iii.23, 340). The "natural price" is, then, the hypothetical, localized, price of a good if there were not all kinds of obstacles preventing the free movement of capital, labor, and goods. That is to say, it comes down to what the world would be like if there were no impediments to the mobility of resources. This situation did not exist in Smith's time (or ours); the natural price can, at best, only be estimated.[10]

The situation of perfect liberty is not a necessary condition for the price of a commodity to be or reach its natural price. Even if there were no complete mobility of resources in an economy, fluctuations in short-run market prices may, for whatever reason, make a commodity occasionally reach its natural price. Smith is clear that except when an economy operates in perfect liberty this is unlikely to happen very often or last very long; "what is sufficient to pay the rent of the land, the wages of the labour, and the profits of the stock employed in raising, preparing, and bringing it to market," is in most non-perfect-liberty-conditions almost always going to be different from and usually *more* than what is said to be the natural price of commodity (I.vii.30, 79).

But how does one go about estimating the natural price of a good? How does one discover what the average rates of rent, wages, and profit are? Moreover, how does one go about figuring out what they would be in non-existing circumstances? Now, it is worth pointing out, to put it crudely, that for Smith, rent and wages rise with the increasing prosperity of society (for explicit statements on wages see I.viii.21–22, 86–87, and on rents see: I.xi.p.1, 264). By contrast, Smith thinks that in rich societies the rate of profit was low (I.ix.20, 113), while in poor societies it would be high, and "it is always highest in countries which are going fastest to ruin" (I.xi.p.10, 266). Smith claims that in prosperous countries, that is, those in which capital had already been accumulated, "mutual competition" among merchants, who have abundant sources of capital, would drive down profit rates (I.ix.2, 105),[11] while poor and declining countries would scare off merchants, thus increasing potential profit for the adventurous few. For Smith high wages and high profits do not tend to go together; he did recognize an exception to this general rule in "the peculiar circumstances of new colonies," where profits, due to relative lack of stock, and wages, due to high growth, could both be high (I.ix.11, 109).[12] All this implies that in Smith's opinion there is, except in new colonies, an inherent conflict over resources between the wage-earning laborers and the profit-oriented merchants (I.viii.11, 83 and I.xi.p.8–10, 265–267).[13]

The high or low rates of land-rent are the *effect* of high or low prices (I.xi.a.8, 162). That is, rents shadow prices. For Smith the rates of rent are the result of haggling between landowners and farmers, influenced by their relative power due to supply and demand. (Of course, Smith repeatedly points out that the legal structure influences the types of leases and land-ownership. I am also ignoring mine and house rents for the sake of brevity.) Wages, however, are not only set by the demand and supply of labor (and the effort, skill, security, public esteem, and probability of success involved, see I.x.b.1–33, 116–128), but they are also influenced by guild policies, fixed wage scales, and various regulations that benefit the merchants and tradesmen at the expense of the workers, who were denied attempts to combine.[14] For Smith wages would be a cause of high or low prices (I.xi.a.8, 162), that is, high wages, a sign of a growing economy, would lead to higher prices, unless, of course, productivity would grow at the same rate (I.xi.o.1, 260). Apparently, Smith does not think that it would be difficult to estimate the average rent. He may be confident about this because the information on rents was (for tax purposes) a matter of public record published in registries (V.ii.c.1-d.9, 828–840, although V.ii.c.21, 834, shows awareness of incentives for fraud on part of lessor and lessee).[15] Smith admits, however, that "[I]t is not easy . . . to ascertain what are the average wages of a labourer even in a particular place, and at a particular time" (I.ix.3, 105; see also the important discussion at I.viii.34, 93–95). At best one can determine what usual (a phrase Smith uses as well) wages are. This does not seem to worry him much. Generally, when Smith makes claims about wages he keeps his sources of information obscure (with a few exceptions, e.g. historical documents at I.viii.34, 94–95, and personal conversation at I.x.b.50, 134).[16]

Figuring out the average rate of profits is even more difficult. For competitive reasons, merchants have a strong incentive to hide their profits (I.vii.21, 77). Moreover, due to price changes and chance (sinking of ships, fires in storehouses, etc.) the rate of "profits of stock" for an individual merchant could fluctuate wildly, "not only from year to year, but from day to day, and almost from hour to hour. To ascertain what is the average profit of all the different trades carried on in a great kingdom, must be much more difficult; and to judge of what it may have been formerly, or in remote periods of time, with any degree of precision, must be altogether impossible" (I.ix.3, p 11). There can be, thus, no doubt that Smith was acutely conscious of the limited accuracy of data available to him. (See his remark on the "somewhat uncertain" quality of "information" at I.xi.o.5, 261.) Smith noted the near-total absence of reliable data and the fudging of the contemporary practitioners of "Political Arithmetick" (roughly, the 18th century version of social science statistics,[17] see WN IV.v.b.30, 534–5 and Letter No. 249 to George Chalmers, 10 November 1758; see also Hume's "Of the Balance of Trade," 310).[18] I return to this issue in Section 3.2.

There is a potential confusion in Smith. When one subtracts wages and rent from the natural price of a commodity, "profit" seems to refer to the margin left over that accrues to manufacturer or trader. This is an understanding of profit that in modern terms is described as the ratio of flow profits to flow costs, or profit margin. But sometimes, as in the quote from WN I.ix.3, 105, Smith seems to be referring to what moderns call the ratio of flow profits to capital stock, or return on investment. The modern conceptual apparatus assumes a distinction between flow and stock.[19] Smith probably assumed that profit margins and rate of profit on stock are connected. It appears he thought that an increase of stock would stimulate competition and increase wages, and drive down profits (I.ix.2, 105). He seems not to have envisioned the possibility that one could have a low margin on an individual commodity, yet still have high rate of return on one's investment or high margins with low returns on investment. Nevertheless, in what follows, I accept Smith's argument at face value. I treat him as saying that profits on stock and profit margins are tightly related.[20]

Inspired, perhaps, by David Hume, who called interest the "barometer" of the state,[21] and Turgot, who called it the "thermometer,"[22] Smith proposes measuring interest rates to indirectly measure the average rate of profit. For Smith, the rate of profit influences the rate of interest: "wherever a great deal can be made by the use of money, a great deal will commonly be given for the use of it; and . . . wherever little can be made by it, less will commonly be given for it" (I.ix.4, 105). In the definition, but not elsewhere (V.iii, 907–947), Smith ignores the effects of government borrowing. Smith thought that in his own time interest rates were about half profit rates.[23] It is only a rough indicator, however, because "The proportion which the usual market rate of interest ought to be to the ordinary rate of clear profit, necessarily varies as profit rises or falls." Smith thinks interest is made up of two components: "insurance" against loss of the capital and "sufficient recompence for the trouble of employing the stock" (I.ix.22, 114).[24] In risky or very stable countries either component may have a different weighting. Of course, various governments have attempted to fix the rate of interest, so Smith warns the reader to focus, on the whole, on market rates, although sometimes those are secret. In general, he thinks that in most countries there are "several very safe and easy methods of evading the law" (I.ix.9, 107; see also II.iv.16, 358). This would make figuring out the exact market rates of interest not a simple task.[25] Nevertheless, Smith thinks that, especially in England, the fixed rates often "follow" the market rates of interest (I.ix.5, 106), so the problem should not be exaggerated.

Moreover, even if the movement of capital were free, the rate of profit is influenced by the existence of monopolies and market barriers that can artificially inflate or lower the rate.[26] So, even if one used market interest rates to get at average profit rates, one is not measuring the natural rate of profit.[27] Finally, Smith notes about the natural rate of profit, rent, and wages that "in every society this rate varies according to their circumstances, according to their riches or poverty, their advancing, stationary, or declining condition" (WN I.vii.33, 80).[28] No wonder Smith never attempts to calculate a natural price in the whole of WN![29]

So what does Smith want to do with this notion of a natural price? Why would he risk the criticism of his close friend, Hume, who upon reading of WN claimed that "I cannot think, that the rents of Farms makes any part of the Price of the Produce, but that the price is determined altogether by the Quantity and the Demand?" (Correspondence, Hume's Letter No. 150 to Smith, 1 April 1776, 186)[30] Smith agrees that this was indeed the case for short run market prices (WN I.vii.8, 73).[31] If even Hume cannot see any use for a natural price, why would Smith introduce this abstract and hard to measure concept?[32]

Let us grant on behalf of Smith that the natural price is a kind of useful fiction. Whatever the metaphysical status of this fiction – I.vii.20, 77 (to be quoted below) makes it tempting to view it something more akin to a center of gravity in physics and less akin to, say, a unicorn – can we say more about it on conceptual grounds? For example, the (average) market price of a good can be below, at, or above the natural price. Smith thinks, however, that most market prices are (well) above the natural price. For if the market price of a good remained below the natural price then workers "will withdraw a part of their labour" (I.vii.13, 75) or farmers and merchants would move into more profitable areas (e.g. I.xi.b.23, 168). Of course, if the market rate dropped below the subsistence rate then the workers would starve and, thus, ultimately reduce the availability of labor.[33] Smith assumes that, in general, market prices will be more frequently above natural prices: "the market price of any particular commodity, though it may continue long above, can seldom continue long below its natural price" (I.vii.30, 79). Smith does not discuss examples where the market price of a good is below a natural price. For Smith prices are nearly always seen falling *to* the natural rate (e.g. I.xi.g.21–22, 219–220).[34] Smith says in a famous passage:

> [B]ut though the market price of every particular commodity is in this manner continually gravitating, if one may say so, towards the natural price, yet sometimes particular accidents, sometimes natural causes, and sometimes particular regulations of police [i.e. public administration], may, in many commodities keep up the market price, for a long time together, a good deal above the natural price (WN I.vii.20, 77).[35]

This passage is central to debates about the degree to which Smith anticipated modern equilibrium theories.[36] That debate misses the reasons why Smith developed his conceptual apparatus and fails to properly understand the logic of Smith's enterprise.[37] Nevertheless, the reading I defend is compatible with attributing an equilibrium analysis to Smith. Because of Smith's use of "gravitating," one could be tempted to hear an echo of Newton's theory of universal gravity in this passage,[38] but the comparison is misleading if only because the natural price is not also gravitating toward the market price, that is, the gravitation is not mutual.[39] Yet, Smith was aware that Newton's theory implied universal, *mutual*, simultaneous attraction ("Astronomy," IV¶67–76, 98–104). Smith explicitly writes about the "mutual attraction of the Planets" at "Astronomy" IV¶67–68, 99.[40] Rather, I argue that for Smith the natural price is "the price of free competition" (WN I.vii.27, 78; see also I.vii.6, 73; I.vii.30, 79),[41] and, without it, the market price will almost always deviate from it.[42]

It is crucial for my argument that Smith informs his readers that there are three types of *reasons* for "*deviations*, whether occasional or permanent, of the market price of commodities from the natural price" (I.vii.32, 80; emphasis added): (1) when regardless of high prices supply is limited due to natural causes (e.g. the vineyards of particular soils in France, I.vii.24, 78); (2) the existence of legal monopolies that keep the market "under-stocked, by never supplying the effectual demand" (I.vii.26, 78); (3) various trade and labor regulations that lower "competition [in a trade] to a smaller number than might otherwise go into them" (I.vii.28, 79). Smith makes it clear that these circumstances can "endure for many centuries" (I.vii.31, 79). For Smith, the difference between the latter two types of cause is just a matter of degree; trade and labor regulations are "a sort of enlarged monopolies" (I.vii.28, 79).

Note that in the quote (I.vii.28, 79) about the third type of reason on why a market price may deviate from the natural price, Smith uses *counterfactual* language. The natural path is one that *would* happen if it were not for obstacles to competition. The discussion of the natural prices is designed to promote the following question: what cause or reasons prevent the market price from falling to the natural price? And the natural response is that, except for a few goods whose supply cannot be increased, human institutions, policies, laws, etc. prevent market prices from falling to natural prices. The discrepancies between market prices and estimated natural prices are caused by human intervention.[43]

Now, a large part of the take-home message of Smith's argument in Books I and II of WN is that the natural price is not only the most efficient, but also the fairest price.[44] It is easy to see part of the argument: not only do existing regulations cause market prices to favor the well-connected few and to raise the price of all goods for all consumers hence lowering their welfare, they also provide false signals; from the vantage point of "equity" (WN I.viii.36, 96)[45] they distort investment decisions. In a way, Smith provides an argument for Montesquieu's claim that "it is competition that puts a just price on goods" (*The Spirit of the Laws*, Part 4, Book 20, Chap. 9; for mention of Montesquieu in WN, see, I.ix.17, 112–113; II.iv.9, 353' IV.ix.47, 684; and V.i.f.40, 775),[46] and a whole host of earlier writers in the Scholastic just price tradition.[47] But, by avoiding "just price" terminology with its Scholastic connotations, Smith can ignore the intellectual baggage associated with it.

So, I agree with Deborah Redman when she claims that Smith "abstracts from the real world to determine a typical – what he terms *natural* – representation of the facts." But this abstraction, which Smith presents in an extremely gentle fashion to his readers, is only the first step. By specifying *in advance* what could be a cause for a deviation of the natural price, Smith allows the "men of learning" among his readers to quantify and exploit discrepancies from these idealizations to improve his theory. Here I mean by the term "idealization" a situation that would hold exactly in certain specifiable circumstances.[48] Smith tells us to expect a gap between his theory (the natural price) and the facts (the market price); it is an invitation not only to determine the nature of and causal role human institutions play in economic life, but also to improve on his theory, if necessary.

2.2. *Newton's Fourth Rule of Reasoning*

Smith's thinking is in accord with a very important feature of Newton's methodology: empirical exceptions to general rules, even minor ones, should be investigated because they open up either the possibility of discovering interesting refinements to general rules or the possibility of formulating a more sophisticated new theory. As Newton writes:

> In experimental philosophy, propositions gathered from phenomena by induction should be considered either exactly or very nearly true notwithstanding any contrary hypotheses, until yet other phenomena make such propositions either more exact or liable to exceptions (*Principia*, Book III, Rule IV).

The Rule says that we should treat well-confirmed propositions as true (or nearly true) until there are deviations that promote new research, which, in turn, will lead us to refine our original propositions or reject them for new ones. That is, Newton accepts that physical inquiry may be *open-ended*. As he writes in the "Preface" to the *Principia*, "the principles set down here will shed some light on either this mode of philosophizing *or some truer one*" (emphasis added).[49]

It goes a bit too far to call Rule IV a principle of the fallibility of induction, as has been argued.[50] It does implicitly accept that the future may bring surprises and new evidence, and, thus, anticipates one of Hume's major insights. But it avoids Hume's skeptical conclusions.[51] Instead, Rule IV is (1) a proposal of how to treat Newton's system – that is, as true until proven otherwise – and (2) an encouragement to find and exploit known deviations from the regularities he has established in order to make them "more exact." It is true that Newton recognizes in the last three words of the first sentence of Rule IV that regularities can have exceptions.[52] But, regardless what Newton means by "phenomena" and "hypotheses," all he is saying in the Rule 4, and this is clearly stated in the second sentence, is that *one must not be distracted by possible differing explanations for the found regularities until one has empirical reason* to do so.

2.3. Smith on Descartes' Neglect of Deviations

I have no direct evidence that Smith found his method by reading Newton, but it is not unlikely.[53] Elsewhere, I showed that Smith was a very astute reader of Newton in the "Astronomy."[54] Nevertheless, as Smith's original editors recognized, in the "Astronomy," Smith's treatment of Newton is not exhaustive. One could reasonably doubt that Smith learned to think about the evidential import of deviations from regularities by reading Newton. I do not have conclusive evidence for this. But this does not mean there is no evidence at all. For, in this section, I present Smith's *criticism* of Descartes' methodology. This shows that Smith was aware of the methodology that I ascribe to him, regardless of its source.

To show the significance, for science – in Smith's philosophy of science – of discrepancies between scientific theories and data, it is useful to remind us of his psychological account of how science works. We learn from the "Astronomy" that for Smith there are two related species of wonder. First, "single and individual objects . . . excite our Wonder when, by their uncommon qualities they make us uncertain to what species of things we ought to refer them" ("Astronomy," 40, II¶5). Second, "Wonder arises from an unusual succession of things. The stop which is thereby given to the career of the imagination, the difficulty which it finds in passing along such disjointed objects, and the feeling of something like a gap or interval betwixt them, constitute the whole essence of this emotion" (II¶9, 42). Both species of wonder have in common that, to an expert,[55] there is a deviation from a pattern we would expect (II¶11, 45).

Now, "new and singular" events ("Astronomy," II¶3, 39) or unusual relations (II¶6, 40) excite wonder in people's imagination and make the mind's customary procession between connecting principles falter; this causes "uncertainty and anxious curiosity" (II¶4, 40) even "discomfort" and "tumult" in the "imagination" (II¶12, 45, 46). The discomfort caused by the appearance(s) of exceptions to general order first motivates inquiry.[56] It is a validation of my general strategy, of connecting remarks in the "Astronomy" with WN, that Smith provides a very similar account in WN (V.i.f.24–26, 767–770, although the emphasis on discomfort is absent), thus suggesting considerable continuity between the two works. It is noteworthy that in the account of WN, Smith discusses both "natural" and "moral philosophy" (V.i.f.26, 767–768), clearly implying that his psychological approach covers both areas. It is this that justifies my appropriation of the material of the "Astronomy" while interpreting WN. Of course, Smith does acknowledge historical differences (natural philosophy came first, see V.i.f.24, 768) and believes that, in contrast to natural philosophy, where "absurd and ridiculous" systems can gain widespread credence, entirely false moral systems would never find any widespread acceptance (*The Theory of Moral Sentiments* (TMS) VII.ii.4.14, 313–314).[57]

Here, I call special attention to a striking passage in the "Astronomy."[58] Smith explains the downfall of the Cartesian system in terms of its inability and unwillingness to deal with the "detailed motions and all the minute irregularities" of the heavenly bodies. In the "Astronomy," Smith points out that Descartes' theory does not explain these deviations from general rules, but attempts to explain them away:

> So far, therefore, from accommodating his [i.e. Descartes'] system to all the minute irregularities, which Kepler has ascertained in the movements of the Planets; *or from shewing, particularly, how these irregularities, and no other, should arise from it*, he contented himself with observing, that perfect uniformity could not be expected in their motions, from the nature of the causes which produced them; that certain irregularities might take place in them, for a great number of successive revolutions, and afterwards give way to others of a different kind: a remark which, happily, relieved him from the necessity of applying his system to the observations of Kepler, and the other Astronomers (IV¶66, 97; emphasis added).

Now one may think that what Smith says here about Kepler is a bit strange because what Kepler had "ascertained" were mostly *regularities* – which regularities Descartes ignored (or rather, he denied that regularities could exist in this domain), contenting himself with irregularities *instead*. But, recall that Kepler's regularities were irregularities from the dominant "rational" view among astronomers when Kepler wrote; Kepler pointed to elliptical rather than circular orbits of planets.[59] Nevertheless, the passage clearly shows that Smith is aware of the importance of pursuing empirical accuracy and exactitude in judging systems.[60] Elsewhere, he criticizes Descartes for claiming that it was not necessary "to suppose, that they [the orbits of the planets] described with geometrical accuracy, or even that they described always precisely the same figure. It rarely happens, that nature can be mathematically exact with regard to figure of the objects she produces" (IV¶64, 95). Of course, the need to accommodate one's theory "to all the minute irregularities" is akin to what we would call careful curve-fitting, but what Smith has in mind is not merely curve-fitting. The passage from IV¶66, 97, also shows he thinks that it is a legitimate requirement on a system that it should provide a *systematic* account of how discrepancies from regularities can arise within it. He means by this that a theory should both explain what would count as evidence for or against it, and what type of deviations from regularities one could expect and explain with it. Smith implies about Cartesian style theorizing that it does not have a feedback mechanism to allow empirical failures to improve one's theory.

Hence, it is not surprising that, in the "Astronomy," Smith calls attention to how deviations from Ptolemy's, Almamon's, and the Alphonsine tables, inspired corrections to Ptolemy's system (IV¶26, 70–71). Moreover, he emphasizes how inquiry gets started in response to perceived "gaps" in chains of events (e.g. II¶8–9, 41–43, IV¶7, 58, and IV¶60, 91). Smith is getting at how the search for discrepancies from expected and clearly specified regularities can lead to refinement of existing or development of new theory. This is very Newtonian.[61] A good theory may even lead to not only a qualitative change in the questions asked, but also to fundamentally different kinds of questions and criteria by which they are judged.[62]

It is useful to draw a contrast with Smith's celebrated contemporary, d'Alembert. (We know that Smith read and personally knew d'Alembert.)[63] In the *Preliminary Discourse to the Encyclopedia* (1751), d'Alembert also advocated that unusual events, or "monsters" (146),[64] required special attention. He even thought they ought to be the topic of a special branch of natural history: "Errors or deviations of nature." But, in the *Preliminary Discourse* d'Alembert was blind to the idea that they could be useful in refining the regularities found in nature. (In fact, the only use d'Alembert saw for "monsters" was "to pass from the prodigies of nature's deviations to the marvels of art," at 146.)[65] So, while d'Alembert emphasized the importance of exactitude in science (95), he missed one of the most important benefits to be derived from it. If the empirical world cooperates, precision and exactitude allow one to get ever more rigorous about deviant data in order to marshal such data as potential evidence for better theories.

3. POSITING A "NATURAL COURSE" OF EVENTS: INSTITUTIONS AND HUMAN NATURE

3.1. The Role of Institutions (1)

The theoretical fiction of a "natural price" not only calls attention to the distorting influences of human institutions, but it also points to an approach that can make evident the causes of the wealth of nations. Adam Smith's science postulates the existence of the natural price and, more broadly, the natural course of economic development. Invoking the language of nature is obviously partly done for rhetorical purposes; to many 18th century readers, deviations from nature will have seemed corrupt and flawed.[66] But discrepancies from the natural course of things also put the spotlight on the causes of wealth formation and retardation: human institutions (recall my discussion above of I.vii.24–31, 78–80).[67] As Smith writes at the start of Book III:

> That order of things which necessity imposes in general, though not in every particular country, is, in every particular country, promoted by the natural inclinations of man. If *human institutions*

had never thwarted those natural inclinations, the towns *could* nowhere have increased beyond what the improvement and cultivation of the territory in which they were situated could support; till such time, at least, as the whole of that territory was completely cultivated and improved (WN III.i.3, 377; emphasis added; cf. III.i.4, 378).

Notice, again, that Smith uses counterfactual language to make his point. In this case, Smith explains that it is the workings of institutions that prevent the natural course of things from taking place. Now, even a casual glance at the chapter heading in Book V "Of the Publick Works and Institutions for facilitating Commerce of the Society," suggests that Smith used the term "Institution" rather widely. For Smith human institutions include roads, bridges, canals, harbors, companies, schools, universities, religious orders/ministries, the monarchy, the armed forces, slavery, taxation policies, and legal arrangements (especially on land and inheritance of property).[68]

In Book III of WN, Smith lays out what he takes the natural, albeit not inevitable, course of civilizations to be; in the quote from III.i.3, 377, necessity only works its course "in general." Smith is also adamant that "the manners and customs" that a government introduces can also cause an "unnatural and retrograde order" even long after the government has changed (III.i.9, 380).

3.2. Human Nature

In III.i.3, 377, Smith also speaks of the "natural inclinations of man."[69] It is important to realize how *weak* Smith's assumptions about human nature are that drive his account.[70] Let us take a brief detour to look at them. People have, according to Smith, a "propensity to truck, barter, and exchange one thing for another" (WN I.ii.1, 25; in TMS, Smith calls attention to many other propensities, see, e.g. I.11.2.5, 33; I.ii.5.2, 42; I.iii.1.4, 44, and IV.2.11, 192).[71] Smith officially remains agnostic whether this propensity is the "necessary consequence of the faculties of reason and speech" or something more fundamental to human nature. And this agnosticism is defended because "it belongs not to our present subject to enquire."[72] That is to say, Smith wants the reader to accept certain aspects of human nature as unobjectionable. One of those things is, for example, that in a (large) commercial society a person must *usually* appeal through speech and other behavior to the self-interest of many strangers to get anything done (I.ii.2, 25–27). To accept this much, Smith believes, one need not argue about anything as complex as human nature, about the inner workings of which the science of his time was still largely ignorant (see "Of the External Senses," EPS, ¶37, 146, and also ¶42, 147–148).[73] Smith thought human nature was not stable enough to be a foundation for, to use Hume's phrase, a "Science of Man."[74] (See also Smith's mention of the "levity and inconstancy of human nature" at WN I.viii.31, 93.)[75] So, even if one believes that TMS develops substantive views about human nature, Smith's argument in WN need not rely on it.

All Smith needs, then, is to find a steady propensity (or set of propensities) that will average out over most people during the course of time. Smith finds this in the propensity to barter, for example, in the service of "bettering one's condition" (see, e.g. II.iii.28, 341).[76] In economic affairs, when we address ourselves to, say, bakers and butchers, we appeal not to their "humanity, but to their self-love, and never talk of our own necessities but of their advantages" (I.ii.2, 27).[77]

Elsewhere I have argued[78] that a crucial assumption of Smith in his account of the development of the "Impartial Spectator" is the fundamental *uncertainty* that each of us has about our *own* judgments (TMSIII.2.24 & III.2.28, 126–127; cf "Astronomy," II¶4, 40). This inner uncertainty is matched by the uncertainty of the theorist. (Recognition of the inconstancy of human nature may drive Smith's vision; cf. the student notes collected in LRBL, Lecture 28, ii 191–192, 171.) For the theorist's fundamental uncertainty about human behavior underlies Smith's system of natural liberty in which "[T]he sovereign is completely discharged from a duty, in the attempting to perform which he must always be exposed to innumerable delusions, and for *the proper performance of which no human wisdom or knowledge could ever be sufficient*; the duty of superintending the industry of private people and of directing it towards the employments most suitable to the interest of society" (WN IV.ix.51, 687; emphasis added). Moreover, the causes driving individual human actions are too diverse (and stubborn!) to be directed from above. As he writes in TMS: "[I]n the great chess-board of human society, every single piece has a principle of motion of its own,[79] altogether different that which the legislature might chuse to impress upon it" (TMSVI.ii.2.17–8, 234).[80] Hence, Smith saw that the problem of state direction of the economy is not only computationally intractable (as suggested by WN IV.ix.51, 687), but that the legislator also has no reliable source of information about most individuals (as implied by TMS, VI.ii.2.17–8, 234). Therefore, for Smith, "[T]he law ought always trust people with the care of their own, Interest, as in their local situations they must generally be able to judge better of it than the legislator can do" (WN IV.v.b, 531; for similar comments: V.ii.c.18, 833). This shows that one reason for Smith's argument in favor of relatively[81] unregulated markets is epistemic: individuals will have better knowledge of their own circumstances than the ruler will.[82] The epistemic weakness of the rulers shows up in other places as well. When in Book V of WN Smith discusses efficient and just ways to collect taxes, he often notes that reliable information is not available, and that it would require an "inquisition" on the part of the magistrate to obtain it (V.ii.f.5–9, 848–50; V.ii.g.4, 853; V.ii.j.2, 867).[83]

An important source of information, that individuals will rely on, is, the market. (It is not the only source because Smith also talks about the importance of knowing the characters of participants in the marketplace as well; see, e.g. II.ii.62, 305–306.) Only the market can, given the right circumstances, provide, to use a modern phrase, an effective signaling system (e.g. IV.v.b.24–25, 533–534). However, Smith does not attribute any magical powers to "the haggling and bargaining of the market," because he notes that it only works "according to that sort of rough equality which, though not exact, is sufficient for carrying on the business of common life" (I.v.4, 49). This quote connects with the wider theme in this paper: notice that here Smith is relying on a distinction between common life and another more exact realm – presumably (mathematical) science. Smith is, in fact, pointing out that markets are good enough for the business of common life, but that the data they provide are insufficient for a more exact enterprise. The concern with exactitude shows up again shortly thereafter: "[A]t the same time and place, therefore, money is the exact measure of the real exchangeable value of all commodities. It is so, however, at the same time and place only" (I.v.19, 55).[84] Smith is aware that the prices provided by market exchange only offer exactitude in a very limited sense. All of this suggests that the "men of learning" of his time, with an interest in constructing an exact science, should not focus exclusively on markets. What is unclear is if Smith thought that this was due to some principled reason about the nature of markets or if this was exclusively due to the limited character of the data provided by the markets in his day. Either way, this provides another reason to think, that in the context of developing a system to account for the phenomena, Smith's focus was not solely on markets but also on other institutions.

The individual actors of WN are themselves deceived or largely ignorant actors whose views of the whole are blocked (e.g. the very first example of WN, in which the division of labor puts different branches of work in different workhouses; I.i.2–3, 14).[85] Often, ordinary folks, do not have an adequate grasp of "abstract" economic notions (I.v.5, 49). Just as in Smith's moral theory people are often self-deceived and partial to themselves (TMS III.iv.1.9–10, 183), in WN, people tend to overestimate their own luck and make decisions on incomplete information (e.g. WN I.x.b.26, 124ff).[86] Moreover, they are open to peer-pressure and bouts of vanity; this is how Smith explains, for example, the maintenance of cartels among employers (WN I.viii.13, 84; see also V.i.f.4, 759–760).[87] Yet, for Smith, people are not just a collection of dunces; in his theory individuals also make sound economic decisions based on their realization that they have limited capacity to track capital and goods.[88]

Earlier I said that Smith claims that the causes driving individual human actions are very diverse. It is tempting to read TMS as an account of what those causes are; it provides a rich phenomenology of the roles sympathy, ambition, vanity, benevolence, custom, fashion, self-approbation, justice, remorse, etc. play in human life.[89]

3.3. The Role of Institutions (2)

Let us return to the main argument. Induced from the "natural inclinations of man," (III.1.3, 377) Smith provides an idealized picture of how societies "naturally" develop.[90] Stock must first be saved in a hunting or shepherding society, before it can be directed to agriculture, then afterwards to manufactures, and finally to foreign commerce (III.i.8, 380).[91] The rest of Book III is an exploration of why and how this natural path was not followed in Europe after the fall of the Roman Empire.[92] In doing this, Smith is put in a position to provide a subtle picture of how wealth is created given certain fairly stable background conditions (e.g. location, climate, geography, etc.). The core of Book III is an account of legal frameworks and political arrangements that retard or encourage the "natural course" of things.[93] Once one pays attention one sees these themes present in Books I-II, also. See, for example, Smith's remark that "China seems to have been long stationary, and had probably long ago acquired that full complement of riches which is consistent with the nature of its laws and institutions. But this complement may be much inferior to what, with other laws and institutions, the nature of its soil, climate, and situation might admit of" (I.ix.15, 111–112; I.viii.24, 89 and IV.ix.40, 679–80).

So, instead of being merely a curious historical/sociological side-show that illustrates Smith's wide range of interests, Book III is on my reading central to the science that Smith attempts to found.[94] It is only a first stab at providing explanations of the comparative and historical performances of various European countries. In Book V, he takes the lessons he has learned, including the law of unintended consequences, and applies them in his proposed design for many institutions.

My reading offers, thus, indirect evidence for Nathan Rosenberg's thesis about the systematic vision underlying Smith's policy recommendations: to provide "an exact, detailed specification of an optimal institutional structure," so that market forces could operate in a beneficent fashion. Rosenberg had argued that, throughout WN, Smith provides "details of the institutional structure, which will best harmonize the individual's pursuit of his selfish interests with the broader interests of society."[95]

3.4. Model, Cause and Process

I found Smith's discussion at WN I.vii.20–32, 77–80 (quoted before) striking because after sketching an abstract "natural" model, Smith systematically laid

out what causes could create "deviations, whether occasional or permanent, of
the market price of commodities from the natural price" (I.vii.32, 80). Future
researchers are in the position to do empirical work on measuring the extent of
these causes. Down the road, this research can stimulate revision, if necessary, to
the ideal model. A small scale revision would be the discovery of causes other than
institutions; this would be welcome, for it would not require wholesale change to
the theoretical structure. It could be accommodated by merely adding the nature
and extent, permanent or occasional, of this newly discovered cause to the list of
possible deviations. One circumstance in which larger-scale revision would happen
is if it turned out that Smith has ignored dominant causes that need to be accounted
for, not merely as causes of deviation, but as elements of the "natural" model; one
could imagine this to be the case if serious empirical flaws were found in his
assumptions about human nature (e.g. when factor owners would systematically
fail to be responsive to available higher sources of income) or if, say, the nature of
exchange changed dramatically in technologically advanced societies.

But even if we ignore the most abstract level of Smith's theory, the
methodological structure of Smith's theory, i.e. postulate a "natural" course and
systematically stipulate causes that can make it deviate, is recapitulated on the
component level (wages, rents, profits, etc.) of his natural price analysis (WN
I.viii-xi.d, 82–193). For example, after presenting a quick account of the origin of
wage-labor (I.viii.1–10, 82–83), Smith provides a general model of the nature
of property-wage relationships and how the circumstances of society effect price
of labor (I.viii.11–57, 83–103).[96] The crucial point is that the "money price of labor
is necessarily regulated by two circumstances; the demand for labour, and the price
of the necessaries and conveniences of life" (I.viii.52, 103; the latter circumstance
acts as a kind of constraint on the former). But shortly hereafter, Smith explains,
while employing counterfactual language, that the model he had just provided is
an idealized one; it only "would be the case in a society where things were left
to follow their natural course, where there was perfect liberty, and where every
man was perfectly free both to chuse what occupation he thought proper, and to
change it as often as he thought proper" (I.x.1, 116). Smith recognizes two different
kinds of causes that can produce deviations from the natural course of things: (1)
those "arising from the Nature of the Employments themselves" (I.x.b, 116–135)
and more important and (2) those "occasioned by the policy [i.e. administrative
rules] of Europe" (I.x.c, 135–159). Each kind of cause gets, in turn, sub-divided
in particular causes all of which receive extensive treatment.

Now, we are in a better position to understand what at least one type of cause is
in Smith's thought: it is the institution or process that can push the natural course
of things from its path. Identifying the operation of such courses is crucial to
Smith's enterprise. There is no reason to presuppose that such causes must be in

strict accord with Hume's (2000) definitions at *Treatise*, 1.3.14.31 (i.e. contiguity of cause and effect, priority of cause over effect, and constant conjunction of cause and event; see also *Treatise*, 1.3, Sections 2, 6, and 15). In fact, it is likely that, according to Smith, the processes that push the natural course of things from its normal path can operate across space and time and even in a simultaneous fashion (cf. Hume's *Treatise*, 1.3.2.7–8).[97] For example, Smith believes that "Commerce and manufactures can seldom flourish long in any state which does not enjoy a regular administration of justice, in which the people do not feel themselves secure in the possession of their property, in which the faith of contracts is not supported by law, and in which the authority of the state is not supposed to be regularly employed in enforcing the payment of debts from all those who are able to pay" (WN V.iii.9, 910). So, while commerce leads to good order, some order is necessary for commerce to flourish. Smith's solution to this problem is to insist that the growth of commerce is a "gradual" and a "slow and uncertain" process during the course of centuries (III.iv.10–23, 418–26). He does not say so, but he implies that the growth of commerce and the rule of law are a concomitant process.[98] In Section 3.6, I show how Smith thinks he can distinguish real from apparent causes.

To briefly summarize: on my reading, Smith offers (a) a "natural" model (based on certain assumptions of human nature, historical change, etc.) of what would be the case under ideal circumstances with (b) a list of factors (stipulated in advance) that will cause deviations from the idealization in order to (c) stimulate research on a part of his readers, both to (d) investigate the nature and extent of these causes, and if they do not turn out to be exhaustive, to what degree there are (e) new causes that need to be incorporated in the model, which, in extremis, (f) may be revised. Smith is starting, then, an open-ended process in which one moves from theory to facts and back. At the same time, Smith's detailed presentation of his idealizations provides a richly layered, systematic structure to help organize, interpret, and understand the phenomena under scrutiny. Smith helps the majority of his readers to make sense of the world they live in, while trying to prevent the "princes" from doing inadvertent harm to the societies they govern.

3.5. Hume vs. Smith on the Introduction of Commerce

By way of contrast to Smith's method, it is worth calling attention to Hume's historical treatment of the origins of commercial society in his essay "Of Commerce." There, Hume suggests we should "consult history" to explain the growth of foreign commerce. He claims it is an empirical fact that in Europe "foreign trade has preceded any refinement in home manufactures." He goes on to suggest that natural endowments such as "soil or climate" influence what commodity gets exchanged. For Hume, the actual historical record suggests, that in most nations, foreign commerce is prior to the expansion of local manufacturing ("Of Commerce," 263–264; recall that for Smith, in the natural course of events, foreign commerce comes after the development of local manufacturing). But he provides no explanatory strategy for thinking that this observation is not merely a contingent fact. Hume provides no theoretical structure for analyzing alternative historical paths. It is for these reasons that I rate Smith's approach as methodologically superior.[99]

In general, Hume thought, "it is the chief business of philosophers to regard the general course of things" and not worry too much about "exceptions" ("Of Commerce," 254–255). Whenever Hume did find a general rule or some law-like relationship it could either be only stated in very vague terms or exceptions to it must be granted immediately. In Hume's theorizing the exceptions to such general rules could not itself provide further evidence in the development of theory; what they pointed to was the contingent nature of human history or the existence of many intervening causes that were not open to systematic investigation.[100]

Nevertheless, I do not want to give the impression that Hume was a casual Empiricist in interpreting history. Hume lets his understanding of human nature *constrain* his interpretations of the historical record. So, for example, before he introduces his discussion of the historical record regarding the relationship between foreign commerce and local manufacture, he points out "Every thing in the world is purchased by labour; and our passions are the only causes of labour" ("Of Commerce," 261).[101]

3.6. Hume's Natural Rate of Propagation and Smith's Digression on Silver

Not unlike Smith, Hume is quite serious about taking the institutional framework and "habits and manners" of a society into account when interpreting the historical record ("Of Interest," 298, and, especially, "Ancient Nations," 381ff). It is worth looking at one of Hume's most sustained efforts at doing so. In his essay "Ancient Nations," Hume points out that, when facts are uncertain, it is appropriate to "intermingle the enquiry concerning the causes with that concerning facts" (381). In this essay, Hume postulates a natural[102] rate of propagation, slightly more than a doubling in every generation of the human species. Hume *stipulates* that "everything else being equal" (vegetation, climate, etc.) this rate can only be achieved under "wise, just, and mild government" with the "wisest institutions" (382). The natural rate is, thus, for Hume an optimal rate. Hume infers what would be the case based on empirical observations of what is the case in, say, the American colonies and the quick rebound in population after plagues as well on facts about human nature (p. 381; as supplied by, for example, Hume's *Treatise*, which had been based on "experiment and observation"). In "Ancient Nations," Hume uses this natural rate to reason from facts to causes as well as from causes to facts. So, for example, if there is reliable information that population is or was increasing in some locale, this is evidence for a mild government with sound economic policy, while he will infer the converse, too. Positing the natural rate, then, allows Hume inferences about the past and present. Acceptance of the relationship between the nature of government and population also provides Hume with an important *constraint* on accepting the facts provided by various literary and political texts. (Alas, Hume does not allow historical facts to help him improve or refute the rule that he employs to interpret history with.) Hume is, thus, self-consciously offering a principled evidential strategy to deal with a situation in which only limited data are available.

In Sections 2.1 and 3.2, while discussing WN I.ix.3, 105 and I.xi.o.5, 261, I made a point of claiming that Smith was acutely conscious of the limited accuracy of data available to him. Of course, understanding how to interpret data may be just as problematic. Smith employs Hume's technique – of moving from causal theory to facts and visa versa – in at least one prominent place in WN.[103] In his very long "DIGRESSIONS CONCERNING THE VARIATIONS IN THE VALUE OF SILVER DURING THE COURSE OF THE FOUR LAST CENTURIES" at the end of the first Book of WN, Smith ingeniously employs his theory about the relationship among increase in aggregate supply (the result of increase in agricultural output, in turn, the effect of improved technology and cultivation), the price of corn (the 18th century word for edible seeds),[104] and the value of silver in order to attack Mercantilism. The "DIGRESSIONS" tries to show that inflation (in the silver price of corn) is not an inevitable consequence of growing national wealth (I.xi.n.1, 255; I.xi.e.30, 207).[105] Smith assumes that an increase in supply caused by technological improvement will cause the value of items that always produce rent to decrease in proportion to the value of items that may or may not afford some rent: "materials of cloathing and lodging, the useful fossils and minerals of earth, the precious metals and the precious stones should gradually become dearer and dearer" (I.xi.d.1, 193; Smith recognizes that changes in supply and demand can alter this relationship; see also I.xi.i.3, 234). Assuming that corn is produced under conditions of constant resource costs "in every stage of improvement" (I.xi.e.28, 206), the silver price of corn should with economic development, thus, decline. Unfortunately, for Smith, this only holds true "if particular accidents" (I.xi.d.1, 193), namely, "the accidental discovery of more abundant mines" do not interfere (I.xi.n.1, 255). So, when the rising nominal corn price can reflect rising silver production, he must have another indicator. Smith has resource to additional assumptions about the trend in the butcher's meat/corn price ratio as economies grow; a rising corn price of meat is, he believes, indicative of "progress of improvement" (I.xi.l.2, 237; I.xi.n.2–3, 256–257).

Based on these relationships, Smith can exhaustively state (I.xi.d.4–6, 194) all "possible combinations of events which happen in the progress of improvement" (I.xi.d.7, 194) as they pertain to the relative prices of silver and corn.[106] With this theoretical framework in place, and the availability of relatively reliable long-running data on the price of corn, Smith is able to impute the value of silver over a long period of time.[107] This, in turn, allows him to make an *empirical* case for the causal claims against the Mercantilists in the "conclusion" of his digression:

> As the wealth of Europe, indeed, has increased greatly since the discovery of the mines of America, so the value of gold and silver has gradually diminished. This diminution of their value, however, has not been owing to the increase of the real wealth of Europe, of the annual produce of its land and labour, but to the accidental discovery of more abundant mines than any that were known before. The increase of the quantity of gold and silver in Europe, and the increase of its manufactures and agriculture, are two events which, though they have happened nearly about the same time, yet have arisen from very different causes, and have scarce any natural connection with one another. The one has arisen from a mere accident, in which neither prudence nor policy either had or could have any share. The other from the fall of the feudal system, and from the establishment of a government which afforded to industry the only encouragement which it requires, some tolerable security that it shall enjoy the fruits of its own labour (WN I.xi.n.1, 255–256).

Smith clearly thinks that his method has enabled him to distinguish *apparent* from *real* causes and to differentiate between natural connections and mere coincidences. Hence, some of his conclusions are offered "with a degree of probability that approaches almost to certainty (I.xi.n.3, 257), while other opinions "scarce, perhaps, deserve the name of belief" (I.xi.h.11, 233). Smith can produce what he takes to be compelling counterfactual arguments because he has an abstract theory about the natural course of events.[108] It is supplemented by crucial assumptions about the relative prices of goods and the "gradual" nature by which certain causes are said to operate in the course of development (e.g. I.xi.g.19, 218). The latter are constraints on his interpretation of the historical data. In "Ancient Nations," Hume has shown the way to this method to interpret the historical record. It is no coincidence that the constraint that is employed on interpreting historical data is of the same kind that, for Smith, enables real growth in wealth: a stable institutional framework that ensures a minimal protection for income earned from labor.

3.7. Some Objections

One could object that the connection between the natural price of Book I and the natural course of things in Book III is tenuous at best. Even if one were to grant that Smith postulated both to stress the importance of institutions and with an eye toward allowing discrepancies from the natural course to provide evidence toward developing better theories, they are not identical situations. After all, the factors that make up a "natural" price, i.e. wages, rent, and profit, only exist in certain economic arrangements or stages of economic development. Specifically, there is no rent in a hunting society (V.i.b.2, 709), and many shepherd societies may not have stable property arrangements. In fact, Smith thinks that civil government is only founded in certain advanced shepherd societies (V.i.b.12, 715).[109] So, the theory being described and defended in Books I-II of WN is only applicable in a limited domain, i.e. societies with property and ones that have at least some freemen – for if all the labor were performed by slaves there would be no wages – and merchants. By contrast, the natural course of things in Book III covers several such domains. (This is not to say that certain aspects of the theory as developed in Books I-II cannot be extended or adapted to cover other periods or levels of development.) The extent of this domain is constrained by features of, say, the legal structure of the society under analysis, as it is in this case of the theory of Book I. But one can imagine that other human institutions – e.g. the existence of different modes of production or the establishment of new categories of income – will structure the contents of the possible generalizations. Because Smith's theory in Books I-II is so context sensitive to the laws and institutions of a society,[110] this may explain why there are, despite many broad qualitative generalizations, no general laws or axioms in WN.[111] This aspect of Smith's theorizing has not been appreciated sufficiently, at least in part, because Smith does not emphasize the context dependent nature of his work.[112] Moreover, Smith's theory is sufficiently broad and abstract that it can be applied to many different kinds of societies.

Another problem, one might think, is that Smith never offers a calculation of the natural price. Moreover, my interpretation clearly implies that such a calculation would be extremely difficult absent the implementation of "system of natural liberty"; on theoretical grounds, the available data are simply too limited (even if statistical techniques were to be improved). Given Smith's general mistrust of "Political Arithmetick" (recall WN IV.v.b.30, 534–5), it is extremely unlikely that Smith would have been attracted to attempting such a calculation. This is a powerful argument, but the absence of such a calculation on the part of Smith can also be explained if we remember that Smith's book has a wider audience than the "men of learning." Such a calculation would appear extremely "abstruse," and its technical difficulty would cause significant *rhetorical* difficulties for Smith's political program, which relied, in part, on the compelling simplicity of the "natural system of liberty." Interestingly, if this system is implemented, the calculations required would also become more tractable. Smith's political project, thus, makes a "science of Man" more possible.

Two further objections present themselves to the reading proposed here. First I cannot provide compelling textual support from WN that my reconstruction of Smith's strategy is accurate. I may be ascribing intentions to Smith's theorizing he did not have. That would devalue the historical significance of my reading, especially if none of Smith's contemporaries or successors saw things this way. Nevertheless, I have shown that, if one wants to learn about evidential strategies in what we call the social sciences, WN is not a bad place to start.

Finally, one could object to my reading that the distinction between natural and market prices is already present in the student notes we have from his "Lectures on Jurisprudence." These provide no evidence that the interpretation I am offering was on Smith's mind then. But this objection is not that worrisome. After all, in his lectures, Smith was not presenting his theory to "men of learning," but to young pupils. Moreover, it would not be the only time that, when it came to the material on prices, Smith changed his mind on important issues between presenting the "Lectures" and publishing WN.[113]

It is a virtue of my reading that I can not only avoid making Smith look confused about something that had been a life-long interest, but also show how Smith can be seen as forward-looking. On my view whole chunks of WN become part of his science and not just interesting asides.

4. SMITH'S PHILOSOPHY OF SCIENCE

In this part, I demonstrate that my interpretation of WN is in the spirit of Smith's views on science. I rely largely on the essays presented in EPS. These texts show that Smith thought: *that scientific theories were in an important sense, research tools; that scientific theorizing was an open-ended enterprise of successive approximations.* If I can prove that then my reconstruction of Smith's strategy in WN gains some additional credibility. I discuss these claims in two different sections. Elsewhere, I argue that for Smith science is an open-ended process.[114] So, here I limit myself to the other elements.

4.1. Machines

For Smith, "philosophy is the science of the connecting principles of nature" ("Astronomy," II¶12, 45); or, as he put it slightly differently elsewhere in the "Astronomy": philosophy should "give some coherence to the appearances of nature" (II¶9, 43).[115] It does this by proposing theories that appeal to the imagination. Smith's "Astronomy" is an examination of what psychological factors play an important role in this process.[116]

In the "Astronomy," Smith claims that the systems of philosophers "in many respects resemble machines . . . A system is an imaginary machine" (IV¶19, 66).[117] In the division of labor that Smith diagnoses, systems are (perhaps, among other things) the products of the philosopher's labour (WN I.1.9, 21–22 and V.i.f.26–34, 769–773). The comparison between machines and the systems of philosophers pertains in Smith's use to their similar pattern of development, that is, that there is a trade-off between simplicity of principles and expansion of application.[118] It is important to note that, for Smith, this relates to the development of an accepted theory. The replacement of one theory with the next, a "revolution" in his own language, is motivated, among other things, by the fact that the new theory has simpler principles and a wider application (of predictions, etc.; "Astronomy," IV¶18–19).[119]

The idea that scientific theories can be compared to machines goes back at least to Bacon, for whom they were, among other things, instruments that guide research.[120] Smith's own usage was probably inspired by Bishop Berkeley, whom, given the attention Smith lavishes on him in "Of the External Senses," Smith apparently had read carefully.

Following Berkeley (Section 65 of *Principles*), we can say that the machine metaphor emphasizes two things: (i) the constructed nature of philosophic systems – they are inventions that change over time, and this is, in fact, one of the major themes of the "Astronomy."[121] Smith also intends the comparison among machines, systems, and languages to imply that the pattern of development is a *gradual* affair, at least until a revolution takes place ("Languages," 223–224). (ii) Systems are effective ways to convey abundant information – they provide efficient explanatory accounts. By attempting to expose nature's "connection principles" and to represent "the invisible chains which bind together all these disjointed objects," natural philosophy is, in Smith's view, designed to appeal to, and calm, people's imagination ("Astronomy," II¶12, 45–46). For Smith, explanation that gains widespread acceptance often seems to consist in proving the existence of a connecting chain from some unusual event, say an eclipse, "to the ordinary course of things" ("Astronomy," II¶9, 43). Of course, the scientific theories that manage to knot together unusual events with the ordinary course of things may themselves be counterintuitive:

For, though it is the end of Philosophy, to allay that wonder, which either the unusual or seemingly disjointed appearances of nature excite, yet she never triumphs so much, as when, in order to connect together a few, in themselves, perhaps, inconsiderable objects, she has, if I may so, created another constitution of things, more easily attended to, but more new, more contrary to common opinion and expectation, than any of those appearances themselves ("Astronomy," IV¶33, 75).

Smith seems to be claiming that it can be a mark of a successful theory that it is unexpected, even surprising. Such a theory, "another constitution of things," itself will almost certainly create a feeling of wonder and surprise.[122] Among "men of learning" this can induce a new round of reflections on the metaphysical or conceptual foundations of such a system. Finally, we can add a third feature that the machine metaphor brings out, harking back to Bacon's use: systems are *tools* to engage in further research.[123]

4.2. Successive Approximations

Smith's account in the "Astronomy" of the successive adoptions of various systems of nature makes clear that the development of all such systems has a fairly predictable sequence: a system is designed by the imagination to provide coherence to the appearances, thus soothing the imagination. As time passes, either irregularities are discovered and successive, gradual modifications are introduced into the system leading toward more complexity (eventually, new requirements are put on the system), or new phenomena are discovered which lead to conflicting accounts or dissatisfaction. This dissatisfaction, combined with the ambition (vanity, etc.) of the philosophers, makes it likely that the system will be replaced by a new system, and so the cycle starts anew.[124]

There is some evidence that Smith viewed his own relationship to previous contributions to political economy as a closer approximation to the truth. In WN, in the process of an extensive, critical discussion of the Physiocratic system, popular in France, he was led to remark:

> This system, however, with all its imperfections is, perhaps, *the nearest approximation* to the truth that has been yet published upon the subject of political oeconomy, and is upon that account well worth the consideration of every man who wishes to examine with attention the principles of that very important science (WN IV.ix.38, 678–679, emphasis added).

Smith greatly admired the Physiocrats; according to Dugald Stewart, Smith's first biographer, Smith would have dedicated WN to Quesnay, "the very ingenious and profound author of this [physiocratic] system" (WN IV.ix.27, 672), if the French physician had lived).[125] There is no doubt, however, that he thought he had advanced beyond the Physiocrats (IV.ix.50, 687).[126]

Perhaps Smith thinks that he had achieved the truth, and no mere approximation to truth, about political economy.[127] WN is obviously written in a confident tone – recall how Smith is willing to assert his views "with a degree of probability that approaches almost to certainty" at I.xi.n.3, 257. Nevertheless, I have showed above that the estimation of a "natural price" can only be achieved through a sort of process of successive approximation. Again, this is very Newtonian. For example, one first employs market prices of wages and rents and interest rates to figure out what the natural price would be in a given set of circumstances. Then, one must imagine how removal or reform of various institutions would impact the profit, wage, and rent rates, etc.

5. CONCLUSION

Then Smith must have hoped that future generations of "men of learning" would see that discrepancies from his postulated natural course of things, themselves could provide evidence for the construction of better theories. Although the principles of his theory are derived from some broad empirical generalizations and ingenious use of counterfactual reasoning, the theory itself can be improved through empirical and historical research. Smith even points to the empirical tools that should make this research possible, even if he himself only partially executes this. His system is not the last word, but the foundation for an ambitious program of research. Meanwhile, it provides grounds for economic reform to benefit the working poor.[128]

There is no denying the scope of Smith's ambitions. Upon the book's publication several commentators explicitly compared his achievement to Newton's.[129] It is not impossible of course that Smith himself thought he had achieved this. (Smith was modest in public.) Without wishing to downplay Smith's achievements as an empirical researcher and theorist, Smith could have hoped that his work was only a start of a new line of research; he expects his theory to be refined by better and more focused empirical data. If my thesis is correct then Smith explicitly designed his theory with this goal in mind. Admittedly, I have read my thesis into the WN in order to make it *coherent*; I have drawn on many apparently disparate elements in the book to do so. Others can give my reconstruction careful scrutiny and use it as a starting point for their research into the methods of WN.

There is a good reason why there is no discussion of methodological and evidential strategies in WN. If Smith had heavily advertised to the "men of learning" the provisional aspect of his project, he could have been fearful that would undermine the political and economic proposals he advocated. What appeals to "men of learning" can undermine rhetorical effectiveness when dealing with princes.

Here, I end by noting that, despite having all of his notebooks burned, Smith made sure that his EPS, which present his most explicit thoughts on scientific method, would be published.[130] As far as I can tell these essays were ignored by later theorists of political economy.[131] Even so, even without EPS, a careful reading of WN can help us figure out what Smith was trying to achieve. We cannot fault Smith that his successors chose not to focus on his strategy to build a science.

NOTES

1. All my quotes are from Adam Smith's *Essays on Philosophical Subjects* (EPS). Edited by W. P. D. Wightman and J. C. Bryce.
2. Schumpeter (1954) and Rothbard (1995) follow Schumpeter and insist that Smith's influence *retarded* the development of economics. Others have accused Smith of plagiarism (Rashid, 1990).
3. All my quotes are from *An Inquiry into the Nature and Causes of the Wealth of Nations* (WN). Edited by R. H. Campbell and A. S. Skinner.
4. For a different, albeit stimulating, approach, see Redman (1997, Chap. 5). I will occasionally offer criticism of Redman's views in my footnotes, but I do not do justice to the richness of her work.
5. My understanding of Newton has been shaped by the writings of and discussion with I. Bernard Cohen, Howard Stein, and George E. Smith (to be cited below).
6. All my references to and quotes from essays by David Hume are to *Essays, Moral, Political, and Literary* (EMPL). Revised edition edited by Eugene F. Miller.
7. The notion of a natural rate looks circular here. I will discuss this below.
8. This is an oversimplification. Strictly speaking it is a composite of rents, wages, profits, and the cost of raw materials and instruments used up but the latter resolves itself ("immediately or ultimately") into one of the three component parts. Smith explicitly rejects the idea that there is a fourth part to the natural rate (WN I.vi.11, 68).
9. Smith wrote in a time when the service part of the economy was not very developed yet, although it is surprising he does not mention it in the early chapters of WN because he later devotes considerable space to banking, insurance, education, and law. For useful comments on the relationship, if any, between "annual produce" and a modern conception of "national income," see O'Donnell (1990, 30ff).
10. One might think that that there were natural prices for some goods in Smith's time. But even if there were free markets in a particular commodity, the factors of production would still be influenced by the obstacles in other markets. For the systemic element in Smith's understanding see references to Skinner (1979, 1996), and my discussion below.
11. Cf. Turgot ([1770] 1889, §XC), where competition is absent.
12. One may be tempted to claim that Smith thought that the *rate* of growth determines the rate of profit, but Smith thought that the unusual circumstance of the American colonies (abundant fertile land, unusually low prices for land, etc.) was an exception that proved the rule. Of course, the rate of growth can influence the rate of profit for Smith.
13. In fact, Smith claims that the political backwardness of the lower classes and the landed classes *vis à vis* the merchant-class is due to their inability to understand their own interests in the context of the State as a whole even though theirs better coincide with it (WN I.xi.p.7–10, 265–267; much of WN is one big lament on how the merchants and tradesmen have hijacked the economic instruments of State to their own advantage). The causes for the failure of the workers and the landholders to properly understand their own interests and

how they are affected by regulations are not identical. Smith thinks that the former often lack basic education and are too overworked to gather and properly analyze the necessary information; Smith speaks of "the torpor of mind" of the common laborer that the division of labor will engender (V.i.f.50, 781). The latter are often spoiled by luxury which makes their minds "incapable of that application . . . which is necessary in order to foresee and understand the consequences of any publick regulation" (I.xi.p.8, 265; see also I.xi.a.1, 223 and V.ii.c.13, 831). For more discussion, see my Schliesser (2004, forthcoming-b) "Adam Smith's Conception."

14. There were probably very few regulations that would aid the workers. As Smith writes, "Whenever the legislature attempts to regulate the differences between masters and their workmen, its counsellors are always the masters. When the *regulation*, therefore, is *in favour* of the *workmen*, *it is always just and equitable*; but it is sometimes otherwise when in favour of the masters" (WN I.x.c.61, 157–158; emphasis added). See Pack (1991, pp. 18, 39), and Schliesser (2002, Chap. 5), for more discussion.

15. Jen Boobar has suggested that Smith's relative optimism on this score may also be due to the fact that many rents were paid in corn, thus, standardizing measurement.

16. Sam Fleischacker called my attention to these examples; see also his 2004 book (pp. 36–44) for more detailed discussion.

17. See Redman (1997, pp. 142–151) for an introduction to the ideas of Petty, King, and Davenant, especially. See also her account of Smith's views on Political Arithmetic (pp. 230–233).

18. In a complex commercial society it is difficult to calculate "real" prices directly without solid data: "the current prices of labour at distant times and places can scarce ever be known with any degrees of exactness." Contrast this with the "exact measure" that nominal prices provide at a given time and place at I.v.19,55. Smith chose the price of corn (the 18th century word for edible seeds) as a second-best way of measuring the real price of things: "Those [prices] of corn, though they have in few places been regularly recorded are in general better known and have been more frequently taken notice of by historians and other writers. We must generally, therefore, content ourselves with them, not as being always exactly in the same proportion as the current prices of labour, but as being the nearest approximation which can commonly be had to that proportion" (WN I.v.22, 56). See Hollander (1973, p. 129, n. 46) and Hueckel (2002, p. 321). For more on Smith's employment of corn as a measure of welfare of the poor, see Schliesser (2002, Chap. 5, II.B).

19. See Mirowski (1982, p. 116), where he cites Tucker (1960, Chaps 4–5).

20. There is another problem in Smith: when he writes about "the profit of stock" he sometimes means the rate of profit and not the total amount of profit. (See Mirowski (1982, Note 10), where G. S. L. Tucker is cited.) In general, the context makes it clear what he means.

21. Cf. Hume's "Of Interest," 303: "And thus, if we consider the whole connexion of causes and effects, interest is the barometer of the state, and its lowness a sign almost infallible of the flourishing condition of a people."

22. Turgot ([1770] 1889, §LXXXIX).

23. Mirowski's (1982) empirical research into the accounting ledgers of 19 British firms of the period lends support for this assertion.

24. Smith is not contradicting himself by claiming, on the one hand, that short term interest rates are determined by the supply and demand of loanable funds, while, on the other

hand claiming, interest rates themselves can be analyzed into two different components. Cf. Turgot ([1770] 1889, §LXXIII), where he insists that interest is a form of compensation for opportunities (of profit or revenue) foregone.

25. Incidentally, at II.iv.17, 358, we learn that the rate of interest influences the price of land, so indirectly at least, interest rates will influence the size of the rent (IV.vii.c58, 611). Moreover, if the natural price of a commodity is the result of adding up its constitutive components then high rent will cause high prices, and so on. I can only give a glimpse of the interconnected relationship of all factors in Smith's system. See Skinner (1979, 1996) for more details.

26. Part of Smith's argument against the Colonial monopolies is that it raises the rate of profit in one sector and advances its interests at the expense of all other sectors by hurting their rate of profit (IV.vii.c.60, 612). Some critics have been puzzled by an element of Smith's argument. For though he clearly shows that other sectors – and consumers in general – are hurt by the monopoly trade, it could be the case that the exorbitant profits from the colonial trade raise the general rate of profit. Smith has no trouble conceding this, while still maintaining his polemic against monopolies. After all, he makes it clear in WN that high rates of profit are, in general, a bad thing. It is only readers that presuppose that Smith is a spokesperson for the profit-seeking class that will see a paradox here.

27. Marx (1963, Part II, p. 229), complains about this.

28. This implies that the natural price of a commodity only changes when the circumstances of a society change, see O'Donnell (1990, pp. 90, 96).

29. Cf. O'Donnell (1990, 10ff., pp. 85, 157, 214–218). O'Donnell accepts Marx's indictment of Smith on this score. The following paragraphs are supposed to give a response.

30. Ricardo and his followers would echo this criticism. Historically, clearing up this confusion may have produced a research program of mathematical economics, but this may not be what Smith intended.

31. O'Donnell (1990, pp. 89, 90) claims that in Smith the market price is the short period, while the natural price is the long period (WN I.vii.4–7, 72–73).

32. Many commentators note the indebtedness of Smith to Petty and the Physiocrats, especially Cantillon and Turgot. Yet neither their *Le prix véritable* nor *Le prix mitoyen* conforms to Smith's understanding of natural price; see Turgot ([1770] 1889, §XXXI and §XXXII). Turgot's notion of *Le Prix fondamental* (see his letter to Hume, March 25, 1767) comes very close because it includes the wages and profits (but not rent). But Turgot views it as a minimum price below which the market price cannot fall; this is not true in Smith's theory. Hume also employs the phrase "natural price" in "Of Taxes" (EMPL, 345) but does so in a casual fashion.

33. Smith does not think this is merely a hypothetical situation (I.viii.26, 92; I.viii.40, 98; V.ii.k.7–8, 872–3; for a discussion of other causes of famine see, IV.v.b.6–9, 526–8). A declining populace would shrink demand and this, in turn (setting off a vicious cycle), would shrink the division of labor, etc. For a contextual discussion of Smith's views on famine, see Rothschild (2001, pp. 73–86).

34. Of course, changes in technology and productivity or supply factors can alter the natural price; see O'Donnell (1990, p. 255, n. 26).

35. A reader suggested that Smith's repeated use of "sometimes" indicated that Smith did not believe that in general the market prices will be more frequently above the natural price than below it. It is true that Smith never claims this explicitly. But in the immediate context of this passage Smith focuses on systematically discussing causes

that raise the market price above the natural price, while he largely ignores those that lower it.

36. Hollander (1973) and O'Donnell (1990) offer conflicting accounts. Cf. Redman (1997, p. 218), for brief, useful comments.

37. While Smith uses imagery that is often suggestive of an equilibrium model, his only explicit mention of the word "equilibrium" is in the context of an *attack* on the Mercantilist (or "Commercial") system (IV.iii.c.2, 489; I want to thank Leonidas Montes for reminding me of this passage). It is by no means clear that he means to endorse an equilibrium conception of the economy there. (Smith's views on population suggest he would have been excited to learn of dynamic dis-equilibrium theories.)

38. See, for example, Redman (1997, p. 219). Cf. Turgot ([1770] 1889 §LXXXVIII and §LXXXIX) on the use of "gravity." See Rothschild (2001, 76ff.) for useful comments on the contrast between Turgot and Smith on general equilibrium.

39. Of course, as Uskali Mäki reminded me, if the central body is several orders of magnitude larger than the other bodies, one may represent the situation as a central body attracting the other bodies. It's not clear how far Smith wants us to push the metaphor.

40. Mirowski (1989, p. 164), while widely read, is highly misleading when suggesting that Smith wanted to divert our attention away from Newton's action-at-a-distance. Not only does Mirowski quote two passages out of context (in which there is no mention of Newton at all), but he also fails to address the passages in which Smith does discuss Newton's principles! One would never know from Mirowski's account that Smith realized that the "Moon may be conceived as constantly falling towards the Earth" and that at IV¶67 he wrote, "He [Newton] demonstrated, that, if the Planets were supposed to gravitate towards the Sun, and to one another." Moreover, Smith singled out Newton's ability to calculate the weights and densities of the Sun and planets for special praise ("Astronomy," IV¶75, 103). And at IV¶68, 99, he comments on Newton's amazing prediction that a mutual attraction between Jupiter and Saturn would be strong enough to perturb their orbits when near conjunction.

41. For useful discussion, see O'Donnell (1990, pp. 58–61, 93–96).

42. Of course, most of WN is a lament about the absence of competition; see T. W. Hutchison (1978, p. 20, n. 27). Hollander (1973, p. 126) points out that Smith's understanding of competition must be distinguished from the modern one in which sellers are "price takers" rather than "price makers."

43. This is not how Smith's discussion of natural price seems to have been understood by successive generations of economists. Rather, economists made determining the natural rates of wages, profit, and rent the object of analysis of economic theory (O'Donnell, 1990, p. 55). Instead of having general validity such theories must assume constant background conditions.

44. Smith did not foresee the possibility that there could be a negative trade-off between efficiency and welfare. In Smith's time most inefficiencies were also welfare-reducing. See Rothschild (2001, Chap. 4), for a discussion of passages that show how for Smith efficiency and fairness are often connected.

45. On the importance of justice in WN, see Brubaker (2002), Berry (1989) and Werhane (1991). The best account of Smith's commitment to natural equality is still Cropsey (1957). See also Schliesser (2002, Chap. 5), and Fleischacker (2004).

46. I quote from Montesquieu (1989). Sam Fleischacker has called my attention to a remark by one of Smith's more prominent students, John Millar: "The great Montesquieu pointed out the road. He was the Lord Bacon in this branch of philosophy. Dr. Smith is

the Newton" (quoted, from Millar, *Historical View of English Government*, 1812 edition, volume II, pp. 429–430). Montesquieu's influence on Smith has yet to be explored in depth.

47. For an ingenious argument to this effect, and with further references, see Young (1986), or Chap. 5 (with Barry Gordon) of Young (1997). Young seems to have been unaware of Montesquieu's statement.

48. Cf. George E. Smith (2002, p. 157).

49. For a more elaborate defense of this point see, George E. Smith (2002) and Stein (2002) both in Cohen and Smith (2002).

50. I take this to be the position of Force (1987, pp. 180–187, especially footnotes 30 and 40). Redman (1997, pp. 79–82), endorses Force's view.

51. I discuss this and other issues relating to Newton's 4th Rule in Schliesser (2004) "The Missing Shade of Blue."

52. I must thank Don Howard and Martin Lin for pressing this point. Newton is also clear about this in the next to last paragraph of the final Query of the *Opticks*. This disarms the practical impact, on scientific theorizing, of what is now known (among philosophers) as the Quine-Duhem thesis. See also my "Galilean Reflections."

53. One might think that to pay attention to empirical exceptions is just obviously sound methodology, and not especially Newtonian. But this is a methodological *achievement* of Newton; in Schliesser (2004) "The Missing Shade of Blue," I discuss how Hume and many natural philosophers before him – including prominent members in the Royal Society such as Boyle – provided arguments that allowed one to dismiss/ignore certain kinds of exceptions to generalization. See also Schliesser (2005a) "Galilean Reflections."

54. See my argument in "Realism in the Face of Scientific Revolutions" (forthcoming-a). It is worth noting that Smith praises Newton's style of presentation in his *Lectures on Rhetoric and Belles Lettres* (LRBL, see ii.132–134), but here I am not concerned with Smith's views on different modes of presentation.

55. This is an important issue in Smith's WN I.i.6–9, 19–22 and I.ii.4, 28–29, where the division of labor causes and *enhances* different talents among different peoples and trades (including philosophers). On such differing skills, see also "Imitative Arts" Annexe, 5, 211–212, and "Of the External Senses," ¶52, 151–152. Cf. Turgot's (posthumously published in 1808–1811) "On Universal History," in Turgot ([1973], 1989).

56. Redman (1997, p. 222, n. 36), points out that Smith's view can be traced back to Hutcheson as presented in *A Short Introduction to Moral Philosophy*. See also Wightman (1975, pp. 55–57), who comments on the relationship to Descartes' account of the passions.

57. All my quotes are from *The Theory of Moral Sentiments* (TMS). Edited by D. D. Raphael and A. L. Macfie.

58. For a very different reading of this passage and Smith's views more generally, see Foley (1976, pp. 33, 214, n. 70).

59. Lauren Brubaker has suggested that Smith's use of "irregularity" may deserve special scrutiny. For in Smith's moral theory, Smith seems to suggest that an irregularity is a *regular* deviation from the expectations of Reason. "Astronomy," IV¶68, 99, seems to support this observation.

60. This is quite evident in the importance Smith's attaches to explaining the significance and ramifications of Cassini's observations (Smith's argument stretches over many paragraphs, see IV¶58–59, 90–91, IV¶64, 95, and IV¶67, 98–99). For an analysis of this see Schliesser (forthcoming-a) "Realism."

61. For more on the "Newtonian Style" see I. B. Cohen (1980). In a series of articles, George E. Smith (2001, 2002), has extended and made precise Cohen's insight. See, for judicious remarks, Wightman (1975, p. 62).

62. I explore this theme in (2005a) "Galilean Reflections."

63. See Smith's "Letter to the Edinburgh Review," 245–256, EPS, and the editors' footnote at TMS, III.2.20, 124.

64. On monsters, see also Daston and Park (1998).

65. Cf. Berkeley, *A Treatise Concerning the Principles of Human Knowledge*: "exceptions from the general rules of Nature are proper to surprise and awe men into an acknowledgment of the Divine Being" (§63).

66. Leon Montes reminded me of a lovely, hyperbolic passage in Becker (1932, p. 63): "Obviously the disciples of the Newtonian philosophy had not ceased to worship. They had given another form and a new name to the object of worship: having denatured God, they deified nature." Smith's own understanding of nature is quite ambivalent (e.g. TMS, III.5.7ff, 166); see Brubaker (2002) for useful comments.

67. For a very different approach, relying on a distinction between Smith as a "philosophical" and "orthodox" historian, see the Editors' "General Introduction" to WN, 54–60.

68. See Redman (1997, p. 125). It is tempting to graft Hume's (2000) distinction between the "natural" and "artificial" onto Smith's approach to institutions (*Treatise*, 3.1.2.9). For Hume education (1.3.9.19), property, honor, custom, civil laws (2.1.10.1), justice (3.3.6.4), and, perhaps, all goal-directed human actions (3.1.2.9 and 3.2.6.6) are "artificial." If Smith thought of "artificial" institutions as deflecting the "natural" course of things then his conception harks back to the traditional (pre-Cartesian) understanding of mechanics, which studied how human artifices change [sic] the course of nature.

69. Lauren Brubaker's dissertation (2002) shows how for Smith human nature is a composite, sometimes an uneasy one, of biological and social factors (both of which are presented as "natural").

70. For very different accounts see Berry (1997) and Otteson (2002, especially Chap. 2).

71. For more on this see Willie Henderson and Waren J. Samuels (ms) "Making Sense of Adam Smith's "Propensity to Truck, Barter, and Exchange." See also Schliesser (2005b).

72. Rothbard (1995, p. 442), ignores this while criticizing Smith.

73. This is discussed in Schliesser (2002, Chap. 3, IV. D).

74. We also find evidence in Smith's students' lecture-notes that he taught: "in no case is the proof of facts from the causes more uncertain than in that of Human actions. The causes of Human actions are motives; And so far is Certain that no one ever acts without a motive ... In proving therefore an action to have happened by proving that its causes subsisted, we must not only prove that one had a motive to commit such an action, but also that it was one that suited his character, and that he had an opportunity to do so. But even when all this is done it does by no means amount to a proof of the action. The character of man is a thing so fluctuating that no proof which depends on it can be altogether conclusive" (Lecture 28, ii. 191–192, 171, LRBL).

75. Cf. Hume's essay "Of Commerce": "Man is a very variable being, and susceptible of many different opinions, principles, and rules of conduct" (and also (Hume, 1975) "A Dialogue" in the Second *Enquiry*).

76. "But the principle which prompts to save is the desire of bettering our condition, a desire which, though generally calm and dispassionate, comes with us from the womb,

and never leaves us till we go into the grave. In the whole interval which separates those two moments, there is scarce perhaps a single instant in which any man is so perfectly and completely satisfied with his situation as to be without any wish of alteration or improvement of any kind. An augmentation of fortune is the means by which the greater part of men propose and wish to better their condition. It is the means the most vulgar and the most obvious; and the most likely way of augmenting their fortune is to save and accumulate some part of what they acquire, either regularly and annually, or upon some extraordinary occasions. Though the principle of expense, therefore, prevails in almost all men upon some occasions, and in some men upon almost all occasions, yet in the greater part of men, taking the whole course of their life at an average, the principle of frugality seems not only to predominate, but to predominate very greatly" (II.iii.28, 341; see the editors' footnotes for further references). Smith avoids making claims about individual human behavior at any given time; all he needs is an average propensity.

77. Smith's famous example may have been inspired by Turgot ([1770] 1889, §LXXIII and §LXXIV). Self-interested behavior in Smith consists of an interplay between a "passion for present enjoyment" and a "desire for bettering our condition," see for discussion O'Donnell (1990, pp. 58, 59).

78. See Schliesser (forthcoming-a) "Realism."

79. Redman (1997, p. 212) claims – without a single citation from Smith's works! – that Smith assumed d'Holbach's *Theory of Motion*. Just because Smith owned a copy of a book by Holbach doesn't mean he adopted his views.

80. The argument in TMS is not only, and maybe not even largely, epistemic; moral and political considerations also enter into Smith's reasoning. The quote in the text is lifted from a passage where Smith worries about "fanaticism" caused by the "spirit of system" or "faction" in turn influenced by the enthusiasm of the masses, see VI.ii.2.15, 232–233. Smith's argument against state direction of the economy is not exclusively epistemic; he also stresses the political dangers of state tyranny, see, for example, WN IV.ii.10, 456.

81. For Smith transactions in the "system of natural liberty" are subject to the "laws of justice" and the Sovereign must protect his sovereigns from "injustice or oppression" (WN IV.ix.51, 687).

82. Haakonssen (1981, pp. 79–82) usefully attributes to Smith an implicit distinction between contextual knowledge and system knowledge, the former being "the knowledge we have of human behavior through the sympathy mechanism," while the latter is "the understanding of things, events, or persons in some sort of functional relationship to a greater 'whole' or system."

83. I thank Gordon Sollars for calling my attention to this feature of WN.

84. For more discussion of this passage see Schliesser (2002, Chap. 5, II. B).

85. For Smith only the philosopher can attempt a view of the whole, yet, "their great abilities, though honourable to themselves, may contribute very little to the good government or happiness of their society" (WN V.i.f.51, 783). This passage is ignored by Redman (1997, p. 230; cf. Fleischacker, 1999, p. 174).

86. For a very interesting analysis, see Caroline Gerschlager's "Adam Smith and Feminist Perspective on Exchange," in Gerschlager and Mokre (2002).

87. In a series of articles, Levy (1999a, b), David Levy has been emphasizing (a) the *social* nature of Adam Smith's vision of economics, and (b) Smith's realization that economic actors can systematically misperceive their own interests, that is, they don't have perfect information. Smith's assumptions were, as Levy points out, not shared by most of the

founders of modern neoclassical economics (who followed Ricardo); see also Levy (1995). For a contrasting view, see Redman (1997, pp. 213, 245), where it is claimed that the basic component in Smith is the individual.

88. Smith thinks that the ability to see one's capital explains why the home trade is more preferable to foreign trade (WN IV.ii.6, 454–455), and why "upon equal, or nearly equal profits, most men will choose to employ their capitals rather in the improvement and cultivation of land than either in manufactures or in foreign trade" (III.i.3, 377–378; see also, III.i.7, 379 and III.iv.19, 423). For other examples that emphasize the ability to observe capital and human beings, see II.ii.62, 305–306. Herbert Simon's work on bounded rationality can be seen as an important descendant of Smith.

89. Many scholars have tried to reconcile TMS and WN – creating a huge industry around the "Adam Smith problem." That is not my project here. The source of this problem is the idea (first propounded by German scholars at the end of the 19th century) that the actors in WN are self-interested (in a very narrow sense) and the actors of TMS are driven by sympathy (mistakenly understood as benevolence; see Montes, 2003b.) This understanding of the problem is now dismissed if only, as Charles Larmore first pointed out to me, because the act of sympathy, that is, imagining oneself in another's position, is crucial to self-interest, particularly in the pursuit of wealth, where we pursue what we think others desires or envy. This is not to say no discrepancies between WN and TMS can be found. See, Otteson (2002), for an effort to revive the Adam Smith problem. In my response, Schliesser (2005b), I offer several examples of the complexity of the WN's moral psychology.

90. Bowles (1986, p. 15) calls this is an a priori picture, but that is only accurate if one could show that Smith's picture of the "natural inclinations of man" is also a priori. Bowles is very critical of Smith because he thinks Smith's approach to history is unempirical. My account defends Smith from this charge.

91. Redman (1997, p. 125, n. 48) usefully employs the (Weberian?) language of "ideal states."

92. D'Alembert's *Preliminary Discourse* also has the structure of postulating a natural development of the arts and sciences through the use of Memory, Reason, and Imagination (in Greek and Roman times), while having to explain that since the Renaissance the order of Enlightenment was Memory (scholarship), Imagination (belles-lettres), and Reason (philosophy).

93. Redman (1997, p. 249).

94. For a very different assessment, see Bryson (1945, p. 86).

95. See Rosenberg (1960, pp. 570, 559). I know of only one work on Adam Smith that has taken up and systematically developed Rosenberg's insights: Muller (1993). Hollander (1973, p. 311) remarks on the importance of Rosenberg's (1960) paper in a footnote without incorporating it into the framework of his discussion of Smith. See Pack (1991) for political aims of WN.

96. That is not all he does. WN, I.viii contains some of Smith's most explicit comments about how important it is to improve welfare of "Servants, labourers and workmen of different kinds, [which] make up the far greater part of every great political society" (I.viii.36, 96).

97. See Schliesser (forthcoming-a) "Realism," for more evidence that Smith rejected Hume's account of causation.

98. Turgot writes: "the spirit of commerce presupposes a property in goods which is independent of every power other than that of the laws" ("On Universal History," Turgot,

1973, p. 73). Although in the main body of the text I emphasize the differences with Hume, Smith's historical narrative is heavily influenced by Hume; see von Hayek (1967, p. 113), and Rothschild (2001, p. 10, for references). See also Rosenberg (1975, 384ff).

99. My analysis provides an explanation for the difference in causal explanatory power that Tieffenbach (forthcoming) has noted between Hume's and Smith's respective theories.

100. For more on this, see Schliesser (2004).

101. In "Of Interest" Hume writes: "There is no craving or demand of the human mind more constant and insatiable than that for exercise and employment; and this seems the foundation of most of our passions and pursuits" (p. 300). See also Hume's invocation of the potent and infallible moral attraction of the interests and passions of men at "Of the Balance of Trade" (p. 313). For more on the role that human nature plays in Hume's economic and historical thinking, see Rotwein (1955) for excellent discussion.

102. Strictly speaking Hume does not call it a "natural rate" (p. 381), although a page later he says, the rate "seems natural to expect."

103. What follows here bears close affinity to the detailed treatment of Hoover and Dowell (2001). In their discussion, they show that Smith's method in the Digression can be understood in terms of J. S. Mill's method of residues. Their conclusions are not very different from those defended here, but my approach avoids this particular anachronism. I thank Harro Maas for calling my attention to this piece.

104. The price of corn is Smith's major approximation to measure the welfare of the working poor. See Schliesser (2002, Chap. 5) for a defense of this claim.

105. For an excellent account, see Hueckel (2000, 323ff).

106. Smith's analysis is focused on long-term prices. Short-term fluctuations indicate supply shocks most frequent in "turbulent and disorderly societies" (I.xi.e.23, 204; Smith has in mind Feudalism here) or changes in weather. Smith must also assume that improvements in the efficiency of producing corn are "counter-balanced" by other costs (such as the price of cattle, "the principal instruments of agriculture"; I.xi.e.28, 206).

107. See O'Donnell (1990, pp. 77–81). O'Donnell is especially clear how this procedure – and added assumptions about the long-run price movements and trade-offs among different commodities see WN, I.xi.i-m, 234–255 – enables Smith to infer "with a degree of probability that approaches almost to certainty" from relative "real" prices of different commodities (i.e. cattle, corn, vegetables, and manufacturers) at what stage of improvement an economy was (I.xi.n.3, 257). For an analysis of Smith's concept of "real price," see Schliesser (2002, Chap. 5, II. B).

108. Cf. Hume's argument in "Of Interest," which turns on an assumption about the proportionate nature of cause and effect (296).

109. For discussion, see Schliesser and Pack (forthcoming).

110. Here's an example from Smith's discussion on price: "[T]hough pecuniary wages and profit are very different in the different employments of labour and stock; yet a certain proportion seems *commonly to take place* between both the pecuniary wages in all the different employments of labour, and the pecuniary profits in all the different employments of stock. This proportion, it will appear hereafter, depends partly upon the nature of the different employments, and partly upon the *different laws and policy of the society in which they are carried on.* But though in many respects dependent upon the laws and policy, this proportion seems to be little affected by the riches or poverty of that society; by its advancing, stationary, or declining condition; but to remain the same or very nearly the same in all those different states" (I.vii.36, 80; emphasis added).

111. See Hutchison (1978, p. 10). He points out (p. 7) that subsequent economists assumed a fairly stable social and political environment.

112. Redman (1997, pp. 219, 220) remarks that Smith's approach is evolutionary, and that the main focus of the 4-stage theory of development is the evolution of institutions.

113. For examples see Brown (1994, pp. 147–175), O'Donnell (1990, pp. 176, 250, n. 10) and Rothbard (1995, pp. 460, 461). Given that Smith's work on "real" prices involved a conceptual innovation (it was not present in LJ, see for discussion, Schliesser, 2002, Chap. 5, II.B) there is no reason why he could not have realized that his early work on natural prices also lends itself to evidential exploitation.

114. See Schliesser (forthcoming-b) "Realism."

115. I don't understand why Redman (1997, p. 114) infers from this that Smith's approach was "atomistic."

116. Although it emphasizes psychological factors, other (social, cultural, political, etc.) factors are not ignored. See Schliesser (forthcoming-b) "Adam Smith's Conception of Philosophy."

117. In contrast to other commentators, I doubt that Smith ever claimed that nature itself is like a machine. One of the most insightful readers of Smith, Skinner (1979, p. 11), erroneously refers to TMS II.ii.3.5, 87, where Smith uses a watch as an example to explicate the difference between efficient and final causation, but where he does not himself claim that the universe is a "great machine." (This passage is treated in Schliesser and Pack (forthcoming).) There are other places that are often cited when the world is a machine view is attributed to Smith: at TMS VII.ii.1.38, 289, Smith talks of the "whole [deterministic] machine of the world"; here he is explicitly summarizing *Stoic* and not his own doctrines. Second, at TMS VI.ii.3.4, 236, Smith uses the phrase, "the immense machine of the universe," but he does so while explaining what *idea* is the "most sublime" object of "human contemplation" (i.e. the Divine Being who produces the greatest possible quantity of happiness); he does not claim that this idea is true. Only once (TMS I.i.4.2, 19) does Smith talk of the "various appearances which the great machine of the universe is perpetually exhibiting." It may well be that Smith took this description of the universe literally (and would be, thus, the only such instance in the whole of Smith's works). However, Brown (1994) has demonstrated that it is important to pay attention to the rhetorical element in Smith's presentation. In this section, Smith is presenting the *common* point of view not his own; he is not describing how the "men of learning" judge. Nowhere in WN does Smith describe the world or universe as a machine; this idea plays no meaningful role in his economic theorizing. Cf. Redman (1997, pp. 218–220).

118. See Lindgren (1969, pp. 909–910), for useful references to "Considerations Concerning the first Formation of Languages" (hereafter "Languages"). For Smith on language, see also Levy (1997) and Berry (1974).

119. I do not understand why Redman (1997, pp. 85 and 214ff., n. 19) seems to agree with Dugald Stewart's claim that Smith ignored the importance of predictions. See, by contrast, Smith's comments on the predictions concerning Halley's comet ("Astronomy," IV¶74, 103). For more on the role of predictions in Smith's understanding of science, see Schliesser (forthcoming-a) "Realism."

120. Redman (1997, p. 226) connects Smith's "Astronomy" with Bacon's Idols in a very interesting way. Hobbes, too, may have been an influence on Smith here; see Cropsey (1957), for an attempt to link Smith to Hobbes.

121. "[[P]hilosophy] is the most sublime of all the agreeable arts, and its revolutions have been the greatest, the most frequent, and the most distinguished of all those that

have happened in the literary world . . . Let us examine, therefore, all the different systems of nature, which, in these western parts of the world . . . have successively been adopted by the learned and ingenious" ("Astronomy," II¶12, 46; see for discussion, Schliesser (forthcoming-a, b) "Realism" and "Adam Smith's Conception").

122. See Skinner (1996, p. 38). It is worth pointing out that Smith's psychological account applies to theory creation and acceptance. For more details, see Schliesser (forthcoming-a) "Realism."

123. Redman (1997, p. 223) has a very different account of why Smith invokes the "machine" metaphor: "it demonstrates how society, like a machine, can be taken apart and explained and shows how it is governed by law." This is not an improbable suggestion. But she admits she does not have a clear statement from Smith to offer as evidence. She does quote an interesting passage from Hume's writings. But her presentation fails to make clear that she is quoting *Cleanthes* in the *Dialogues concerning Natural Religion*! It is by no means obvious that we should attribute his views to Hume, let alone Smith. I do think it is a view that can be safely attributed to Turgot, see his letter to Hume, March 25, 1767.

124. See Skinner (1979, pp. 26–29), for a more detailed account of this.

125. Stewart "Account of the Life and Writings of Adam Smith, L. L. D.," §III¶12, 304, EPS.

126. For Smith's relationship to the Physiocrats, see Skinner (1996, pp. 123–142). Smith calls the Physiocrats a "sect" the members of which have an admiration of Quesnay, their leader, not inferior "to that of any of the ancient philosophers for the founders of their respective systems" (WN IV.ix.38, 679).

127. The language of approximation also shows up in Smith's discussion of prices: "[W]e must generally, therefore, content ourselves with them, not as being always exactly in the same proportion as the current prices of labour, but as being *the nearest approximation* which can commonly be had to that proportion" (I.v.22, 56; emphasis added). But in context this is not a claim about successive approximation.

128. See Schliesser (2002, Chap. 5), Pack (1991), Rothschild (2001).

129. Recall the passage quoted from John Millar. See, for example, Governor Thomas Pownall's (1776) *Letter to Adam Smith, being an Examination of Several Points of Doctrine laid down, in his Inquiry* (reprinted in the Correspondence, Appendix A, 337–376) or Montes (2003a).

130. Amazingly, Redman (1997, pp. 187, 188) claims that Smith's method was "ambivalent" and "to a casual reader . . . proof of contradiction," and quotes a passage from TMS (VII.iii.2.6, 319) without making clear that Smith is discussing Hobbes and Cudworth. (Redman invokes the same passage at p. 209.)

131. Redman (1997, p. 227) offers some evidence to qualify this assertion a bit. Also, Laura Snyder called my attention to the following letter from Whewell to Richard Jones, 23 September 1822 to be found in the Whewell Papers Add.ms.c.51 f.15: "I still meditate doing something about the History of the Metaphysics of Mechanics though as yet it is only intention. Something like Smith's History of Astronomy but with more historical facts."

ACKNOWLEDGMENTS

Independent of my research, Leonidas Montes arrived at a parallel and complementary understanding of Adam Smith's relationship to Newton. Not only does Montes (2003a) provide me with generous recognition, but this paper has benefited from correspondence with him. I am also indebted to Dan Garber, Charles Larmore, Sam Fleischacker, David Levy, Uskali Mäki, Spencer Pack, Warren Samuels, Nathan Rosenberg, Harro Maas, Howard Stein, Alessandro Pajewski, Christopher Berry, Joe La Porte, Jen Boobar, and several anonymous referees as well as audiences at the University of Amsterdam, The Summer Institute for the Preservation of the History of Economics at George Mason University, the contemporary philosophy workshop at The University of Chicago, and, especially, the EIPE Seminar at Erasmus University, Rotterdam, for many thoughtful comments. I owe a special debt of gratitude to Sonja Amadae, who first put me on the Newton-Smith trail, Mark Blaug, who provided me with generous and insightful comments at the EIPE Seminar, and, especially, I. B. Cohen for sharing his notes on the Isaac Newton-Adam Smith connection with me. The usual caveats apply.

REFERENCES

Becker, C. (1932). *The heavenly city of the eighteenth-century philosophers*. New Haven: Yale University Press.

Berkeley, G. ([1734] 1998). *A treatise concerning the principles of human knowledge*. In: J. Dancy (Ed.). Oxford: Oxford University Press.

Berry, C. J. (1974). Adam Smith's *Considerations* on language. *Journal of the History of Ideas, 35,* 130–138.

Berry, C. J. (1989). Adam Smith: Commerce, liberty and modernity. In: P. Gilmour (Ed.), *Philosophers of the Enlightenment*. Edinburgh: Edinburgh University Press.

Berry, C. J. (1997). *Social theory of the Scottish enlightenment*. Edinburgh: Edinburgh University Press.

Bowles, P. (1986, February). Adam Smith and the 'Natural Progress of Opulence.' *Economica, 53*(209), 109–118 [Reprinted in Wood (1994), Vol. VI].

Brown, V. (1994). *Adam Smith's discourse: Canonicity, commerce, and conscience*. London: Routledge.

Brubaker, L. (2002). *Adam Smith and the limits of enlightenment*. A dissertation submitted to Committee on Social Thought at The University of Chicago.

Bryson, G. (1945). *Man and society: The Scottish inquiry of the eighteenth century*. Princeton: Princeton University Press.

Cohen, I. B. (1980). *The Newtonian revolution*. Cambridge: Cambridge University Press.

Cohen, I. B., & Smith, G. E. (Eds) (2002). *The Cambridge companion to Newton*. Cambridge: Cambridge University Press.

Cropsey, J. (1957). *Polity and economy: An interpretation of the principles of Adam Smith*. The Hague: Martinus Nijhoff.

D'Alembert, J. le Rond. ([1963] 1995). *Preliminary discourse to the encyclopedia of Diderot*. Trans. Richard N. Schwab with the collaboration of Walter E. Rex. Chicago: UCP.

Daston, L., & Park, K. (1998). *Wonders and the order of nature: 1150–1750*. New York, NY: Zone Books.

Fleischacker, S. (1999). *A third concept of liberty: Judgment and freedom in Kant and Adam Smith*. Princeton: Princeton University Press.

Fleischacker, S. (2004). *Adam Smith's wealth of nations: A philosophical companion.* Princeton: Princeton University Press.

Foley, V. (1976). *The social physics of Adam Smith.* West Lafayette, IN: Purdue University Press.

Gerschlager, C., & Mokre, M. (Eds) (2002). *Exchange and deception: A feminist perspective.* Boston-Dordrecht-London: Kluwer Academic Publishers.

von Hayek, F. A. (1967). The legal and political philosophy of David Hume. In: *Studies in Philosophy, Politics, and Economics* (pp. 106–132). London: Routledge.

Henderson, W., & Samuels, W. J. (ms.). *Making sense of Adam Smith's 'propensity to truck, barter, and exchange'.*

Hollander, S. L. (1973). *The economics of Adam Smith.* Toronto: University of Toronto Press.

Hoover, K. D., & Dowell, M. E. (2001). Measuring causes: Episodes in the quantitative assessment of the value of money. In: J. L. Klein & M. S. Morgan (Eds), *The Age of Measurement* (pp. 137–161). Annual Supplement to Vol. 33 of *History of Political Economy.* Durham: Duke University Press.

Hueckel, G. R. (2000). On the "insurmountable difficulties, obscurity, and embarrassment" of Smith's 5th Chapter. *History of Political Economy, 32*(2), 317–345.

Hume, D. (1975). *Enquiries concerning human understanding and concerning the principles of morals* (3rd, revised Selby-Bigge ed.). P. H. Nidditch (Ed.).

Hume, D. (2000). *A treatise of human nature.* D. F. Norton & M. J. Norton (Eds). Oxford: Oxford University Press.

Hutchison, T. W. (1978). *On revolutions and progress in economic knowledge.* Cambridge: Cambridge University Press.

Levy, D. M. (1995). The partial spectator in the wealth of nations: A robust utilitarianism. *European Journal of the History of Economic Thought, 2*(2), 299–326.

Levy, D. M. (1997). Adam Smith's rational choice linguistics. *Economic Inquiry, XXXV*(3), 672–678.

Levy, D. M. (1999a). Adam Smith's katallactic model of gambling: Approbation from the spectator. *Journal of the History of Economic Thought, 21*(1), 81–92.

Levy, D. M. (1999b). Kattalactic rationality: Language, approbation and exchange. *American Journal of Economics and Sociology.*

Lindgren, J. R. (1969, November/December). Adam Smith's theory of inquiry. *Journal of Political Economy, 77*(6), 897–915.

Marx, K. (1963). *Theories of surplus value* (3 vols). Moscow: Progress Publication.

Mirowski, P. (1982). Adam Smith, empiricism, and the rate of profit in 18th century England. *History of Political Economy, 14*(2), 178–198.

Mirowski, P. (1989). *More heat than light: Economics as social physics, physics as nature's economics.* Cambridge: Cambridge University Press.

Montes, L. (2003a). Smith and Newton: Some methodological issues regarding general economic equilibrium theory. *Cambridge Journal of Economics, 27*, 723–747.

Montes, L. (2003b). Das Adam Smith problem: Its origins, the stages of the current debate, and one implication for our understanding of sympathy. *Journal of the History of Economic Thought, 25*, 63–90.

Montesquieu, Charles de Secondat, baron de (1989). *The spirit of the laws.* A. M. Cohler, B. C. Miller & H. S. Stone (Trans. & Eds). Cambridge: Cambridge University Press.

Muller, J. Z. (1993). *Adam Smith in his time and ours: Designing the decent society.* New York: Free Press.

O'Donnell, R. (1990). *Adam Smith's theory of value and distribution: A reappraisal.* New York: St. Martin's Press.

Otteson, J. (2002). *Adam Smith's marketplace of life*. Cambridge: Cambridge University Press.

Pack, S. J. (1991). *Capitalism as a moral system: Adam Smith's critique of the free market economy*. Brookfield, VT: Edward Elgar.

Rashid, S. (1990). Adam Smith's acknowledgments: Neo-plagiarism and the wealth of nations. *The Journal of Libertarian Studies, IX*(2), 1–24.

Redman, D. (1997). *The rise of political economy as a science: Methodology and the classical economists*. Cambridge, MA: MIT Press.

Rosenberg, N. (1960). Some institutional aspects of the wealth of nations. *Journal of Political Economy, 68*, 557–570.

Rosenberg, N. (1975). *Adam Smith on profits – paradox lost and regained*. In: Skinner and Wilson (1975).

Rothbard, M. N. (1995). *An Austrian perspective on the history of economic thought*. Brookfield, VT: Edward Elgar.

Rothschild, E. (2001). *Economic sentiments: Adam Smith, condorcet, and the enlightenment*. Cambridge, MA: Harvard University Press.

Rotwein, E. (1955). *David Hume: Writings on economics*. Madison: University of Wisconsin.

Schliesser, E. (2002). *Indispensable Hume: From Isaac Newton's natural philosophy to Adam Smith's "Science of Man."* Dissertation submitted to the Philosophy Department, The University of Chicago. DAI, 63, No. 11A (2002) p. 3969, ISBN: 0–493–89859-X.

Schliesser, E. (2004). The missing shade of blue, reconsidered from a Newtonian perspective. *Journal of Scottish Philosophy, 2*(2), 164–175.

Schliesser, E. (2005a, March). Galilean reflections on Milton Friedman's *The Methodology of Positive Economics*: With thoughts on *Economics in the Laboratory, Philosophy of the Social Sciences. 35*(1).

Schliesser, E. (2005b). Adam Smith's theoretical endorsement of deception: A response to James Otteson's *Adam Smith's Marketplace of Life*, to appear in *Adam Smith Review* (Vol. 2).

Schliesser, E. (forthcoming-a). Realism in the face of scientific revolutions: Adam Smith on Newton's copernicanism. *British Journal of History of Philosophy*.

Schliesser, E. (forthcoming-b). Adam Smith's conception of philosophy. In: L. Montes & E. Schliesser (Eds), *New Voices on Adam Smith*. London and New York: Routledge.

Schliesser, E., & Pack, S. (forthcoming). Adam Smith's Humean criticism of Hume's theory of the origin of justice. *Journal of History of Philosophy*.

Schumpeter, J. A. (1954). *History of economic anylysis*. E. B. Schumpeter (Ed.). New York: Oxford University Press.

Skinner, A. S. (1979). *A system of social science: Papers relating to Adam Smith*. Oxford: Clarendon Press.

Skinner, A. S. (1996). *A system of social science: Papers relating to Adam Smith* (2nd ed.). Oxford: Clarendon Press.

Smith, A. (1982). *Essays on philosophical subjects*. W. P. D. Wightman & J. C. Bryce (Eds), Indianapolis: Liberty Fund (reprint of the Glasgow edition of the works and correspondence of Adam Smith; Vol. 3, Oxford: Oxford University Press, 1980).

Smith, A. (1984). *An inquiry into the nature and causes of the wealth of nations*. R. H. Campbell, A. S. Skinner & W. B. Todd (Eds), Indianapolis: Liberty Fund (reprint of the Glasgow edition of the works and correspondence of Adam Smith; Vols. 2, Oxford: Oxford University Press, 1976 and reprinted with minor corrections in 1979).

Smith, G. E. (2001). The Newtonian style in Bk II of the *Principia*. In: J. Z. Buchwald & I. B. Cohen (Eds), *Isaac Newton's Natural Philosophy*. Cambridge, MA: MIT Press.

Smith, G. E. (2002). The methodology of the *Principia*. In: Cohen and Smith (pp. 138–173).

Stein, H. (2002). Newton's Metaphysics. In: Cohen and Smith (pp. 256–307).

Turgot, A. R. J. ([1770] 1889). *Reflections on the formation and distribution of riches*. New York: Macmillan.

Turgot, A. R. J. (1973). *Turgot on progress, sociology and economics: A philosophical review of the successive advances of the human mind, on universal history [and] reflections on the formation and the distribution of wealth* (Translated, Edited and with an Introduction by R. L. Meek). Cambridge: Cambridge University Press.

Werhane, P. H. (1991). *Adam Smith and his legacy for modern capitalism*. Oxford: Oxford University Press.

Wightman, W. P. D. (1975). Adam Smith and the history of ideas. In: Skinner and Wilson.

Young, J. T. (1986). The impartial spectator and natural jurisprudence: An interpretation of Adam Smith's theory of natural price. *History of Political Economy*, *18*(3), 365–382. [Reprinted in John Cunningham Wood (1994), VI, 62–79.]

Young, J. T. (1997). *Economics as a moral science: The political economy of Adam Smith*. Cheltenham, UK: Edward Elgar.

INEQUALITY OF WHAT AMONG WHOM?: RIVAL CONCEPTIONS OF DISTRIBUTION IN THE 20TH CENTURY☆

Robert S. Goldfarb and Thomas C. Leonard

ABSTRACT

Distribution concerns who gets what. But does "who" refer to the personal distribution of income among individuals or the functional distribution of income among suppliers of productive factors? For nearly 150 years, Anglophone distribution theory followed the Ricardian emphasis on functional distribution – the income shares of labor, land, and capital. Only beginning in the 1960s, and consolidated by a research outpouring in the early 1970s, does mainstream economics turn to the personal conception of distribution. This essay documents Anglophone (primarily American) economics' move from functional to

☆The authors have benefitted from conversations with and/or suggestions from Steve Baldwin, Rachel Boaz, Bryan Boulier, Barry Chiswick, Carmel Chiswick, Joseph Cordes, Edwin Dean, David Greenberg, Daniel Hamermesh, Pam Labadie, David Lindauer, Ben Okner, Don Parsons, David Pritchett, Malcolm Rutherford and Stephen Smith in the course of writing this paper. We also benefitted from comments during presentations at the Eastern Economic Association meetings March 2002, the History of Economics Society meetings July 2003, and during seminar presentations at George Mason University, George Washington University, and the University of Maryland Baltimore County.

A Research Annual
Research in the History of Economic Thought and Methodology, Volume 23-A, 75–118
Copyright © 2005 by Elsevier Ltd.
All rights of reproduction in any form reserved
ISSN: 0743-4154/doi:10.1016/S0743-4154(05)23003-1

personal distribution, and tries to illuminate something of its causes and timing.

The produce of the earth – all that is derived from its surface by the united application of labour, machinery, and capital, is divided among three classes of the community; namely, the proprietor of the land, the owner of the stock or capital necessary for its cultivation, and the labourers by whose industry it is cultivated. . . . To determine the laws which regulate this distribution, is the principal problem in Political Economy . . ..

> David Ricardo (1821, p. 5).

The traditional 'theory of income distribution' is concerned exclusively with the pricing of factors of production . . .. It has little to say about the distribution of income among the individual members of society, and there is no corresponding body of theory that does. This absence of a satisfactory theory of the personal distribution of income and of a theoretical bridge connecting the functional distribution of income with the personal distribution is a major gap in modern economic theory.

> Milton Friedman (1953, p. 277).

Student: "I have not learned anything in my graduate economics courses thus far about the distribution of income across individuals and families. What courses would address that?" Professor: "Economists study functional distribution of income. If you want to study size distribution, go to the sociology department . . ."
Paraphrase of an actual conversation[1] between a faculty member and graduate student at a leading Ph.D. program in Economics, circa 1968.

1. INTRODUCTION

Few questions in economics are more venerable than "who gets what?" Aristotle worried about the distributive consequences of exchange, as did Aquinas. Ricardo saw the division of the wealth of nations as more important than its causes.[2] Marx is unimaginable without distribution, as are the Progressive-Era (roughly 1890–1920) American economists who dared to imagine the state as an agent of progressive redistribution.

But does that "who" refer to the personal distribution of income across individuals or the functional distribution across suppliers of productive factors? For nearly 150 years, Anglophone economics followed David Ricardo (1815) and conceived of distribution as referring to the functional role in economic production. Moreover, functional roles were identified with membership in one of the three great socioeconomic classes of early 19th-century Britain – workers, landlords and capitalists. The functional approach to distribution survives the marginal revolution in economics, an industrial revolution, the development of welfare economics, the Great Depression, the advent of macroeconomics, the creation of welfare state, the mathematizing of neoclassical economics, several generations of prominent economists arguing that economics should rightly be concerned with the distribution of well being across individuals, and the erosion of the sharp class divisions that for Ricardo gave his distribution theory a social reference.

Beginning only in the 1960s, and consolidated by a research outpouring in the early 1970s, does the Anglophone profession turn to distribution across persons (and families and households). The new emphasis on the size distribution of income (SDI) also seems to coincide with a decline in research dedicated to distribution by productive function. By the late 1970s, mainstream economics is no longer comparing the income of labor with that of capital; it is comparing a poor family's (or a minority family's) income with the income of more fortunate families. Both this shift from a functional to a personal conception of distribution, and its timing have gone largely unexplored in the literature of 20th-century economics. This essay documents Anglophone (primarily American) economics' move from functional to personal distribution, and tries to illuminate something of its causes and timing.

The paper divides into two parts: Sections 1–7 present a time-line of the development of interest in, and research on, the size distribution of income, while Sections 8–12 analyze why the development took so long in coming. Section 2 provides a bare sketch of distribution circa 1900, as a way of setting the "initial conditions" for our history. Section 3 sets out some aspects of distribution research over the period 1900–1946. Section 4 considers an important strand of research developed in the annual volumes of the Conference on Research in Income and Wealth, an NBER-associated institution, from 1939 through the late 1950s. One focus is upon the evolving responses in these volumes to the question "for what purposes do we want personal income distribution data?" Section 5 of the paper considers the (mostly unheeded) contributions of Friedman and Kuznets in calling for greater attention to the personal distribution. Section 6 discusses the development of human capital theory and its advancement of theorizing about size distribution. Section 7 documents the eruption of size distribution articles and books, circa 1970, culminating with Sahota's (1978) Journal of Economic Literature (JEL) survey of theories of size distribution, which documents the arrival of personal distribution research. Sections 8–12 of the paper offer some speculation on the causes and timing of the move to a greater focus on the size distribution of income, considering factors that promoted and hindered the change.

1.1. Some Preliminaries: Questions of Interest

This essay considers the "who" of "who gets what," but distribution concerns four other questions that bear on our inquiry. First, "what do they get" asks a mostly empirical question about what is being distributed, and statistical techniques for characterizing its dispersion.[3] Second, "why do they get what they get" is a theoretical question, an attempt to explain the economic (and sometimes legal) causes of a given distribution. Third, "does the dispersion of what they get have real economic consequences of its own," treats distribution as a cause, rather than just an effect. It asks whether too much inequality causes adverse economic outcomes, as when the inability of the poor to borrow decreases the rate of economic growth (Aghion & Bolton, 1997).[4]

Ultimately, all of these lines of inquiry are joined to the fourth and ancient question of distributive justice – who *should* get what. More than any subject in political economy, distribution entangles matters of fact with ethical judgment. Surely all economists who have considered the question "who gets what?" have a view of "who *should* get what?" The confusion of "what is" with "what should (or should not) be" is a special occupational hazard for scholars of distribution.

2. INITIAL CONDITIONS: RECEIVED VIEWS OF DISTRIBUTION CIRCA 1900

To set the stage for our story, which focuses on 20th-century developments, we offer a sketch of distribution theory circa 1900, a moment when marginal productivity theory is building upon classical distribution theory.[5]

In classical political economy, the product is divided among three claimant groups, the suppliers of productive factors whose functional roles are identified with membership in the laboring, landowning or capitalist classes. Ricardo effectively models distribution as a kind of division, with the three shares determined by different processes. Landlords pay capitalist-tenant farmers their marginal products, and retain what is left of output as rent. The wages portion of payments to tenant farmers is determined "exogenously"; wages above subsistence increase worker fertility, which increases population hence labor supply, which, in turn, lowers wages toward subsistence, with opposite effects when wages fall below subsistence (Ricardo, 1821, p. 94). Thus are payments to capital the residual after farmers get their wages and landlords get their rent. With growth, the diminishing marginal productivity of labor and capital applied to (increasingly less productive) land ensures that payments to capital and rent are antagonistic – the landlords' share increases at the expense of the capitalists' share.

In the 1890s the marginal productivity theorists, John Bates Clark (1891), John A. Hobson (1891), Knut Wicksell (1893), Philip Wicksteed (1894), and others made Ricardian diminishing marginal productivity into a general principle for determining the value, hence the income shares, of *all* productive factors.

What workers and capitalists get is determined by the value of their respective contributions to output. Thus, did marginal productivity theory more closely join value theory – the determination of price – to the theories of production and distribution. Marginal productivity theory also recast the question of who should get what: a general theory of factor pricing, which regards all inputs as contributing value to output, tends to make all productive factors commensurate.

However, key elements of Ricardo's distribution scheme remained intact. In particular, marginal productivity theory carried over the Ricardian emphasis on distribution as a matter of productive function, and the identification of suppliers of productive factors with membership in the laboring, landowning or capitalist classes.[6] Clark, for example, insisted that, though "the issue [of unfair distribution] is personal . . . it is settled by a knowledge of purely functional distribution" (1899, p. 7). The emergence of the marginal productivity theory of distribution did little to change the tradition of "submerg[ing] the theory of personal income distribution within the grander themes of Labour, Capital and Land" (Shorrocks, 1987, p. 824).[7]

This one-sided emphasis on functional distribution did not pass without prominent criticism. Edwin Cannan (1905) argued that "poverty is a question of persons rather than of categories" (1905, p. 362). Irving Fisher's *Elementary Principles of Economics* (1912) argued that, with respect to the personal distribution of income, "no other problem has so great a human interest as this, and yet scarcely any other problem has received so little scientific attention" (cited in Dalton, 1920, p. 147). Hugh Dalton (1920, p. vii) wrote:

> While studying economics at Cambridge in 1909–1910 . . . I gradually noticed that most 'theories of distribution' were almost wholly concerned with distribution as between 'factors of production.' Distribution as between persons, a problem of more direct and obvious interest, was either left out of the textbooks altogether, or treated so briefly, as to suggest it raised no questions. . . .

Equally trenchant protests can be found in Allyn Young (1917, p. 484) and Thomas Carver (1901).[8]

Europe, with its longer history of income taxation, its broader income tax base, and a more fully developed welfare state, offered American distribution scholars a somewhat more established literature on which to draw.[9] There was Pareto's (1897) pioneering empirical work on personal income distribution, and his famous inference – which he ultimately called a "loi naturelle" – that income inequality was stable across time and place.[10] And there was an established literature proposing alternative (to Pareto's slope coefficient) statistical measures of income inequality, such as Corrado Gini (1912) and M. C. Lorenz (1905). Even so, U.S. personal income distribution data were fragmentary and slow to be developed.

3. ASPECTS OF DISTRIBUTION RESEARCH, 1900–1946

3.1. Division of Labor Between Empirical and Theoretical Researchers

Early on, there emerges a kind of professional division of labor in American distribution scholarship. The economists and statisticians who first heeded the call for more study of the personal income distribution were empirical researchers – their mandate was measurement.

The empirical scholars were concentrated in government statistical offices, and in the emergent private research organizations – the Conference Board, Brookings Institution, and, above all, the National Bureau of Economic Research. Their published work mostly appeared in government publications (such as the *Monthly Labor Review* and *Survey of Current Business*), statistical journals (such as the *Journal of the American Statistical Association*), and the house journals or series of the private organizations.

The National Bureau of Economic Research, founded to supply empirical evidence on leading economic issues, was the principal organization in and around which the empirical distribution scholars gathered. The National Bureau made the two volumes of *Income in the United States: Its Amount and Distribution* (King et al., 1922; Mitchell et al., 1921) its very first publications: Frederick Macaulay wrote the distribution section, and Willford I. King, a pioneering distribution scholar, wrote the section on income by source of production.[11]

The National Bureau study emphasized the challenge of early work in personal income distribution – the difficult problems of definition (e.g. what counts as income, what is the appropriate income-receiving unit) and of measurement, especially data collection, data comparability across heterogeneous primary sources, and techniques for measuring and characterizing income dispersion.[12] The lack of reliable primary data proved especially challenging. There were good data from the new Federal personal income tax, but tax-return data were, until the second World War, confined to the upper reaches of the income distribution. In 1918, the last year covered in the National Bureau study, over 90% of those with income paid no Federal income taxes (Mitchell et al., 1921, p. 134).[13]

Thus, when in 1939, C. L. Merwin produced a monograph-length survey of the (American) field for the National Bureau's Conference on Income and Wealth, he found only eight previous studies of the personal distribution of income and wealth worth evaluating: King's (1915) earlier work, two quite rudimentary precursors, Macaulay's section of the National Bureau Study, some unpublished work by King, two studies by Maurice Leven that were part of a large Brookings (1933–1934) survey (discussed below), and the vast 1935–1936 Study of Consumer Purchases, supervised by Hildegaard Kneeland of the BLS and sponsored by the National Resources Planning Board.[14]

After a careful evaluation, and an acknowledgment of the empirical challenges faced by these pioneers in the empirical study of personal income distribution, Merwin judges the literature "too crude and inaccurate to allow measuring temporal and spatial differences in the inequality of distribution – differences that must be known if changes in the relative welfare of different social groups, in tax burden and in taxable capacity, in the volume of savings and in the pattern of consumer demand are to be analyzed." Merwin even questions whether "existing distributions give a true picture of the relative welfare of the different strata in society," and he concludes by asking, why "do we not have better and more adequate data?" (1939, p. 74.) Simon Kuznets's discussion of Merwin, which offers some conjectures on why the personal income distribution data are so poor, took it as given that there was "no information collected during these decades on a sufficiently comprehensive scale to make possible an acceptable distribution of income or wealth by size among individuals or families" (1939, p. 85).

Merwin's survey ignored a related if now obscure empirical literature on the income and expenditures of poor families. This "family budgets" literature was heavily empirical, had a strong Institutionalist character, and much of the research was carried out by women economists (Kyrk, 1923; Peixotto, 1929; Reid, 1934).[15] It certainly belongs in the category of empirical work with a distributional emphasis.

But the family-budgets literature differed from empirical distribution scholarship "proper" in both focus and motive. The family-budget scholars did not study income dispersion per se, but focused on low-income families (and on consumption expenditures in particular). The family-budget scholars' motivation was to document poor families' standards of living because Progressive and Institutionalist theories of wage determination tended to regard wages as determined more by a worker's need or standard of living, than by, as per the neoclassical view, the value of a worker's productivity. Cost-of-living studies were thus deemed essential to the policy task of setting minimum wages or determining mothers' pensions. These different emphases may or may not explain the relative neglect of the family-budgets literature by the protagonists at the National Bureau, but it is clear that, even among distribution scholars well disposed to empirical work and to Institutionalist themes, the family-budgets work was seen as occupying an intellectual space somewhat outside empirical distribution scholarship proper.

With respect to the *theory* of distribution, the family-budget literature was all but invisible. As the evidence presented later in the paper suggests, contemporaneous distribution theory essentially ignored all work in personal income distribution in favor of the functional distribution.

3.1.1. Depression-Era Distribution Theory, Seen from 1946

Distribution theory, which then constitutes the bulk of mainstream American research concerned with distribution, remained almost entirely functional in orientation. In 1946 the American Economic Association gathered prominent papers in distribution for its *Readings in the Theory of Income Distribution*.[16] The volume reprints articles originally published from 1929 through 1946, and represents a who's who of Depression-Era luminaries in economics: Simon Kuznets, J. M. Clark, Kenneth Boulding, Chamberlin, Kalecki, Cassels, Stigler, Joan Robinson, Oscar Lange, Dennis Robertson, Lionel Robbins, A. P. Lerner, Lorie Tarshis, John Dunlop, Hayek, Frank Knight, Keynes, Hicks, and R. A. Gordon.

What is notable for our purposes is that 31 out of the 32 papers conceived of distribution as functional. Mary Jean Bowman's article on the graphical analysis of personal income distribution is the only exception. Simon Kuznets's contribution, "National Income," devotes 10 of its 40 pages to the personal distribution, and argues, in a lonely voice, that the personal income distribution is "an indispensable complement of national income estimates if they are to throw any light on the welfare of the nation" (p. 34).[17,18] Though the editors, Bernard Haley and William Fellner, concede that personal income distribution "gives rise to problems of great significance" (p. xi), they flatly state that "distribution theory in the usual sense relates mostly to the functional income distribution." Thus, when the editors argue that "the present state of the theory of income distribution is generally considered unsatisfactory, and it is rightly so considered," they are not referring to the paucity of work on personal distribution. They refer, rather, to the weakness of the theoretical link between the marginal productivity theory of factor pricing and the theory of income distribution, a weakness due especially to the lack of an adequate theory of labor supply.

The only *Readings* contributors who even consider the personal distribution, Bowman and Kuznets, emphasize its empirical, "what do they get" aspects. Kuznets's (1933) paper laments "the gap between what . . . is measured and what ought to be measured" (pp. 42–43), while, in 1945, Bowman looks forward to the better data that will arrive with the 1945 sample census.

Several years later, at an AEA session on income distribution, Fellner (1953) reiterated: "by contemporary distribution theory we presumably mean a qualified marginal productivity theory. . . ." (484). "Distribution theory," George Garvy said at an AEA session the following year, "deals with functional shares in national income" (1954, p. 236). "[E]conomic analysis provides a reasonably good theory of the functional distribution of income," writes D. Gale Johnson in 1954, "and nothing that can be called a theory of the personal income distribution . . ." (249).

The intellectual division of labor among distribution scholars thus persists well into the 1950s. The study of the personal income distribution remains the province of the measurement-oriented researchers organized around the NBER and in the government agencies, while distribution theory remains entirely functional, and, within neoclassical economics, essentially an adjunct of marginal productivity theory.

Distribution scholars become less specialized in the late 1950s. This change comes from better data, a concomitant evolution in the view of what personal distribution data are for, and, perhaps most conspicuously, from the development of a new theory of why persons get what they get – human capital theory. We examine this change by considering, first, the empirical work of the NBER's Conference on Research in Income and Wealth, and second, the development of human capital theory.

4. THE CONFERENCE ON RESEARCH IN INCOME AND WEALTH, 1939–1958[19]

The Conference on Research in Income and Wealth, a collaboration of the NBER and several leading universities, was founded in 1936 to advance the cause of measurement in economics. In 1937 the Conference began publishing an approximately annual series entitled *Studies in Income and Wealth*, still in publication today. The Conference was a major force in developing and analyzing income distribution data, and the *Studies* series provides a remarkable record of how data availability and analyses progressed over the mid-century period. Many of the annuals from the 1940s through the 1960s include papers, and sometimes entire volumes, about the personal distribution of income. Two themes interweave throughout the *Studies*: what income distribution data are available, and what the data should be used for.

4.1. Data Availability

In its early years, the Conference was concerned principally with the quality and meaning of national income accounting data. Its 1939 survey of personal income distribution information echoes Kuznets's lament of 1933 about data quality. Recall Merwin's (1939) summary of the literature as "too crude and inaccurate," even unable to offer "a true picture of the relative welfare of the different strata in society, even at a given moment" (p. 74), a judgment seconded by Kuznets (1939).[20]

The fifth volume of the *Studies*, entitled *Income Size Distributions in the United States* (1943) states that the Conference has, since its inception, "considered one of its major objectives to be the improvement of basic data on income and its distribution . . . Because the need for more data was especially pressing in the field of the distribution of personal income by size, the Conference has centered attention on this field." Attention notwithstanding, however, "It has . . . become increasingly clear that the failure to coordinate the various studies made the data far less useful . . . (due to) differences in concepts, coverage, and methods of . . . presentation."

The data on income and its distribution gradually improve, on three fronts especially. First, the decennial U.S. Census began asking income questions in 1940.[21] It is intriguing to note that, as Kuznets reports, the advocacy for income questions in the 1940 Census came not from economists, but from population statisticians interested in economic effects upon differential fertility (Kuznets, 1939, p. 91, Note 1). The 1950 Census provides still higher quality and more extensive income data than any previous source.[22] Second, beginning in 1948, income questions were permanently added to the Current Population Survey of households. And, third, during World War II, the Federal income tax base vastly expands, which would offer a much broader picture of the income distribution. In 1944, 47 million persons filed income tax returns, as compared with 26 million in 1941, 5 million in 1935 and 4 million in 1929 (Goldsmith et al., 1954, p. 1). Volume 23 of the *Series* (1958), entitled *An Appraisal of the 1950 Census Income Data*, documents the advances in data sophistication and quality achieved by the late 1950s. Still, as late as 1951, Dorothy Brady (1951, pp. 3–4) could write, with reason, in volume13:

> One sentence summarizes aptly and completely present knowledge of the size distribution of income: we know little more than that the data are deficient in both quality and quantity, that income is very unequally distributed, and that a high standard of living cannot be attained on the average income. This much we knew 30 and more years ago.

4.2. Why Do We Want Personal Income Distribution Data?

Different reasons for the uses of distribution data arise over time as its quantity and quality increase. Early empirical work in income distribution, influenced by Pareto, focused on characterizing the extent and stability of income inequality. During the Depression, however, American economists began to ask, "does the distribution of income have economic effects of its own," especially on savings and consumption behavior. A four-volume Brookings study argued yes. As reviewer Arthur Burns put it: "the central argument of the work is simple. The chronic retardant of economic progress is our [unequal] method of distributing income" (1936, p. 477). Influenced by John A. Hobson's (1910) underconsumption hypothesis, Harold

Moulton (1935) argued in *Income and Economic Progress*, the fourth Brookings volume, that consumer spending had not increased proportionately with the rise in national income, resulting in what Burns characterized as "persistent underconsumption." [23] What is worse, the higher savings were not finding their way into more spending on capital goods, so that business investment was also falling.

Not all distribution scholars shared this Hobsonian, proto-Keynesian view that greater inequality reduces growth by increasing savings. But the idea that important macroeconomic effects could be caused by the personal distribution itself clearly emerges in the *Series* literature (see, for example, Merwin, 1939, Kuznets, 1943, Preface, 1946, 1951). A particularly striking statement is found in Hollander's (1952) introduction to volume 15:

> We are still seeking to understand the response of consumption and saving behavior to various stimuli. We know, of course, that they are particularly sensitive to income: this, in fact, has been the reason for our interest in income and income size distribution for many years (p. 2).

The idea that distribution could be a causal variable proved important, opening a line of research that continues to this day.[24]

Dorothy Brady's (1951) paper, the same one that laments distribution data deficiencies, discusses two related policy questions. The first, which becomes central during the 1960s Great Society Era, concerns the definition and measurement of poverty. Redistributing income to the poor requires knowing who the poor are, which, in turn, raises the question of how redistribution affects economic growth. The second question, which is taken up earlier in the economics literature, concerns the relationship between economic growth and income dispersion, a relationship that Simon Kuznets influentially addressed in 1955.

There is a striking shift in the *Series* papers evident by the late 1950s. The focus is less on income inequality as something objectionable – for its injustice or for its adverse effects upon growth – and more on explaining why incomes vary in the first place. George Garvy's (1952) paper, entitled "Inequality of Income: Causes and Measurement," is one of the first to signal the coming shift in theoretical emphasis. Garvy argues against focusing on measures of inequality relative to some equality norm. He urges instead a more analytical, and less normative, focus: "the problem really is to identify, isolate, and then measure the various factors that determine relative income positions, not to 'measure' inequality" (p. 27).

Thomas Atkinson (1958) sounds a similar note in his short introductory article to Volume 23 entitled "Some Frontiers of Size-Distribution Research." Atkinson argues that economists should ask what are "the determinants of income for the individual?" (p. 36), which he views as the "the key to many of our size distribution problems." In 1958, Atkinson finds little progress on the determinants of income dispersion since Kuznets and Friedman's *Income from Independent Professional Practice* (1945).

5. CALLS-TO-ARMS: FRIEDMAN-KUZNETS, 1953–1962

Two major figures in the profession, Friedman and Kuznets, called for greater attention to the personal distribution of income, featuring it in their own research in the 1950s.

5.1. Kuznets

Simon Kuznets is a central figure in our story. He made a important contribution to the development of income distribution statistics through his intellectual leadership of the Conference on Income and Wealth. Kuznets's work with Milton Friedman, *Income from Independent Professional Practice* (1945) was a path-breaking study of the income distributions of these groups. Gary Becker (1964) among others cites it as an important precursor to the development of human capital theory.[25]

Kuznets's third contribution came to be known as the Kuznets Curve. His 1955 Presidential Address to the American Economic Association, entitled "Economic Growth and Income Inequality," proposed an inverted-U relationship between growth and inequality. Income inequality is hypothesized to increase in the early stages of economic growth, and then decrease in its later stages. Kuznets's paper provoked a large and decades-long literature that developed to examine this hypothesis.

Several points are worth noting about the 1955 article. First, "[d]espite its name, Kuznets never actually drew such a curve. He was content to offer a verbal conjecture about how income equality might move, and to use a tale of compositional shifts and some common sense to suggest explanations" (Lindert, 2000, pp.172–173). Second, the article's major emphasis does not seem to be the existence of such a curve. Instead, it is to explain why, in the U.S., England and Germany, "the relative distribution of income . . . has been moving toward equality . . . particularly since the 1920s" (p. 4). This is a puzzle for Kuznets because "there are at least two groups of forces in the long-term operation of developed countries that make for *increasing* inequality" (p. 7). He posits factors – especially compositional shifts in population and production sectors – that might contribute to explaining the puzzle. The other part of the Kuznets Curve, that inequality widens at the early stages of development, Kuznets considers only briefly.

Third, Kuznets expresses some doubts whether the pattern of widening then narrowing income dispersion also applies to developing countries. Despite Kuznets's own qualms, the Kuznets Curve became "perhaps the dominant strand in the income distribution and development literature" (Kanbur, 2000, p. 797).

Fourth, several authors express major misgivings about the immense influence the Kuznets Curve has had on the income distribution literature. Lindert (2000) asserts that it has "to some extent tyrannized the literature on inequality trends" (p. 173), while Kanbur (2000) suggests that "in a strange way the framework . . . may have become a straightjacket which inhibits fresh thinking" (p. 800).[26]

Kuznets's conjecture was influential in part because it framed the future debate over how best to reduce income inequality – through economic growth or through government tax-and-transfer redistribution. For a full generation after WWII, the American economy grew rapidly and income inequality fell, consistent with Kuznets's hypothesis. This lent some credence to the view that growth not redistribution was the best means to reduce income inequality.[27]

The strong economic growth and decreasing income inequality of the post-War era may help explain why distribution scholars moved away from an emphasis on income distribution as a determinant of consumption and savings, and toward a new interest in explaining, theoretically, why individuals get what they do. For example, as we noted above, distribution scholars writing in the NBER volumes increasingly called for a theoretical explanation of the determinants of the personal distribution of income.

5.2. Friedman

In the second epigraph of this essay, from his "Choice, Chance, and the Personal Distribution of Income" (1953), Friedman decries the lack of a theory of the personal distribution of income, echoing his Progressive-Era antecedents. Sahota (1978) describes Friedman's (1953) paper as the opening salvo of the "individual choice" theory of personal income distribution – the theory that individuals have a say in their future incomes.

Drawing on his earlier work with Leonard Savage, Friedman explains income dispersion (and its skewness) by positing differences across individuals in their attitudes toward risk. Friedman's paper is a precursor to modern human capital theory because it sees the individual as optimizing (and doing so with known probability distributions, hence insurable risk), and because it asserts that individuals have some choice, admittedly bounded by the gifts of nature, parents, society and luck, in the determination of their future location in the income distribution.

Friedman reproduced the essay in his 1962 graduate text *Price Theory: a Provisional Text* in a chapter on the size distribution of income. In 1976, Friedman produced a new version of the text, entitled *Price Theory*, containing four new chapters. The size distribution chapter reappears, but it is preceded by a new chapter with the title "The Relation Between the Functional and Personal Distribution of Income." This new chapter provides a broader and more thorough introduction to issues surrounding the size distribution.

5.3. But Was Anyone Listening?

Yet despite this call from two of the profession's leading figures, theoretical interest in the personal distribution of income still received relatively little attention. Some evidence is provided by Kaldor's widely-cited and reprinted 1955 article "Alternative Theories of Distribution." Title notwithstanding, the article is entirely concerned with functional distribution. There is not a single mention in the article of the personal distribution of income. In Section 12, we examine how Kaldor's theory of distribution worked to embed the Ricardian functional emphasis.

6. HUMAN CAPITAL THEORY OF THE INCOME DISTRIBUTION EMERGES, CIRCA 1960

Why human capital theory, which has a long history in political economy, ultimately flowers only at the very end of the 1950s, and in Columbia-Chicago garb, presents an interesting puzzle in the history of economics.[28] What is indisputable is that human capital theory, when it did flower, provided a long missing *neoclassical* explanation for why persons get what they do. Human capital theory helped fill Friedman's "major gap in economic theory" by arguing that individuals could affect their income levels, and therefore their locations in the income distribution, by the investment choices they made with respect to schooling, training and so forth. In so doing, it directly spawned major analytical work on income distribution questions.[29] In his 1976 JEL survey, Mark Blaug could write: "(T)he human capital research program has . . . boldly attacked certain traditionally neglected topics in economics, such as the distribution of personal income" (p. 849).

The personal distribution and human capital are, as Jacob Mincer (1970) points out, "intimately connected," since income differentials are what measure the costs and returns to investments in human capital. Both Becker and Mincer, two of the major figures in the doctrine's development, made the personal distribution central. Mincer's (1957) doctoral dissertation was entitled "A Study of Personal Income Distribution"; his 1958 JPE paper drawing on his dissertation was entitled "Investment in Human Capital and Personal Income Distribution"; and his 1970 JEL survey paper was entitled "The Distribution of Labor Incomes with Special Reference to Human Capital Accumulation."[30] Becker's (1967) Woytinsky Lecture, incorporated into later editions of his book *Human Capital*, was entitled "Human Capital and the Personal Distribution of Income."[31]

6.1. The Content of Human Capital Theory

Complete expository coverage of the insights of human capital analysis about the size distribution of income is far beyond the scope of this review. Instead, we provide a summary sketch, based on a number of Mincer's contributions, Becker's (1967) Woytinsky lectures and his book *Human Capital*.

The basic idea is that individuals can make forward-looking investments that enhance their future earnings power. This implies, among other things, that an individual's current income reflects investment decisions he or she made in the past, and more broadly, that an individual's current income can be affected and has been affected by that individual's prior choices.

Two things are required to put analytical and empirical meat on this basic skeleton. First, the nature of human capital investment must be conceptualized in a way that permits empirical measurement. Second, the effect of investment on earnings must be modeled. The measurement requirement was approached in several ways. Initially, years of schooling were used as a measure of formal schooling investment. Later, various measures of labor market experience, including Mincer's famous measure of experience as "age minus schooling minus six," were adopted to capture the possibility of post-school on-the-job training.[32]

The second requirement, involving the modeling of how investment might affect earnings, developed from Becker's so-called "general earnings function," which provided an algebraic expression for how past investments influence current earnings.[33] Mincer's so-called "simple schooling equation," which expressed log earnings as a linear function of years of schooling (the coefficient on schooling providing an estimate of the rate of return to schooling), could be shown to be a special case of Becker's general earnings function (Mincer, 1970, p. 9).[34]

This earnings-function-based way of proceeding, while it yields many important insights, fails to make explicit use of the typical supply-demand dichotomy so helpful in much of economic theorizing. Indeed, Sahota (1978) indicates that one objection to human capital theory has been that it is "a partial and piecemeal theory . . . until very recently, a supply theory" (p. 16).

However, an alternative formulation in Becker's Woytinsky lecture (1967) sets forth a human capital approach which is embedded in the supply-demand dichotomy. He uses supply and demand curves for human capital investment for an individual to show how these influences interact to determine the individual's human capital investment. Differences across individuals, which generate different incomes over time, are produced by differences in the demand and supply functions facing different people. However, as Sahota (1978, p. 17) notes, the determinants of the supply and demand functions are treated as exogenous.

This approach generates both general and concrete results about the income distribution. We have already indicated the crucial premise, that size distribution was something to be explained – a dependent variable-and that the explanation should embed the idea that individuals could affect their income levels, and therefore their locations in the income distribution, by the investment choices they made. As Blaug (1976) puts it: human capital theory's original goal was to demonstrate "that a wide range of apparently disconnected phenomena . . . are the outcome of a definite pattern of individual decisions, having in common the features of foregoing present gains for the prospect of future ones."

In so doing, Blaug suggests, human capital theory also "discovered novel facts, such as the correlation between education and age-specific earnings, which have opened up entirely new areas of research in economics" (p. 850). Mincer (1976) makes the remarkable claim that as much as half of the total variation in observed earnings can be attributed to "the distribution of schooling and post-school investment" (Mincer, 1976, p. 151). The human capital approach also offered explanations for the positive skewness of the distribution of earnings (see Sahota, 1978, pp. 13–14 for a useful summary). Human-capital-theory-inspired earnings equations have become a staple of the labor economist's repertory, a standard way of "explaining" wage variation. Sherwin Rosen (1992) has referred to the ubiquitous use of a particular form of the earnings equation[35] as the "Mincering" of labor economics.[36]

6.2. The Emergence of Microdata Sets

Modern human capital theory's emergence in the 1960s generated a wave of empirical studies. Early work was limited to the use of grouped data, rather than microdata. Becker and Chiswick (1966), for example, included regressions of the log of earnings on years of schooling, using published Census table cell averages as observations (pp. 365–367). By the early 1970s, however, the data situation had changed in a big way. James Smith's "Introduction" to Volume 39 in the *Studies in Income and Wealth* series (James Smith ed., 1975) gives the following description:

> With respect to data, the decade of the sixties saw a rich harvest of microdata, reflecting the desire of policymakers to estimate in advance and measure in retrospect the consequences of social programs. Early in the sixties, the Board of Governors of the Federal Reserve System produced the Survey of Financial Characteristics of Consumers.... By mid-decade, the Department of Labor was at work on the National Longitudinal Surveys, and the Office of Economic Opportunity had begun work on the Surveys of Economic Opportunity (1966 and 1967). The Office of Economic Opportunity in conjunction with the Survey Research Center... also began collecting data (for)... the Panel Study of Income Dynamics. Microdata from all these studies were made available to researchers. Near the end of the decade, Internal Revenue Service... tapes of tax returns... became available to researchers (p. 1).

Smith argues that the "renewed interest in the distribution and determinants of income and wealth" is data-inspired: "In large measure, the resurgence of researcher interest in personal distributions... has resulted from the increased availability of microdata and the sustained methodological efforts of Orcutt and others demonstrating (its) superiority (in) the estimation of many... models of behavior" (p. 1).

6.3. Stigler as a Barometer

The ascendancy of human capital theory, which was fueled by the interactive benefits of new theory in conjunction with new data, marks the neoclassical conquest of labor economics, one of the last Institutionalist redoubts in American economics. American neoclassical economics now began to claim, as it could not at mid-century, that the market for people is like the market for goods.

George Stigler's revisions to his quintessentially neoclassical *The Theory of Price* text reflect these changes in the economics of distribution. The 1941 and 1946 editions have no chapter on income distribution.[37] The revised edition of 1952 adds a chapter entitled "The Distribution of Income," which signals its worthiness as a subject of study. Mirroring the distribution scholarship of the day, Stigler's chapter is empirical; one major message is a cautionary tale whose moral is that the data can mislead with respect to actual inequality.[38]

By 1960, Stigler could write, in "The Influence of Events and Policies on Economic Theory" (1965, p. 22): [O]ne can predict that certain problems will affect economic theory and others will not. The problem of personal income distribution will eventually receive much theoretical attention, since it is a problem of all economies and all times." The 1966 edition of Stigler's text revises the size distribution chapter, which now opens with an observation akin to those made by Becker and Mincer, and by Friedman before them: "of all the major topics discussed in this book," the size distribution "has been studied least" (p. 288). The 1966 chapter also draws a figure, which plots annual net earnings against age for college vs. high school graduates, that would now be recognized as a typical human capital diagram, though there are no accompanying cites to that literature. Stigler says, "If the men in an occupation were of identical ability and worked equal periods and with equal intensity, the present value of their life time earnings would be equal (chance factors aside), but their earnings in any one year . . . would display substantial dispersion" (p. 290). Stigler's position on inequality is unchanged, but human capital, with its lifetime income focus and its stress on years of formal education, has invaded Stigler's text.

6.4. Human Capital Theory Makes Labor Productivity Endogenous

The marginal productivity theorists of 50 years prior argued that productivity determines the factor's price. But what determined productivity? For half a century, students of distribution ordinarily appealed to genetic, cultural, familial and material inheritance. Distribution scholars might emphasize different kinds of inheritance, but all took productivity to be exogenous, something one was given. So-called ability theories tried to reconcile their view that human talents are normally distributed – a view that was propounded in Francis Galton's *Hereditary Genius* (1869) – with the fact that the personal income distribution was right skewed (roughly) log-normally distributed.[39] The stochastic theories of income distribution, which regarded future outcomes as the product of luck, tried different stochastic processes to produce a given frequency distribution of income (e.g. Gibrat, 1931). But most of these traditional approaches to income distribution assumed that human capital was always and everywhere a gift. What the new theory argued was that human capital could also be acquired. It thereby made labor productivity endogenous, which not only directs attention to distribution across individuals, but also insists that a person's place in the distribution is not (wholly) an accident of birth.

6.5. Resistance to the Move to SDI

American economics gradually drags the study of labor relations under the tent of neoclassical price theory. Human capital theory and the growing availability of micro-data increase attention to personal income distribution, as manifested in the extraordinary outpouring of personal income distribution research in the early 1970s that we discuss below. At the same time, however, heterodox traditions in economics, especially the Cambridge U.K. tradition, resist the neoclassical expansion in ways that are important for distribution theory. In fact, in the 1950s, when distribution is nearly moribund in mainstream American economics, distribution enjoys something of a revival on the left, as part of its return to classical theories of growth.

The post-Keynesian and neo-Ricardian theories of distribution developed largely at Cambridge harken back to the Ricardian triad – they insist upon, by their very structure, a functional conception of distribution. An American example is Sidney Weintraub's *An Approach to the Theory of Income Distribution* (1958), a Post-Keynesian effort to connect distribution theory with contemporary developments in the theory of the firm, and the macroeconomic determination of income and employment. Weintraub's book contains no treatment of the personal distribution of income; indeed, it lacks any reference to personal distribution in its table of contents or index.

A more influential example, mentioned above, was Nicholas Kaldor's widely cited 1955 article, "Alternative Theories of Distribution." Kaldor does two things. First, he proposes a taxonomy of distribution theories – Ricardian, Marxian, neo-classical/marginalist, and Keynesian. The second thing his article develops is his own "Keynesian" theory of distribution. For Kaldor, distribution theory is *understood* to mean "functional distribution," just as it is in the American neoclassical tradition at this time.

But the Cambridge tradition is hostile to the marginal productivity theory of pricing, and, even more so, to the marginal productivity theory of income distribution. The Cambridge School rejects neoclassical economics' general theory of factor pricing, and instead appeals to the Ricardian tradition of different theoretical explanations for labor and capital income, respectively. Kaldor's model explains growth and functional shares by recourse, first, to different marginal propensities to save – savings out of profits are higher than those out of wages – and, second, to the assumption that investment's share of total spending is invariant (1955, p. 95).

The American neoclassicals embrace marginal productivity theory, with its microeconomic emphasis on the allocation of resources. The Cambridge School emphasizes the Keynesian macroeconomic determinants of growth. In invoking Ricardo, the English Cantabridgians revived the classical conception of distribution not as the byproduct of a factor pricing process, but as a matter of division between socioeconomic classes.[40] Thus, the American neoclassicals and the Cambridge School are fundamentally opposed in their conception of how value theory relates to distribution, and would become still more adversarial over the national production function. Nonetheless, until human capital theory made headway in neoclassical economics, these adversaries, who disagreed on so much, agreed that distribution was a functional affair.

7. AN ERUPTION OF SIZE DISTRIBUTION RESEARCH, CIRCA 1970

After three generations of prominent Anglophone economists lamenting the paucity of research on the personal income distribution, the dam bursts circa 1970. In just a few years, more economists would write books, monographs, and survey articles on the personal income distribution than in the preceding half century. What is more, the outpouring came from many different corners of the discipline. Distribution scholars such as Anthony Atkinson (1970, 1975), Martin Bronfenbrenner (1971), Harold Lydall (1968), and David Champernowne (1973), made important contributions, but they were joined by leading figures in the profession. There is Amartya Sen's *On Economic Inequality* (1973), Jan Tinbergen's *Income Distribution* (1975), Harry Johnson's *The Theory of Income Distribution* (1973), James Meade's *The Just Economy* (1976), Arthur Okun's *Equality and Efficiency: The Big Trade-off* (1975), James Tobin on limiting inequality (1970), Kenneth Boulding on the personal distribution (1975), Lester Thurow's *Generating Inequality* (1975), the human capital research of Becker (1967), Mincer (1970), and Barry Chiswick (1974), and early work of Alan Blinder (1974) and Joseph Stiglitz (1969).

This outpouring is not monolithic in approach, scope, or even in its emphasis upon the personal distribution. Some earlier efforts, such as Bronfenbrenner (1971) and Johnson (1973), remain more functional in coverage. Some are surveys rather than original research, and some are more philosophical in spirit. But the change in research emphasis, and its suddenness, measured in historical terms, are striking nonetheless.

While the distinction is far from iron-clad, some of these contributions are primarily surveys, while others make new theoretical or empirical contributions. Because surveys typically attempt to provide overviews of the field, it is instructive to compare those written near the beginning of the period – Reder (1969), Johnson (1973), and Bronfenbrenner (1971) – with Sahota's (1978) survey, which is published after the major 1970s outpouring of books and articles on the subject. Specifically, we will first indicate what size distribution issues are addressed in Reder-Johnson-Bronfenbrenner, to show how they view the field. We will then consider Sahota's (1978) view of the state of size distribution analysis. The contrast between the Sahota overview and what Reder-Johnson-Bronfenbrenner present is instructive, providing an indication of how the field had developed during the 1970s.

7.1. Reder

Reder's (1969) survey appears as a chapter in the *Studies in Income and Wealth* series. He starts by quoting Stigler about the "absence of a developed theory of the size distribution of income." He then asserts the contrary proposition that "there are a good many bits and pieces of theory lying around in the literature that can . . . be fitted into a mosaic called 'The Theory of Income Size Distribution" (p. 205). The purpose of economic theory in this context is to "provide hypotheses as to the direction and, where possible, the extent to which changes in structural parameters alter the size distribution of income or some component" (pp. 205–206). Reder concentrates on the determinants of the distribution of earnings.

While Reder's discussion touches on a large number of the "mosaic's" pieces, he devotes much of his attention to a few specific topics. The most striking example is his focus on the distinction between "temporary" and "permanent" workers, and how their differential risks of unemployment might translate into differential effects on earnings concentration. This discussion which takes up more than 20% of the survey's pages, is an extension of his previous work, well-known to an earlier generation of labor economists, on factors influencing the skilled/unskilled wage differential (see, for example, Reder, 1962). Much of the rest of the survey reads like a set of interesting but diffuse comments on various literatures, especially human capital theory. Someone looking for a compact overview of the essentials of a theory of income size distribution would not find it easy to extract from Reder's survey.

7.2. Bronfenbrenner

While Reder's survey is an article, both Bronfenbrenner (1971) and Johnson (1973) produced books. Moreover, both authors devote most of their attention to functional distribution, but also discuss the personal distribution. Bronfenbrenner frames his book as a "reformulation and restatement" of the income distribution literature. He notes that "(T)he major distribution problem, for general economists (economic theorists), past and present, has been *functional*. . . . The secondary distribution problem has been *personal*" (p. 27). His book contains 17 chapters. Of the 15 that follow the two introductory chapters, only one, "Topics in Personal Income Distribution," is entirely devoted to size distribution issues.

Compared to Reder's survey, Bronfenbrenner's chapter seems a more systematic and comprehensive overview of size distribution issues, as indicated by the chapter's five subsections. The first subsection "Statistical Measurement of Inequality, "reviews and criticizes various measures of the distribution, paying special attention to Pareto's "law," Lorenz curves and Gini coefficients. The second subsection, "Distribution Formulas and Their Generation," discusses how statistical processes might generate some empirical functions (distributions) that mimic certain features of actual income distributions. Bronfenbrenner notes that income and wealth distributions typically include relatively few large values; that is, they are skewed to the right or positively skewed. Among the statistical processes that can generate this are Gibrat's approach, which yields a lognormal distribution. This distribution "does in fact fit many income distributions quite closely" (p. 53). A number of ways of generating Pareto distributions, which fit upper ranges of the income distribution well, are discussed. The names here include Lydall and Herbert Simon. A "more general" Markov chain process, and how it might be rationalized, is also discussed. The next section, "Explanations for Skewness," starts by asking how, if ability is normally distributed, incomes might still be positively skewed. Besides the statistical explanations in the previous section, Bronfenbrenner mentions a number of economic explanations: Friedman's (1953) "attitudes toward risk" framework and the human capital approach each get a paragraph. Finally, the effects of inherited "income-bearing property" on skewness and the upper tail of the income distribution are considered. The final two subsections of the chapter consider poverty, and whether there has been "an income revolution," a sizable decrease in the income share of the upper 1 or 5 or 10% of the population in recent decades.[41]

7.3. Johnson

Harry Johnson's (1973) contribution is less of a systematic overview, and more of a set of simple illustrative modeling exercises and big-think critiques to give readers a sense of what the important issues about size distribution (as Johnson sees them) might be. Johnson's book is "based on the notes of the course in the theory of distribution and related matters . . . (Johnson had) been giving at the University of Chicago for some eight years" (Preface; no page number). Like Bronfenbrenner's book, Johnson's is largely concerned with the functional distribution; "(N)evertheless, we shall touch on the theory of personal distribution of income developed especially within the last seven or eight years under the impetus of the 'War on Poverty' " (p. 1). Of the book's 18 chapters (235 pp), two chapters (30 pp) are devoted to the size distribution. The second of these two chapters focuses on "the poverty problem." Our discussion concentrates on the first of the two chapters, since it contains most of the analytical content relevant to our topic.[42]

Johnson starts by pointing out that functional distribution "may have little to do with" personal distribution, the latter involving either individual or family distributions. The two major forces determining size distribution are inheritance (broadly construed to include genetic and cultural inheritance), and investment in factor accumulation. Social concern about distribution has two distinct sources: concern about inequality (dispersion of income around the mean), and concern about poverty. Serious data problems arise, Johnson argued, when trying to "validate the demonstration of inequality or of poverty" (p. 207).

Johnson's treatment contains several simple but informative modeling exercises. The first, "A Simple Fisherian Model of Measured Inequality with Actual Equality," presents a stylized example showing that a world whose underlying characteristic is complete "over-life" equality can generate cross-section measures suggesting extreme inequality.[43] A second simple model shows the effects of allowing (probabilistic) movements between income groups. One implication of both models seems to be that simple measures of income distribution fail to reveal the true underlying characteristics of the personal distribution. Moreover, actual inequality may be far less than apparent (measured) inequality.

There is no choice behavior in either of these models. The next section incorporates choice under certainty. The focus here on the effects of individual choice, including human capital investment, on the income distribution (an aspect "frequently ignored by social critics") and how taxation affects these choices. A number of striking Chicagoesque claims about the effects of taxation are derived.[44] The final section of the chapter is entitled "Uncertainty of Income Prospects and Differing Attitudes toward Risk." It uses an analysis based on Friedman's (1953) article to explore the implications of attitudes toward risk for the earnings of occupations with different risk characteristics.

The Johnson overview treatment seems a cautionary warning about simplistic interpretations of cross-section data, and suggests some of the conceptual modeling intricacies that would be involved in deriving income distribution findings in a world in which individuals are making maximizing choices faced with uncertainty and human capital investment possibilities.

7.4. Sahota

The Reder/Bronfenbrenner/Johnson contributions provide a sense of what perceptive observers viewed as the state of personal distribution analysis in the

Table 1.   Sahota Bibliography Distributed by Time Period of Citation.

Time Period	Number of Citations
1975–1978	81
1970–1974	108
1965–1969	39
1960–1964	40
1955–1959	21
1950–1954	9
1945–1949	5
1900–1944	14
Pre-1900	9
Total	326

early 1970s.[45] Sahota's (1978) survey appears on the heels of the personal income distribution outpouring. Comparing Sahota to Reder/Bronfenbrenner/Johnson provides an indication of the major changes in the literature that developed during the 1970s.

One striking contrast has to do with focus. Bronfenbrenner's and Johnson's treatments of the personal distribution are embedded in discussions mainly concerned with the functional distribution. Even the Reder article, which focuses on personal distribution only, speaks of little bits and pieces of theory that need to be "assembled" into a "mosaic." By the late 1970s however, Sahota could review a vast personal distribution literature, and one rich enough for Sahota to produce a "taxonomy of distinctly identifiable theories" (p. 2). His ten categories are: ability theories; stochastic theories; individual choice theory; human capital theory; theories of educational inequalities; inheritance theories; life cycle theories; public income redistribution theories; "more complete" theories; and theories of distributive justice.[46]

The 326-item bibliography in Sahota's article[47] suggests how rich an SDI literature has developed by the late 1970s. Table 1 below presents the distribution of Sahota's citations by time period. As the Table indicates, 189 of the 326 cites are from 1970 or later, and only 37 come from before 1955.[48]

8. WHAT LED TO THE SWITCH TO SDI, AND WHY DID IT TAKE SO LONG?

Part I of this paper has presented evidence that the major blossoming of research into personal income distribution took place in the 1970s. In this second part of the paper, we ask: why did it occur when it did, and why was it so long in coming?

9. WHAT LED TO THE SWITCH TO SDI?

In speculating about the factors that promoted (or impeded) the blossoming of economic research into the personal distribution of income, we will consider state activity, theory development, data collection, and the *zeitgeist*, among other things. The relationships between these causal factors are complicated and subtle, and our conjectures, confined as they are to a fraction of a paper, must be tentative. We offer these ideas as informed (and, we hope, provocative) speculation upon the sorts of developments that influenced the trajectory of research interests among economists considering distribution.

9.1. The Welfare State and Redistribution

The American welfare state expanded significantly in the 1960s Great-Society era, and played an increasingly influential role in determining who gets what. The Federal government redistributed a greater share of national income, by design and as a byproduct of policy. Family income inequality reaches postwar lows in the late 1960s and early 1970s. To apply its view of who should get what, the state needed to know who got what in order to effect progressive redistribution via tax and transfer. On the transfer side, especially, an expanded welfare state required good personal distribution data. The "War on Poverty" demanded data on incomes in the lower tail of the income distribution. A functional distribution concept could not shed any light on poverty issues, as it had virtually nothing to say about the distribution of income by individual, family or household at its lower end.

Theory mattered too, to understand how to transfer resources to poor families while minimizing dead-weight losses, and to predict whether income subsidies, wage floors, or payments-in-kind best advance poor families' well being. Means-tested programs like Medicaid are not the only examples: universal programs like Social Security and Medicare are also mildly redistributive.

Nor is the size distribution of personal income all that mattered circa 1970. With the successes of the civil rights and women's rights movements, government increasingly considered the income and well being of groups defined by race, sex, ethnicity, and family structure. These demographic concerns, "first cousins" to concerns about poverty per se, could not be addressed with a functional conception of distribution. To cut the data demographically, one needs to estimate a size distribution of personal income.[49]

On the tax side, the personal income distribution had long been of interest to public finance students of the incidence and burden of the tax system. The issue of "who pays the taxes" implies a concern with the distribution of tax burden by income class, especially with respect to the income tax.[50] Optimal taxation, the distribution of the income-tax burden, and the War on Poverty all clearly demanded knowledge of the personal income distribution.

This bare sketch can only gloss the complicated and subtle causal relationships between policy, theory and data collection. A more redistributive state creates direct demand for personal distribution data. More indirectly, the state may call upon economists to evaluate its programs, and economists witnessing the expansion of the government's attempts to redistribute might view it as important to explain why income was distributed as it was (and, perhaps, to warn against redistribution with excessively high efficiency costs). The causality can also run the other way: economic research and the collection of government statistics can, of themselves, influence government policy. We are proposing only that these interactions were especially active and mutually reinforcing during the Great Society era.[51]

9.2. The Functional Distribution No Longer Explains the Sources of Income Inequality

The economists who contributed to the personal distribution outpouring increasingly regarded the functional distribution as disguising rather than revealing the sources of inequality. The significance of factor shares for inequality is "nowadays rather limited," said Alan Blinder (1974, p. 1), given that "disparities in wages dominate all other causes of inequality" (1974, p. 125). Mincer (1970) makes the same point: there is more inequality among wages earners – those the functional approach lumps under "L" – than there is in total income. Taking the long view, economic historian Peter Lindert (1986) compares the U.K. shares of the Ricardian triad (rents, profits, wages) with those of the top 10% and bottom 90% of the personal income distribution, for 1867 and 1972–1973. Two things stand out. In Victorian England, virtually all land was owned by the top decile and land rents made up 13% of national income. A century later, the top decile gets almost no income from land rents, which also cease to be economically significant, and "the share [the top decile] gets from other property income is not that different from the share that property contributes to the poorer 90%" (1986, p. 1155).

The classical economists simply identified wage earners with the poor. In the early 20th century, Pigou acknowledged that the functional distribution was less adequate than the personal, and felt obliged to argue that "no great error is introduced if we identify the income of the poorer classes with the receipts of the factor labor" (Pigou, 1912, pp. 78–79, cited in Dalton, 1920, p. 147). By 1970, the traditional identification of labor income with poverty was long past tenable. Because the returns to human skill had increased so much relative to other productive resources, wage differences among workers contributed more to income inequality than any other cause. "While this simple equation of factors and [income] quantile ranks had some validity back when the classical economists wrote ... it was," says Lindert, "obsolete long before it was abandoned" (2000, p. 172). Thus, economists investigating inequality were drawn to explore the sources of wage inequality, a task the functional distribution obscured rather than illuminated.

9.3. Why Do They Get What They Get: Human Capital Theory

It seems clear that the development of human capital theory – which offered a theory of human skill acquisition – played an important enabling role in the circa 1970 blossoming of personal distribution research. Not only could income distribution questions be addressed using the human capital framework, but it actually generated, by its very logic, a focus on income distribution questions. Human capital theory offered an account of income inequality consistent with the actual sources of income differences, and created demand for more empirical work. Though human capital theory focuses on individuals, it does not say who should pay for investment in individual skills, and thus could be made congruent with the idea that government should invest in its disadvantaged citizens.

9.4. What Should They Get: The Revival of Distributive Justice

The "what should they get" question has always loomed behind interest in distribution. But in the early 1970s, distributive justice was enjoying an important revival, thanks to the influence of John Rawls's (1971) *A Theory of Justice*, and the vast literature it generated. Rawls's book almost single-handedly revived distributive justice within political philosophy, and, moreover, did so in a recognizably economic language.[52] Rawls was an egalitarian, but he wrote within a Liberal/contractarian framework that made the individual – not his productive class – the unit of appraisal. Rawls, as with the vast majority of his interlocutors, was concerned with distribution across persons. His principles of justice rested upon the notion that individuals devising a social contract would have no knowledge of the productive resources – human and tradeable – that they would in fact individually possess. Distribution was thus in the intellectual air, and many leading scholars conceived of distribution as applying to individuals not groups, and certainly not groups defined by productive function.

10. WHY DID THE SWITCH TO SDI TAKE SO LONG?

Why did this blossoming of personal distribution research occur as late as it did, three generations after Pareto's pioneering work, 50 years after the NBER's maiden publication, and following decades of prominent lamenting over the functional conception's inadequacy? We cannot provide a definitive answer, but we do offer some suggestive conjectures in two categories: first, factors that slowed the impact of the SDI-promoting trends just identified, and, second, factors that worked to maintain an interest in the functional approach to distribution.

11. FACTORS SLOWING SDI-PROMOTING TRENDS

11.1. Why Did the Development of Good Data Take So Long?

The inexorable improvement of the data combined with large reductions in calculating costs seem to be "obvious" contributing factors to the outpouring of personal income distribution research. The information available for measuring size distribution in the U.S. improved markedly during the 1950s and 1960s, and was accompanied by massive improvements in data processing technologies.

There is indirect evidence for the stimulating effects of lower data processing costs. In "Progress and Microdata," Andrew Oswald (1991) reviews all full-length articles in the Economic Journal (EJ) from 1959 through 1990 in order to examine the following claim: "Compared with today, did a previous generation have journals full of practical articles based on data for real firms and real people?" Oswald finds that the percentage of EJ articles using empirical microdata grew from 5% during 1960–1969 to 17% during 1980–1989, using a 3-year moving average. However, the increase from 5 to 17% is not smooth. There is, in fact, a spike that occurs from 1973 to 1980, after which the percentage of empirical articles does not change much.[53] The spike in microdata-oriented research occurs across many fields in economics-not just within distribution – and is thus consistent with the notion that "cheaper data and computing" helped promote more research in the personal distribution.

But why did the development of good income distribution data take so long? Given that data supply is at least partly endogenous, why didn't the effective demand for income distribution data produce better data before the 1950s and 1960s?

Merwin's answer in 1939 was that many American citizens, instinctively distrustful of the state, and perhaps concerned about tax liability, were disinclined to provide income and consumption data to government surveyors. Merwin speculated that this attitude was "probably fostered by democratic institutions that aim to exalt free enterprise, individualism and personal liberty-all with a minimum of government interference" (p. 75).

Kuznets (1939), who agreed with Merwin's assessment that personal distribution data were seriously inadequate, disagreed with Merwin's explanation for it. Kuznets argued that the data, bad as they were, were improving owing to the fact that citizens increasingly saw the government more as an ally than as an adversary. The Great Depression had raised serious doubts about effectiveness of "free and individualistic economic organization," less assurance of large production growth in the future, and less belief that one's economic fortune is largely due to individual ability. Thus were Americans, Kuznets argued, increasingly adopting "an attitude . . . that makes the provision of income information a natural and acceptable step designed to help public authorities in dealing with commonly recognized economic problems" (p. 92).

But Kuznets also emphasized that better data would be the natural byproduct of an expanded welfare state – the number of Federal income tax returns were not increased tenfold from 1929 to 1946 in order to improve personal income distribution data, but those better data were produced as a byproduct. Once a government institutes "a graduated income tax, social security legislation, laws concerning wages and hours, etc . . . it [enters] fields of administrative activity whose byproducts are large bodies of data on distribution of income by size," Kuznets argued. In effect, Kuznets proposed, once the welfare state acquires a legitimacy sufficient to expand its administrative functions, as it did so conspicuously in the New Deal Era, it generates SDI data almost in passing (p. 92).

11.2. Distribution Ethics May Not Specify an Acceptable Gini Coefficient[54]

A second impediment to the development of the personal income distribution concept may have come from the modern economist's endemic discomfort with normative questions. Some of this is simply part of the neoclassical *ethos*: since the failure of welfare economics in the 1920s and 1930s, many American economists have felt ambivalent concerning normative questions, of which "who should get what" is an example par excellence (Atkinson & Bourguignon, 2000).[55]

Even economists willing to engage with moral philosophy found ambiguities when trying to apply theories of distributive justice to real, live income distributions. Part of this ambiguity is a matter of precision. A distributive ethics ordinarily does not designate a morally acceptable point (or range) of income inequality.[56] A second aspect of the ambiguity arises from the fact that not all theories of distributive justice pertain to the entire income distribution. Take, for example, the view that a decent society is one that provides for its poor. In practice, this means there is a floor, or safety net below which no one shall fall, but there is no income ceiling, or other ethical constraint on income dispersion. A society with no poverty can be deemed just without knowledge of the entire distribution. More generally, "help the poor" is an injunction ethically distinct from "narrow the income distribution," even if, in practice, the former will tend to promote the latter.

Were there developments circa 1970 that might have reduced the difficulty of applying theories of justice to actual income distributions? Two such developments suggest themselves. First, Atkinson (1970) devised a means for ranking Lorenz curves that crossed, thereby providing a method for identifying and gauging the *normatively-relevant* inequality characteristics of a particular distribution. Atkinson helped inspire Amartya Sen (1997) and others who developed the literature that derives welfare measures from income distributions.[57]

Second, the "War on Poverty" focused attention on measures of poverty, which require determining a "poverty line." A literature developed in the 1960s in the U.S. about how to measure poverty, which included the empirical notion of poverty lines. Such measures are inevitably contested, but, as a practical matter, drawing a poverty line is more straightforward than determining which sets of income distributions are ethically acceptable.

12. FACTORS GENERATING CONTINUING INTEREST IN FUNCTIONAL DISTRIBUTION

Even in the face of the numerous factors promoting a move to the personal income distribution, the functional distribution enjoyed some countervailing support of its own: (1) its pragmatic role in neoclassical macroeconomics; and (2) its centrality to the Cambridge School and to other heterodox views of economic relations.

12.1. The Aggregate Production Function

The neo-classical production function of the national economy, a macroeconomic entity, has its origins in marginal productivity theory. It was originally devised as part of a microeconomic explanation of a firm's demand for productive factors. But when Paul Douglas, a student of John Bates Clark, set out to provide some evidence for marginal productivity theory, his data, employment (L), and capital (C), were aggregate at the national level. Douglas asked the mathematician Charles Cobb to devise a functional form that would provide a decent fit to the painstakingly assembled macroeconomic data (1899–1922) and that would also yield constant factor shares of output, a widely accepted stylized fact.[58]

Though beset with difficulties, the Cobb-Douglas functional form proved to be a useful formulation for American neoclassical economists willing to aggregate the firm's production function into a macroeconomic production function.[59] The national production function has had a somewhat checkered history. Robert Solow (1966) characterized it as follows: "I have never thought of the macroeconomic production function as a rigorously justifiable concept. In my mind it is either an illuminating parable, or else a mere device for handling data, to be used so long as it gives good empirical results, and to be abandoned as soon as . . . something better comes along" (1966, pp. 1259–1260).

But it never was completely abandoned, in part because its analytical properties proved so useful to modern macro theory. For example, modern macro theory aims to develop a "relatively simple, relatively aggregated" way of describing and analyzing the economy. In such approaches factor shares are convenient as a shorthand way of dealing with returns within the economy. Real business cycle models, for example, pay attention to factor shares. Moreover, macro modeling approaches often use the concept of the representative agent. In order to get into personal-distribution-type issues, one must get away from the representative agent, and build heterogeneity into the consumer side of the model. While heterogeneity is sometimes introduced to deal with particular macro-empirical puzzles, it is very difficult to build in heterogeneity in a simple but general way.

The national production function caused a conspicuous and prolonged dust-up with Cambridge School partisans. In the so-called "Cambridge Controversies," Joan Robinson and other Cambridge, England economists denied the very possibility of measuring aggregate capital. This issue commanded attention for decades, and was still of great interest in the late 1960s and after.[60]

12.2. Individuals vs. Social Classes

The issues underlying the Cambridge Controversy ran deeper than the technical matters of whether interest rates price capital or whether heterogeneous capital goods could meaningfully be aggregated. The deeper disagreement concerned whether individuals or classes were the appropriate unit of analysis. American neoclassical economists adopted marginal productivity theory, with its general theory of factor pricing, and its microeconomic emphasis on the allocation of resources. The Cambridge School, in reviving Ricardo, adopted the classical conception of distribution, which has the different factors' shares determined not as the byproduct of a general factor pricing process, but by theoretically distinct processes, an approach that carries with it the classical vestige of distribution as a matter of division between socioeconomic classes. These very different approaches to the problem of "why do they get what they get" led to (or perhaps embedded) very different conceptions of the appropriate "who" (in "who gets what?") as the relevant unit of analysis.

The Cambridge School, like the Progressives, Fabians, Institutionalists and other predecessors on the Left, did *not* reason as follows: (1) We want to help the poor; (2) we don't have enough data to know who exactly is poor, but labor is poor, and therefore a decent proxy for poverty; ergo (3) let's help labor. Instead, their reasoning was: (1) We want a fairer distribution of income; (2) the market is unfair because capital gets more than it deserves, indeed, capital gets more *because* labor gets less; ergo; (3) redistribute from capitalists to workers.

The Cambridge School did not regard labor as deserving *because they were poor*. In principle, poverty could be eliminated and the functional distribution would still be unfair. The Cambridge School regarded labor as a class as deserving because they were being unfairly exploited. *Thus, it is not that workers' poverty is unfair, but that the unfairness of capitalism explains workers' poverty.* The Cambridge School view was that income distribution is the product of the intrinsic opposition of (class) interest in production, that workers are poor because capitalists are rich. It thus regards the functional distribution as the distribution concept of greatest importance. As Avi Cohen and Geoff Harcourt put it in their recent review of the Cambridge Controversies: for the "English" Cantabridgians, "social class (position within the division of labor) becomes the fundamental unit of analysis" (2003, p. 208).[61] The group of economists who were most committed to the idea that modern economies were unjust in their distribution, were also committed, by the same deep assumptions, to the functional distribution.

13. CONCLUSION

This essay documents American economics' 20th century move from a functional to a personal distribution of income, and has speculated on what caused the change and why it happened as late as it did. Among the interesting features our narrative has considered are: the role of the Conference on Research on Income and Wealth in encouraging the development of better data, and in adducing new uses for income distribution data; the changing rationale for the study of personal income distribution among its proponents; Kuznets's and Friedman's call for more research decades before the outpouring of personal income research in the 1970s; the impetus of better data, lower-cost data processing, human capital theory, War-on-Poverty and other redistributive programs, the obsolescence of the functional distribution with respect to income inequality, and the intellectual vogue in distributive justice in pushing scholarship toward the personal conception of distribution; and, apparent handicaps notwithstanding, the functional distribution's ongoing role as a pragmatic tool in the representative-agent models of neoclassical macroeconomics, and as a concept central the Cambridge School and to other heterodox views of capitalist economic relations.

NOTES

1. This anecdote was recounted to Goldfarb by a Ph.D. economist who witnessed the conversation. The anecdote helped to suggest the topic of this paper.

2. "Political Economy," Ricardo wrote to Malthus, "you think is an enquiry into the nature and causes of wealth – I think it should rather be called an enquiry into the laws which determine the division of produce of industry among the classes who concur in its formation. No law can be laid down respecting quantity, but a tolerably correct one can be laid down respecting proportions. Every day I am more satisfied that the former enquiry is vain and delusive, and the latter only the true objects of the science" (Letter dated 9 October 1820, *Works* Sraffa Edition Vol VIII, pp. 278–279, Cited in Kaldor, 1955, p. 54, Note 4).

3. Since well-being is famously difficult to measure, the distribution of income (or, less frequently, consumption or wealth) commonly stands in for the distribution of well-being in the large The "they" in question may be different persons or groups. Income distribution trends can measure a cohort over time, or can measure a section of the distribution comprised of persons or groups that vary over time – such as the "middle quintile" of the income distribution.

4. "Inequality" can refer neutrally to an income distribution that is not uniform, but it also has come to connote a undesirable departure from income equality (see Allyn Young, 1917). This terminological ambiguity illustrates how, in the study of distribution, ethical judgments tend to encroach upon factual descriptions, a point also made by Atkinson and Bourguignon (2000).

5. Because these ideas are well-documented in an extensive secondary literature, we present only the barest sketch, eschewing interpretive subtleties. For histories of the 19th-century production and distribution theories, see for example Cannan (1917 [1894]), which covers 1776–1848, and Stigler (1941), which pertains to 1870–1895. See also Hollander (1903).

6. Critics like Henry George, whose several editions of *Progress and Poverty* (1879) motivated Clark to develop his marginal productivity theory of distribution, likewise retained the Ricardian view that distribution is a matter of productive function.

7. Progressive-Era American economics was slow to adopt marginal analysis; it remained only partially integrated into the disciplinary fabric well into the 1920s. Marginal productivity theory is not even mentioned in leading American textbooks until E. R. A. Seligman (1905). See the discussion in Howey (1972).

8. Carver, for example, argued that "The right of the present social order to exist depends on the laws which govern not functional, but personal distribution. Our only interest in

functional distribution is due to the light which it throws on the vastly more important question of personal distribution" (1901, p. 579).

9. See, for example, Josiah Stamp (1919) and Arthur Bowley (1920).

10. Pareto proposed that, at least for relatively high incomes, the distribution of income could be described by the formula $\ln N = C - \alpha \ln Y$, where Y is income and N is the number of persons with income above Y, and α, which $= 1.5$, is the coefficient of inequality. (For more on Pareto's Law, see Persky, 1992).

11. See King's (1915) *The Wealth and Income of the People of the United States.*

12. Wesley Clair Mitchell writes in the preface to the first volume of the NBER's *Studies in Income and Wealth*: "Every candid investigator who has tried to make, or use properly, estimates of national income realizes how difficult it is to know just what the results mean. Those who have not struggled with the highly technical problems that crop up in the work can scarcely appreciate their intricacy, or how considerable are the differences in results . . . produced by . . . slightly different definitions" (1937, pp. vii–viii).

13. The data Pareto used to construct Pareto's Law were derived from European incomes well above the mean. The Federal income tax was established by the 16th Amendment to the Constitution, ratified in 1913. The annual *Statistics of Income*, which reports data from tax returns, commences in 1916.

14. See Stapleford (2003) for an exhaustive and illuminating account of the 1935–1936 survey of consumer purchases.

15. We are indebted to Malcolm Rutherford for drawing our attention to this literature, and for the insight that Margaret G. Reid, a student of Hazel Kyrk's, was a colleague of Theodore Schultz's, and that Jacob Mincer and Gary Becker were exposed to Reid's work on the household during her tenure at Chicago.

16. In the 1940s, the American Economic Association sponsored the "Blackiston Series of Republished Articles in Economics" which were "designed to make accessible in its successive volumes the most useful articles and essays in the various fields of economic analysis and policy." *Readings in the Theory of Income Distribution* was Volume Three in the series, and was reprinted as late as 1963. In selecting content, editors Bernard Haley and William Fellner, with the help of Fritz Machlup, "consulted approximately 30 professional economists . . . known to have an interest in the theory of distribution" (p. xi).

17. There are 7 articles under the heading "Production Function and Marginal Productivity," 8 under "Wages," 7 under "Interest," 4 under "Profit," and 2 under "Rent." The Bowman article appears under the heading "Concept of Income and Distribution," along with two articles on National Income/National Product and JM Clark's entry, "Distribution," which says, flatly: "economic theory has for a long time concerned itself with functional distribution only" (p. 58).

18. The volume also contains a bibliography assembled by Frank Norton, Jr. The section on "Personal Distribution of Income and Wealth" contains 80 citations. 5 of these are in Italian; 8 in *the Survey of Current Business* (6 of these by Edward Denison); 20 are from the NBER's *Studies in Income and Wealth*; 3 are Conference Board publications.

19. Appendix 1, available from the authors, gives an extended description of the data analysis concerns and contents in the 9 volumes from Vol. 3 (1939) to Vol. 23 (1958) dealing wholly or in part with income distribution issues. In the text we limit ourselves to brief observations about Vol. 5 (1943) and Vol. 23 (1958).

20. We discuss Merwin's and Kuznets's conjectures on why the data were so poor in Section 11.

21. "In 1940 the Census of Population for the first time contained questions on income, but unfortunately not in detail. Each person 14 years of age or older, except inmates of specified institutions, on April 1 was asked how much he had received in 1939 in money wages and salaries up to $5,000, and whether he had received other income of $50 or more" (*Series*, 1943, p. 61). The chapter notes that, before the 1940 Census was administered, "certain political opposition to the income questions received front page notice." (p. 67) It goes on to wonder how this might have affected responses to the income questions.

22. The 1950 Census included three questions about income. One asked about the amount of wages or salaries in 1949, the second about amount of income earned on the individual's "own business, professional practice, or farm," and the third asked about amount of income from "interest, dividends, veteran's allowances, pensions, rents or other income (aside from earnings)" (Goldfield, 1958, pp. 55–56).

23. Hobson was on the faculty of the Robert Brookings Graduate School in its first year, 1924–1925 and influenced scholars there for some years (Rutherford, 2001, pp. 16–17).

24. Today's research focuses on credit market imperfections and political economy effects. Credit-market imperfections can make it difficult for the poor to borrow, which leads to sub-optimal investment, retarding growth (Aghion & Bolton, 1997). The political economy story argues that when inequality drives the median voter below average income, he votes for tax and regulatory redistribution that causes sub-optimal investment in human and physical capital, retarding growth (Persson & Tabellini, 1994).

25. Becker says in *Human Capital* (1964, p. 7, Note 2): "In addition to the earlier works of Smith, Mill, and Marshall, see the brilliant work (which has greatly influenced my own thinking about occupational choice) by M. Friedman and S. Kuznets. . . ."

26. One of Kanbur's gripes is that the Kuznets curve viewpoint is a "reduced form" approach that discourages detailed examination of what has actually happened in specific economies, tending to "overlook the rich texture of actual relationships . . . which can be revealed in detailed case studies of the development process" (Kanbur, p. 797).

27. This was not the case in less developed countries, which is consistent with development economics' ongoing interest in distribution.

28. David Lindauer noted that a 1935 QJE paper by J. R. Walsh (1935) entitled "Capital Concept Applied to Man" lays out a good deal of the basic human capital theory that appears in the 1960s. Dan Hamermesh independently suggested that a major precursor laying out human capital ideas is Dublin and Lotka *The Money Value of a Man* (1930). Becker cites both of them in *Human Capital* (see 1964, Notes 2, p. 7 and 20, p. 148). The issue, analogous to our size distribution question, is why, as Lindauer put it, "Becker was enormously influential; Walsh made no impact." Sahota notes that there was a previous and much older "treatment of human skill within the capital-theory framework," which he calls " '(t)he old vintage' theory of human capital," going back to Adam Smith (1776) through Alfred Marshall (1890), a literature that "has been extensively surveyed by Bernard F. Kiker (1968)." (1978, p. 11). Becker, in the same footnote that cites Walsh and expresses his intellectual debt to Kuznets and Friedman (1945), also acknowledges the influences of Smith, Mill and Marshall (1964, p. 7, Note 2). Mill viewed educational expenditures as investment, and believed that they would have economically observable effects. On this last point and for a useful discussion of the early literature in human capital, see Teixeira (2003).

29. T. W. Schultz's work is often cited as contributing importantly to the 1960s birth of human capital research at Chicago. Blaug (1980, p. 224) notes that "The birth of human

capital theory was announced in 1960 by Theodore Schultz," and Sahota (1978, p. 11) refers to the 1960s development as being "under the inspiration of Theodore W. Shultz." Becker also cites Schultz as a key influence (1964, p. 7, Note 2).

30. Mincer reports that his dissertation on wage differentials was directly inspired by Friedman's dissertation and Kuznets and Friedman (1945) on professional incomes (Teixeira, 2003, p. 307).

31. Both Becker and Mincer remark on the long neglect of the personal distribution. Becker (1967, reprinted in 1993, p. 109) explains that economists "neglected the study of personal income distribution during the last generation" because they lacked a theory "that both articulates with general economic theory and is useful in explaining actual differences among regions, countries and time periods." By general economic theory, Becker means neoclassical economics' maximization-cum-equilibrium method. He then goes on to try to show that "emphasizing investment in human capital" allows development of "a theory of income distribution that can satisfy both desiderata" (p. 109).

Mincer (1970) indicates that the study of the functional distribution, rather than size distribution, "continues to flourish in the literature despite the blurring of . . . social class identifications and despite the recognition that under modern conditions the variance in labor incomes is the dominant component of total income inequality. Remote links exist between the functional and size distributions of income, but (the functional distribution of income) approach does not address itself to the distribution of labor incomes" (1970, p. 3).

32. The subtraction of the six is to account for the years before schooling begins. See Rosen (1992) for a useful discussion of Mincer's contributions. A later innovation possible only on data sets that included information on tenure at the firm was to enter this firm-specific tenure as a separate variable additional to the one measuring general labor market experience. This was to try to capture the separate effect of firm-specific training. The distinction between general on-the-job training and firm-specific on-the-job-training was one of Becker's (1964) important conceptual contributions. For a discussion of some difficulties with the interpretation of the firm tenure variable, see Hutchens (1989).

33. The term "general earnings function" is used by Mincer (1970, p. 8), attributing the function's development to Becker (1964). The general earnings function can be written in several related forms. One useful version (Becker & Chiswick, 1966, p. 359) showed an individual's earnings E_n in year n (gross of that year's cost of investment) as equaling the sum of the "raw" earnings X_n the individual would have obtained in the absence of any human capital investment, plus a series of terms, each term being the net investment cost C_{ij} of a particular human capital investment i (schooling, for example) in year j, multiplied times the rate of return r_{ij} on that type of investment in year j:

$$E_n = X_n + \sum r_{ij} C_{ij}$$

Empirical implementations usually express the dependent variable in logs. The transformation to logs is discussed in for example Becker and Chiswick (1966, p. 363) and Mincer (1970, p. 7).

34. A number of the specific empirical applications of the general earnings function make the assumption that the rate of return r is identical across categories of investment. One important example is the assumption in Mincer's simple schooling equation that r is identical for different schooling levels. This assumption is contradicted by numerous studies (see, for example, Blaug, 1976, pp. 838–839).

35. This equation has log of earnings as the dependent variable. Schooling is entered linearly as an explanatory variable. Labor market experience, measured as age minus schooling minus six, is entered as both linear and squared terms.

36. Nothing as influential as human capital theory could escape criticism, and its theory and empirical implementations have been widely criticized. Usefully critical discussions from the mid to late 1970s include Blaug (1976), Sahota (1978) and Rosen (1977). Appendix 2, available from the authors, sets forth a number of these criticisms, and evaluates how serious they look from today's perspective.

37. The first edition was entitled *The Theory of Competitive Price*.

38. Data on lawyers' income by age and size of community is used to illustrate that these two variables can generate considerable extraneous dispersion. In his example, "controlling" for these two sources of variation makes a Lorenz-curve measure of inequality look less unequal by more than 1/3. He goes on to discuss hours differences, differences in training, and so forth.

39. H. L. Moore (1911), for example, posited that ability was normally distributed, and sought empirical evidence for what he saw as the implication: that wages were also normally distributed.

40. Kaldor open his article with: "According to the Preface of Ricardo's Principles, the discovery of the laws which regulate distributive shares is the principal problem of political economy. The purpose of this paper is to present a bird's eye view of the various theoretical attempts, since Ricardo, at solving this 'principal problem.' "

41. While the rest of the volume is mostly about the functional distribution, there are scattered additional discussions directly relevant to size distribution. For example, Bronfenbrenner considers the relation of the functional to the personal distribution, noting the difficulties with making statements that relate changes in the importance of labor's share to changes in the size distribution.

42. The book also includes Johnson's reading list. "The Personal Distribution of Income" section contains 6 articles: Roy (1951), Friedman (1953), H. P. Miller (1963), Mincer (1958), Becker (1967), and Reder (1969). Only the Friedman article is required. The entire reading list consists of two texts (a Johnson volume on two sector general equilibrium models, and Bronfenbrenner, 1971). Of the 91 additional articles and books listed, 18 are required.

43. Johnson's model assumes a static population, "in which all babies born have exactly the same natural capacities, and all adults do exactly the same work. The minute a baby is born, it goes into an orphanage for rearing. The orphanage . . . debits the child with the costs of its upbringing until it reaches the age of fifteen, at which point it becomes a member of the labor force" (p. 207). During its working life, it pays off its debts to the orphanage, and saves for retirement. The interest rate is zero, and individuals consume the same amount at every age.

In this world, the lifetime income and consumption pattern of every individual is identical. But a cross-section of the income distribution at any point in time "permits us to make such shocking observations as 'the top 26 2/3% of income earners receive 60% of the total income,' and 'one third of the population received no income whatsoever' – gross inequality in the first case, widespread and shameful poverty in the second" (p. 208).

44. For example, "(T)he theory of the impact of income taxation applied only to measured cash income in the presence of nonpecuniary advantages . . . of various occupations suggests . . . that society will tend to be relatively overpopulated with people anxious to do

good . . . as contrasted with people . . . concerned only to maximize their monetary returns from economic activity" (p. 216).

45. Appendix 3, available from the authors, reviews Blinder (1974), Thurow (1975) and Atkinson (1970), important examples of the substantial contributions to the personal distribution outpouring of the 1970s.

46. The first two categories contain important contributions that go back many decades, and the existence of the first four categories is recognized by earlier authors such as Bronfenbrenner. However, the treatment in Sahota documents contributions in the first two categories throughout the 1960s and 1970s. Of more significance, Sahota devotes considerable attention to the importance for SDI of the third and fourth categories – especially to human capital theory. Bronfenbrenner had devoted one paragraph each to human capital theory and individual choice theory.

47. Sahota's bibliography numbers each entry. The numbers run from 1 to 324. However, there is a 215a and a 254a, so the actual number of items is 326.

48. By way of comparison, Reder's 1969 article contains 40 citations (the bibliography is numbered 1 to 41, but number 7 is missing). Thirty-one of these are from 1955 or later. Only 18 of the 40 Reder cites are in Sahota, though the overlap in authors cited is larger.

49. We owe this point to David Colander.

50. The 1975 Conference on Research on Income and Wealth volume (Smith, 1975) exploiting microdata to analyze tax-related issues is an example of this emphasis and concern. The concern with the distribution of tax burden by income class is a long-standing tradition in public finance, displayed for example in Richard Musgrave's well-known graduate public finance text of 1959.

51. Though beyond the scope of this paper, it might be possible to empirically assay the relationship between the extent of income redistribution and the volume of theoretical research and data development dedicated the personal income distribution topics. One option would be to compare the US, this paper's focus, with the continental European states, which are earlier to develop a tax-incidence literature, for example, and which also seem to have a concomitantly earlier development of SDI data. And do, for example, data collection efforts lead or lag the redistribution programs? The history of European approaches to personal income distribution is, more generally, an interesting topic for future research.

52. We owe this idea to Tyler Cowan.

53. The 1970–1979 average is 15%, "close" to the 17% average for 80–89. Actually there is a small rise from around 1968 to 1971, a drop to 1973 then a much larger rise.

54. We owe this point to Royal Brandis, who expressed the matter roughly as follows: Even if you had personal distribution numbers, there is the "so what" question of how you turn these numbers into findings about economic justice?

55. But not all. See Ray Fair (1971) "The Optimal Distribution of Income" and the literature it responds to, cited therein.

56. And, even if it did, considerations of justice are not exhausted by an examination of a given distributional outcome. As Robert Nozick (1974) argued contra Rawls, an evaluation of consequences doesn't exhaust our ethical concerns; there is also the justness of the process by which individuals come to their location in the income distribution.

57. The Atkins index proved quite influential because it better connected the welfare and income-distribution literatures. Note that the Atkinson index requires the analyst to specify, as an input, a parameter known as the level of "inequality aversion."

58. Keynes called the constancy of labor's share "a bit of a miracle" (1939, p. 48). Kaldor argued that ". . . no hypothesis as regards the forces determining distributive shares could be intellectually satisfying unless it succeeds in accounting for the relative stability of these shares in the advanced capitalist economies over the last 100 years or so, despite the phenomenal changes in the techniques of production, in the accumulation of capital relative to labor and in real income per head" (1955, p. 24). Solow (1958, p. 618) was more skeptical: "like most miracles, this one may be an optical illusion."

59. The Cobb and Douglas (1928) formulation ($P = AL^k C^{1-k}$) imposed constant returns to scale, the index numbers used for labor and capital were somewhat fishy (C was capital capacity, not capital employed), and the data were collinear. Most problematically, Cobb and Douglas assumed that if their estimate of labor's share (k) was near to the actual k provided by a direct measure of labor's share, then the Cobb-Douglas assumptions were thereby validated. The problem is that other functional forms (such as $P = aL + bC$), with quite different assumptions, can also generate the same estimate of labor's share. So, a decent fit for labor's share does not, by itself, validate the Cobb-Douglas assumptions, as pointed out by Simon and Levy (1963).

60. A major breakthrough about how to overcome the conceptual measurement-of-capital difficulties was the methodology appearing around 1967 in the work of Hall and Jorgenson (1967), and Hall (1968) (see also Diewert, 1980, a paper given at a conference in the early 1970s). They showed how a theoretically-defensible measure of aggregate capital could in fact be derived and used. The fact that their papers appeared in 1967 and later shows that a focus on factors and their shares was still of great interest in the late 1960s and well into the 1970s. Ed Dean suggested this point to us. For a useful discussion of the development of measures of capital input, see Dean and Harper (2001, pp. 62–63).

61. The American neoclassical economists, in contrast, said that workers are poor because buyers don't attach a high value to the labor services the poor have to sell. Poor workers are not cheated in the process of production and exchange, as critics had it, they are cheated in the birth lottery, which under-endowed them, and perhaps by market failure, which permitted socially sub-optimal investment in poor workers' human capital.

REFERENCES

Aghion, P., & Bolton P. (1997). A theory of trickle-down growth and development. In: H. Chenery & T. N. Srinivasan (Eds), *Handbook of Development Economics* (Vol. 2, pp. 949–1003). Amsterdam: North-Holland.

American Economic Association (1946). *Readings in the theory of income distribution*. Homewood, IL: Irwin (Richard D.).

Atkinson, A. (1970). On the measurement of inequality. *Journal of Economic Theory, 2,* 244–263.

Atkinson, A. (1975). *The economics of inequality* (2nd ed., 1983). Oxford: Clarendon Press.

Atkinson, A., & Bourguignon, F. (2000). Income distribution and economics. In: A. Atkinson & F. Bourguignon (Eds), *Handbook of Income Distribution* (Vol. 1, pp. 5–58). Amsterdam: Elsevier.

Atkinson, T. (1958). Frontiers of size-distribution research. In: *Conference on Research in Income and Wealth. An Appraisal of the 1950 Census Income Data. Studies in Income and Wealth* (Vol. 23, pp. 29–38). Princeton, NJ: Princeton University Press.

Becker, G. (1964, and third edition, 1993). *Human capital*. Chicago: University of Chicago Press.
Becker, G. (1967). Human capital and the personal distribution of income: An analytical approach. Woytinsky lecture No. 1. University of Michigan Institute of Public Administration, Ann Arbor, MI. Reprinted in 3d edition of his Human Capital (1993), pp.108–158.
Becker, G., & Chiswick, B. (1966). Education and the distribution of earnings. *American Economic Review, 56*(2), 358–369.
Blaug, M. (1976). The empirical status of human capital theory: A slightly jaundiced view. *Journal of Economic Literature, 14*(3), 827–855.
Blaug, M. (1980). *The methodology of economics*. Cambridge: Cambridge University Press.
Blinder, A. (1974). *Toward an economic theory of income distribution*. Cambridge, MA: MIT Press.
Boulding, K. (1975). The pursuit of equality. In: J. D. Smith (Ed.), *The Personal Distribution of Income and Wealth. Studies in Income and Wealth* (Vol. 39, pp. 11–28). New York: Columbia University Press.
Bowley, A. L. (1920). *The change in the distribution of the national income, 1880–1913*. Oxford: Clarendon Press.
Bowman, M. J. (1946). A graphical analysis of personal income distribution in the United States, in American Economic Association. In: W. Fellner & B. Haley (Eds), *Readings in the Theory of Income Distribution* (pp. 72–99). Homewood, IL: Irwin (Richard D.).
Brady, D. (1951). Research on the size distribution of income. In: *Conference on Research in Income and Wealth, Studies in Income and Wealth* (Vol. 13, pp. 3–55). Princeton, NJ: Princeton University Press.
Bronfenbrenner, M. (1971). *Income distribution theory*. Chicago: Aldine.
Burns, A. F. (1936). The Brookings inquiry into income distribution and progress. *The Quarterly Journal of Economics, 50*(3), 476–523.
Cannan, E. (1894). *A history of the theories of production and distribution in English political economy from 1776 to 1848*. London: Rivington, Percival & Co.
Cannan, E. (1905). The division of income. *The Quarterly Journal of Economics, 19*(3), 341–369.
Carver, T. N. (1901). Review of John Bates Clark's The Distribution of Wealth: A theory of wages, interest and profits. *The Quarterly Journal of Economics, 15*(4), 578–602.
Champernowne, D. G. (1973). *The distribution of income between persons*. Cambridge: Cambridge University Press.
Chiswick, B. R. (1974). *Income inequality: Regional analyses within a human capital framework*. New York: NBER.
Clark, J. B. (1891). Distribution as determined by a law of rent. *Quarterly Journal of Economics, 5*(3, April), 289–318.
Cobb, C., & Douglas, P. (1928). A theory of production. *American Economic Review Papers and Proceedings of the 40th Meeting of the American Economic Association, 18*(1), 139–165.
Cohen, A., & Harcourt, G. (2003). Whatever happened to the Cambridge capital controversies? *Journal of Economic Perspectives, 17*(1), 199–214.
Conference on Research in Income and Wealth (1937, 1939, 1946, 1947, 1948, 1951, 1952). *Studies in Income and Wealth* (Vol 1, 1937), (Vol 3, 1939), (Vol 7, 8, 1946), (Vol 9, 1948), (Vol 10, 1947), (Vol 13, 1951), (Vol 15, 1952).
Conference on Research in Income and Wealth (1943). Income size distributions in the United States. *Studies in Income and Wealth* (Vol. 5). Princeton, NJ: Princeton University Press.
Conference on Research in Income and Wealth (1958). *An appraisal of the 1950 census income data (Vol. 23), of studies in income and wealth*. Princeton, NJ: Princeton University Press.

Conference on Research in Income and Wealth (1964). The behavior of income shares: Selected theoretical and empirical studies. *Studies in Income and Wealth* (Vol. 27). Princeton, NJ: Princetom University Press.

Dalton, H. (1920). *Some aspects of the inequality of incomes in modern communities.* New York: E. P. Dutton.

Dean, E., & Harper, M. (2001). The BLS measurement productivity program. In: C. Hulten, E. Dean & M. Harper (Eds), *New Developments in Productivity Analysis, NBER Studies in Income and Wealth* (Vol. 63, pp. 55–84). Chicago: University of Chicago Press.

Diewert, W. I. (1980). Aggregation problems in the measurement of capital. In: D. Usher (Ed.), *The Measurement of Capital. NBER Studies in Income and Wealth* (Vol. 45, pp. 433–528). Chicago: University of Chicago Press.

Dublin, L., & Lotka, A. (1930). *The money measure of man.* New York.

Fair, R. (1971). The optimal distribution of income. *The Quarterly Journal of Economics, 85*(4), 551–579.

Fellner, W. (1953). Significance and limitations of contemporary distribution theory. *The American Economic Review, 43*(2), 484–494.

Fisher, I. (1912). *Elementary principles of economics.* New York: Macmillan.

Friedman, M. (1953). Choice, chance and the personal distribution of income. *Journal of Political Economy, 61,* 277–290.

Friedman, M., & Kuznets, S. (1945). *Income from independent professional practice.* New York: NBER.

Galton, F. (1869). *Hereditary genius.* London: Macmillan.

Garvy, G. (1952). Inequality of income: Causes and measurement. Conference on Research in Income and Wealth. *Studies in Income and Wealth* (Vol. 15, pp. 25–47). Princeton, NJ: Princeton University Press.

Garvy, G. (1954). Diminishing inequality in personal income distribution: Relation to functional distribution and factor compensation. *The American Economic Review Papers and Proceedings of the Sixty-sixth Annual Meeting of the American Economic Association, 44*(2), 236–253.

George, H. (1879). Progress and Poverty: An inquiry into the cause of industrial depressions, and of increase of want with increase of wealth – The remedy. San Francisco, CA: W. M. Hinton & Co.

Gibrat, R. (1931). *Les inegalites economiques.* Paris: Sirey.

Gini, C. (1912). *Variabilita e mutabilita.* Bologna.

Goldfield, E. (1958). Decennial Census and Current Population Survey Data on Income. Conference on Research in Income and Wealth: An Appraisal of the 1950 Census Income Data. *Studies in Income and Wealth* (Vol. 23, pp. 39–63). Princeton, NJ: Princeton University Press.

Goldsmith, S. (1958). The Relation of Census Income Data to Other income Data. Conference on Research in Income and Wealth: An Appraisal of the 1950 Census Income Data. *Studies in Income and Wealth* (Vol, 23, pp. 65–107). Princeton, NJ: Princeton University Press.

Goldsmith, S., Jaszi, G., Kaitz, H., & Liebenberg, M. (1954). Size distribution of income since the mid-thirties. *Review of Economics and Statistics, 36*(1), 1–32.

Hall, R. (1968). Technical change and capital from the point of view of the dual. *Review of Economic Studies, 35*(1), 35–46.

Hall, R., & Jorgenson, D. (1967). Tax policy and investment behavior. *American Economic Review, 57,* 391–414.

Hobson, J. A. (1891). The law of the three rents. *The Quarterly Journal of Economics, 5*(3), 263–288.

Hobson, J. A. (1910). *The industrial system; an inquiry into earned and unearned income.* London: Longmans Green.

Hollander, J. H. (1903). The residual claimant theory of distribution. *The Quarterly Journal of Economics, 17*(2), 261–279.

Hollander, E. (1952). Introduction. Conference on Research in Income and Wealth. *Studies in Income and Wealth* (Vol. 15, pp. 1–8). Princeton, NJ: Princeton University Press.

Howey, R. S. (1972). The origins of Marginalism. In: R. D. Collison Black et al. (Eds), *The Marginal Revolution in Economics* (pp. 15–36). Durham, NC: Duke University Press.

Hutchens, R. (1989). Seniority, wages and productivity: A turbulent decade. *Journal of Economic Perspectives, 3*, 49–64.

Johnson, D. G. (1954). The functional distribution of income in the United States, 1850–1952. *The Review of Economics and Statistics, 36*(2), 175–182.

Johnson, H. (1973). *The theory of income distribution*. London: Gray-Mills.

Kaldor, N. (1955–1956). Alternative theories of distribution. *Review of Economic Studies, 23*(2), 83–100.

Kanbur, R. (2000). Income distribution and development. In: A. Atkinson & F. Bourguignon (Eds), *Handbook of Income Distribution* (Vol. 1, pp. 791–842). Amsterdam: Elsevier.

Keynes, J. M. (1939). Relative movements of real wages and output. *The Economic Journal, 49*(193), 34–51.

Kiker, B. (1968). Human capital in retrospect. University of Carolina Bureau of Business and Economic Research, Columbia, SC.

King, W. C., Knauth, O. W., & Macaulay, W. I. (1922). *Income in the United States: Its amount and distribution 1909–1919 (Detailed Report)* (Vol. 2). New York: NBER.

King, W. I. (1915). *The wealth and income of the people of the United States*. Macmillan, NY.

Kuznets, S. (1939). Comment (on Merwin). Conference on Research in Income and Wealth. *Studies in Income and Wealth* (Vol. 3, pp. 85–93). Princeton, NJ: Princeton University Press.

Kuznets, S. (1943). The Why and How of Distributions of Income by Size. Conference on Research in Income and Wealth: Income Size Distributions in the United States. *Studies in Income and Wealth* (Vol. 5, pp. 5–33). Princeton, NJ: Princeton University Press.

Kuznets, S. (1946). National income in American Economic Association. In: W. Fellner & B. Haley (Eds), *Readings in the Theory of Income Distribution* (pp. 3–43). Homewood, IL: Irwin (Richard D.).

Kuznets, S. (1955). Economic growth and income inequality. *American Economic Review, 45*, 1–28.

Kyrk, H. (1923). *A theory of consumption*. Boston: Houghton Mifflin.

Lindert, P. H. (1986). Unequal English wealth since 1670. *Journal of Political Economy, 94*(6), 1127–1162.

Lindert, P. H. (2000). Three centuries of inequality in Britain and America. In: A. Atkinson & F. Bourguignon (Eds), *Handbook of Income Distribution* (Vol. 1, pp. 167–216). Amsterdam: Elsevier.

Lorenz, M. O. (1905). *Methods of Measuring the Concentration of Wealth Publications of the American Statistical Association, 9*(70), 209–219.

Lydall, H. F. (1968). *The structure of earnings*. Oxford: Clarendon Press.

Meade, J. E. (1976). *The just economy*. London: Allen & Unwin.

Merwin, C. L. Jr. (1939). American Studies of the Distribution of Wealth and Income. Conference on Research in Income and Wealth. *Studies in Income and Wealth* (Vol 3, pp. 4–84). Princeton, NJ: Princeton University Press.

Miller, H. P. (1963). Trends in the Income of Families and Persons in the United States 1947–1960. U.S. Bureau of the Census Technical Paper No. 3. GPO, Washington, DC.

Mincer, J. (1957). *A study of personal income distribution*. (Ph.D. dissertation, Columbia University.)

Mincer, J. (1958). Investment in human capital and personal income distribution. *Journal of Political Economy, 66,* 281–302.

Mincer, J. (1970). The distribution of labor incomes: A survey with special reference to the human capital approach. *Journal of Economic Literature, VIII,* 1–26.

Mincer, J. (1976). Progress in human capital analyses of the distribution of earnings. In: A. Atkinson (Ed.), *The Personal Distribution of Incomes* (pp. 136–192). London: Allen & Unwin.

Mitchell, W. C., King, W. I., Macaulay, F., & Knauth, O. W. (1921). *Income in the United States: Its amount and distribution 1909–1919 (Summary)* (Vol. 1). New York: Harcourt Brace.

Moore, H. L. (1911). *Laws of wages: An essay in statistical economics.* New York: Macmillan.

Moulton, H. G. (1935). *Income and economic progress.* Washington, DC: Brookings Institution.

Musgrave, R. (1959). *The theory of public finance.* New York: McGraw-Hill.

Nozick, R. (1974). *Anarchy, state and utopia.* Oxford: Basil Blackwell.

Okun, A. (1975). *Equality and efficiency: The big tradeoff.* Washington, DC: Brookings Institution.

Oswald, A. (1991). Progress and microeconomic data. *Economic Journal, 101*(404), 75–80.

Pareto, V. (1897). *Cours d'economie politique professé à l'Université de Lausanne.* Paris: F. Rouge.

Peixotto, J. (1929). *How workers spend a living wage.* Berkeley, CA: University of California Press.

Persky, J. (1992). Retrospectives: Pareto's law. *Journal of Economic Perspectives, 6*(2), 181–192.

Persson, T., & Tabellini, G. (1994). Is inequality harmful for growth? *The American Economic Review, 84*(3), 600–621.

Pigou, A. C. (1912). *Wealth and welfare.* London: Macmillan.

Rawls, J. (1971). *A theory of justice.* Cambridge, MA: Harvard University Press.

Reder, M. (1962). *Wage differentials: Theory and measurement, in aspects of labor economics.* Princeton, NJ: Princeton University Press (for the NBER).

Reder, M. (1969). A partial survey of the theory of income size distribution. Conference on Research in Income and Wealth. *Studies in Income and Wealth* (Vol. 33, pp. 205–254). New York: Columbia University Press.

Reid, M. G. (1934). *The economics of household production.* New York: Wiley.

Ricardo, D. (1815). *Essay on The influence of a low price of corn upon the profits of stock* (2nd ed). London: John Murray.

Ricardo, D. (1821). *Principles of political economy and taxation* (3rd ed.). In: P. Sraffa (Ed.), *The Works and Correspondence of David Ricardo* (Vol. 1). Cambridge: Cambridge University Press.

Rosen, S. (1977). Human capital: A survey of empirical research. In: R. Ehrenberg (Ed.), *Research in Labor Economics* (Vol. 1, pp. 3–38). Greenwich, CT: JAI Press.

Rosen, S. (1992). Distinguished Fellow: Mincering labor economics. *Journal of Economic Perspectives, 6*(2), 157–170.

Roy, A. D. (1951). Some thoughts on the distribution of earnings. *Oxford Economic Papers, 3,* 135–146.

Rutherford, M. (2001). Walton Hamilton, Amherst, and the Brookings Graduate School: Institutional Economics and Education. Manuscript.

Sahota, G. (1978). Theories of personal income distribution: A survey. *Journal of Economic Literature, XVI,* 1–55.

Seligman, E. R. A. (1905). *Principles of economics, with special reference to American conditions.* New York: Longmans Green and Co.

Sen, A. (1997, first edition 1973). *On economic inequality.* Oxford: Oxford University Press.

Shorrocks, A. (1987). Inequality between persons. In: J. Eatwell, M. Milgate & P. Newman (Eds), *The New Palgrave: A Dictionary of Economics* (Vol. 2, pp. 821–824). New York: Macmillan.

Simon, H. A., & Levy, F. K. (1963). A note on the Cobb-Douglas function. *The Review of Economic Studies, 30*(2), 93–94.

Smith, J. (1975). Introduction. In: J. Smith (Ed.), *The Personal Distribution of Income and Wealth. NBER Studies in Income and Wealth* (Vol. 39, pp. 1–8). New York: Columbia University Press.

Solow, R. (1958). A skeptical note on the constancy of relative shares. *American Economic Review, 48*(4), 618–631.

Solow, R. (1966). Review of John Hicks's *Capital and Growth. American Economic Review, 56*(5), 1257–1260.

Stamp, J. C. (1919). The wealth and income of the chief powers. *Journal of the Royal Statistical Society, 82*(4), 441–507.

Stapleford, T. A. (2003). *"The most important single statistic": The consumer price index and american political economy, 1880–1995*. Ph.D. dissertation. Harvard University.

Stigler, G. (1941). *Production and distribution theories, 1870–1895*. New York: Macmillan.

Stigler, G. (1946, 1952, 1966). *The theory of price* (2nd ed, revised ed, 3rd ed). New York: Macmillan.

Stigler, G. (1965). *The influence of events and policies on economic theory (1960)*. Reprinted in Essays in the History of Economics. University of Chicago Press, Chicago.

Stiglitz, J. (1969). The distribution of income and wealth among individuals. *Econometrica, 37*, 382–397.

Teixeira, P. (2003). *The "human capital revolution" in economic thought*. Ph.D. dissertation. University of Exeter.

Thurow, L. (1975). *Generating inequality*. New York: Basic Books.

Tinbergen, J. (1975). *Income distribution*. Amsterdam: North Holland.

Tobin, J. (1970). On limiting the domain of inequality. *Journal of Law and Economics, 13*(2), 263–277.

Walsh, J. R. (1935). The capital concept applied to man. *Quarterly Journal of Economics, 49*(2), 255–285.

Weintraub, S. (1958). *An approach to the theory of income distribution*. Philadelphia: Chilton.

Wicksell, K. (1893). *Über Wert, Kapital und Rente*. Jena: G. Fischer.

Wicksteed, P. H. (1894). *Essay on the co-ordination of the laws of distribution*. London: Macmillan.

Young, A. (1917). Do the statistics of the concentration of wealth in the United States mean what they are commonly assumed to mean? *Publications of the American Statistical Association, 15*(117), 471–484.

INTRODUCTORY NOTES TO THE STUDY OF THE HISTORY OF ECONOMIC THOUGHT (SET II)

Warren J. Samuels

The first set of introductory notes to the graduate study of the history of economic thought, and the reasons for their use, was published in Volume 22-B (2004). Subsequently, while distributing the first set in my graduate courses, I initiated a largely new, second set of introductory topics, using a new outline for presentation in each course of lectures on further introductory ontological, epistemological and hermeneutic topics that went beyond the materials in the first set. For several years, I lectured using in part an outline of my 1991 essay (cited below). That outline is reproduced here as Set II.1. The notes published below as Sets II.2 and II.3 are composites, as to content and sequence of topics, of subsequent successions of lectures. Whereas the set of notes published in Volume 22-B was distributed to students with only casual accompanying remarks, these served for me as the basis of lectures and were not distributed. No set of notes published here indicates the comments I made, from course to course, when distributing the first set of notes on the first day of class. One difference between II.1 and II.2–3 is the increasing attention to historiographic topics vis-à-vis discourse-analysis topics with the passage of time. The common elements are, first, the social construction of reality, in two senses: the literal creation of society and the interpretations given that creation; second, the distinctions between truth and belief system, and between truth and validity; third, the continuing relevance therefore of epistemology and

A Research Annual
Research in the History of Economic Thought and Methodology, Volume 23-A, 119–133
Copyright © 2005 by Elsevier Ltd.
All rights of reproduction in any form reserved
ISSN: 0743-4154/doi:10.1016/S0743-4154(05)23004-3

ontology alongside the rhetoric of economics; fourth, the relations of epistemology and language to policy; and fifth, the importance of limits. During this period of time conflict had erupted between advocates of the rhetorical and epistemological approaches to the history of economic thought. I was teaching that both approaches to the meaningfulness of ideas were important.

The problem is that several sets of notes were developed. All served only as the basis of lectures; none were entirely closely followed. Emendations, changing from year to year, were added to the typed/printed original of each before, during and/or after class. The notes reproduced below, therefore, are composites. They were constructed to remind me of what I wanted to say. They should be seen as indicative of the topics and themes presented during the first period or two of each course. Alas, the materials were not dated. (II-5 is an exception: it was given the last period of the course and was dated.)

For many years, just prior to taking up Marshall in my lectures, I presented a dual interpretation of the situation as of c.1890. One part of the interpretation is the heritage of dissonance. The second part is the search for disciplinary identity. The notes for these lectures, heavily amended over the years is publish below as Set II.4.

On the other hand, I recall having only rarely given a retrospective or integrative "concluding" lecture. My files contain the notes for only two such ventures. One is dated: Fall 1990. It is Set II-5. The other, undated, is Set II-6.

Only mildly corrective editing has been undertaken.

It had long been my practice to distribute reprints and new manuscripts to more fully acquaint students with what I do as an historian of economic thought and as a methodologist. Included, therefore, in distributed materials during the period when notes such as these were used, were the following:

" 'Truth' and 'Discourse' in the Social Construction of Economic Reality: An Essay on the Relation of Knowledge to Socioeconomic Policy," *Journal of Post Keynesian Economics*, vol. 13 (Summer 1991), pp. 511–524.

"In (Limited but Affirmative) Defence of Nihilism," *Review of Political Economy*, vol. 5 (April 1993), pp. 236–244.

"The Roles of Theory in Economics," in Philip A. Klein, ed., *The Role of Economic Theory*, Boston: Kluwer, 1994, pp. 21–45.

"Richard Reeve's Study of the Kennedy Presidency: Implications for Studying Economics and the History of Economic Thought," *History of Economics Review*, no. 23 (Winter 1995), pp. 108–116.

"Some Thoughts on Multiplicity," *Journal of Economic Methodology*, vol. 2 (December 1995), pp. 287–291.

"My Work as an Historian of Economic Thought," *Journal of the History of Economic Thought*, vol. 18 (Spring 1996), pp. 37–75.

"Postmodernism and Knowledge: A Middlebrow View," *Journal of Economic Methodology*, vol. 3 (June 1996), pp. 113–120.

"The Work of Historians of Economic Thought," *Research in the History of Economic Thought and Methodology*, vol. 15 (1997), pp. 181–197.

"Some Problems in the Use of Language in Economics," *Review of Political Economy*, vol. 13, no. 1 (2001), pp. 91–100.

INTRODUCTORY LECTURES (SET II.1)

"TRUTH" AND "DISCOURSE" IN THE SOCIAL CONSTRUCTION OF ECONOMIC REALITY: THE RELATION OF KNOWLEDGE TO SOCIOECONOMIC POLICY

Introduction
   Desire for confident knowledge
   Produced belief systems re: metaphysics, epistemology, discourse
   Late 20th century critique of positivism
   Conflict between epistemology and rhetoric in economics
   Purpose: sensible resolution, sensitive to desires, issues, and critiques

Tour de Horizon

Toward Synthesis and Resolution

1. *Epistemology*
   Epistemology too important to be discontinued and disregarded: problem of
      credentials of knowledge
   Quest for absolutist, prescriptivist epistemology has failed
   Credentialism rather than prescriptivism; methodological pluralism plus
      individual choice
   Serious attention to limits of preferred epistemologies
   Knowledge = Truth difficult to produce
   Making credentials clear: strengths and limits
   Emphasize, and give effect to, key role of criticism
   Positivism as shifting ideology of science: discomfort

2. *Discourse*
   Meaning in social sciences a matter of discursive as well as epistemological
      character: modes of discourse, stories, groups of metaphors
   Language constitutes network of beliefs, paradigms, theories, etc.
   Approaches to discourse analysis have their own limits
   Self-referentiality problem: hermeneutic circle

3. *Social Construction of Reality*
Economy as matter of social construction: social construction of its
meaning/social construction of economy itself: former may not be true but it
is the basis of debate and policy
Definitions of reality are instrumental in policy making and thereby in
reconstruction of reality
Economy as artifact, a matter of social reconstruction in part through creation
and deployment of language, discourse; ergo, object of control and
manipulation
Idea of social construction of reality is inescapably political; power = choice,
especially re: social construction of reality
Idea of social construction of reality also itself a conceptualization of reality
Deal with phenomenological, not ontological, reality
Diverse definitions of complex and kaleidoscopic reality

Conclusion
Affirm both epistemology (credentialist) and discourse analysis
Skepticism of claims to prescriptive conclusiveness
Eclectic and agnostic re: epistemological and discursive nature of economics;
tolerate ambiguity and open-endedness
Key role of choice re: supplementary premises
Operative psychological mechanisms need to be understood: (1) identification,
and privileging; (2) allocative economics of the intellect, and privileging
Re: laxity, relativism, nihilism, indiscipline, malaise, cynicism: not "anything
goes," but rejection that only one thing goes: pluralism and openness, not
self-deception re: limits: tolerance, recognition of human choice
Psychic-balm desire for absolutes
"Truth" (T) not necessary for rational criticism: Truth principally a name given
to what we accept as confident knowledge
Reason even more important, since can no longer assume or pretend that what
we believe actually mirrors nature or constitutes unequivocal facts: simple
facts/interpretive meaning
Learn to live with radical indeterminacy, ambiguity, social construction of
reality (not economy given by nature)

INTRODUCTORY LECTURES (SET II.2)

HISTORY OF ECONOMIC THOUGHT: INTRODUCTORY NOTES

I. Objectives of course
a. use "Introduction" handout

b. coverage of course: use Outline
II. Introductory orienting themes
  1a. history of economic thought/theory
    b. history of thought-theory/history of economics as intellectual discipline
    c. further facets:
      * pure theory of price
      * problem of order
      * economic role of government
      * pure model/reality – yet always abstraction
      * fact as theory-laden; theory as interpretation of "facts" (evidence)
  2. multiple interpretation of economy and of history of economic thought: individuals, theories, schools, and of economics itself [ubiquity of multiplicity]
  3. hermeneutic circle problem: choice of standpoint
  4. duality of approaches to doing economics:
    1. analysis of resource allocation within given system/analysis of system per se
    2. "economic theory"/theory of economic order
      a. modern economics a function of modern economy
    3. actual economic system/model of abstract pure a-institutional system
      a. market/institutions
    * Shackle: three levels or orders of economic theory:
      a. theory of actual economic arrangements
      b. theory of pure conceptual entities
      c. theory relating a to b
  5. nature of object of study: independent of man or artifact subject to social construction of reality
  6. ontology/epistemology/substance
  7. definition of reality/a story(ies)
    a. e.g. people as in self-interest:
      * a definition of reality
      * a tautology
      * a limiting assumption
    b. approaches: Whig/critical/hermeneutic
  8. language/reality
  9. false dichotomies
  10. role of obfuscation
  11. matrix approach
  12. some related concepts:
    dialectic

general interdependence
general equilibrium
cumulative causation
overdetermination
13. further notes on methodology, and on truth and discourse

INTRODUCTORY LECTURES (SET II.3)

HISTORY OF ECONOMIC THOUGHT

Introductory Lectures

Objectives of course
    Objectives per se
    Course outline: coverage of course
    "Introduction" handout
    "Work of Historians of Economic Thought"
    "My Work as an Historian of Economic Thought"

Introductory Orienting Themes
    History of ideas
    History of economic thought/theory
    History of economic thought-theory/history of economics as intellectual,
        professional discipline
    Pure model/reality – yet always abstraction
    Fact as theory laden; theory as interpretation of "facts" (evidence)
    Multiple interpretation of economy and of history of economic thought:
        individuals, theories, schools, and of economics itself: ubiquity of
        multiplicity
    Hermeneutic circle problem: choice of standpoint
    Duality of approaches to doing economics:
        Analysis of resource allocation within given system/analysis of system per
        se
        "Economic theory"/theory of economic order
            Modern economics a function of modern economy
    Shackle: three levels or orders of economic theory:
        Theory of actual economic arrangements
        Theory of pure conceptual entities
        Theory relating first to second
    Nature of object of study: independent of man or artifact subject to social
    construction of reality

Conceit of truth
Ontology/epistemology/substance
Definition of reality/a story(ies)
   As in self-interest:
      A definition of reality
      A tautology
      A limiting assumption
   Approaches: Whig, critical, hermeneutic
      Kuhn, Lakatos
Language/reality
False dichotomies:
   Non-interventionism/laissez faire vs. reform
      Fundamental nature of government, with legal change of law as problem
      Propositions as attitude vs. reality
         Functional re: social construction of reality
      Problem not government vs. no government, but which interests is
         government to protect and which it will inhibit
   Polity vs. economy
      Legal-economic nexus
Role of obfuscation of role of public purpose
   Inter-individual interrelationships/rights, etc.
      Necessity of basis for choice: public purpose
   Obfuscation of fundamental role of government as mode of social control
      re: public purpose
   Obfuscation of selective adoption of status quo as natural, given, etc.

Supplementary Themes
   Two traditions:
      Economic Theory
      Theory of Economic Order/Policy
   Two approaches to "market": "The Market"
      Pure abstract conceptual a-institutional market
      Market as function of and giving effect to institutions/power structure that
         operates through it

Overview of history of value and price theory: Introductory notes on value and
   price
   Value as metaphysical notion; price as theoretical and empirical
      Nature as metaphysics: ultimate and absolute basis of price
      Theoretical: short run and long run [Marshall]

Empirical: market price
Intrinsic vs. extrinsic value
　　Just price: intrinsic value/cost/conventional price/re social
　　　status/competitive price
Demand and supply model
Marshall:
　　Marriage: two blades of a scissor
　　Short and long run prices
　　From focus on value to focus on price
　　　Price as temporary resting point in dance of demand and supply: relativist
　　　Objective, and normative [function of valuation], not absolutist
1. Reasonable value: Commons re working rules of law and morals
4. Social value: non-market valuation

Historiographic problems
　Authorial intention vs. reader interpretation:
　　Latter inevitable
　Meaning as function of context/environment of author vs. presentist
　　interpretation of past on basis of present
　Multiplicity of interpretation
　Matrix approach to meaning
　"Problems of Language in Economics"
　Modern economics as function of modern economy
　　Fact
　　Diverse reactions
　　Critical role of power structure and system
　　Taking system for granted: dangerous
　　Different modes of institutionalizing generic systems
　　Precursive ideas
　Matrix approach
　Some related concepts: dialectic, general interdependence, general
　　equilibrium, cumulative causation, over-determination

Further as to methodology, and on truth and discourse
　Diverse meanings of individualism: emphases on utilitarian happiness, on the
　　form which liberty takes, on thinking of rights as private in nature, on
　　conceiving of individual human beings as ultimate independent units, on
　　oppositions between the individual and the social and between the social and
　　the natural, on rights vs. privileges, on a movement to secure individual
　　human beings greater play of personal desires, on comprising a progressive

factor in human history, on being constituted of laissez faire in matters of
economic policy, on political democracy, and so on
Diverse critiques of Classical (Ricardian) economics:
  Marxian: incomplete re: exploitation and class
  Neoclassical-Austrian: incomplete-wrong re: marginal utility and consumer
    sovereignty
  Keynesian: incomplete/wrong re: instability and income mechanism
  Institutionalism: incomplete/wrong re: institutions, preconceptions
  Physiocratic and Romantic: wrong re: natural and desirable social order
Implications of foregoing:
  Selective perception
  Defense of social system and structure
    Evolution of social system and structure
  Value/price: philosophical/scientific realism/determinism
    Foreclosure of process
    Artifactual and social construction of reality
  Social construction of reality
    Hierarchic individualism and use of government re: social construction of
      reality
    Selective perception plus social structure plus policy as function of
      definition of reality (including values as part of reality per se): yield use
      of government re: social construction of reality

SET II-4

A HERITAGE OF DISSONANCE

1. The problem of Identity: Economics by 1890
  Identity Crisis: Diversity yields confused identity
    Conflicts and problems as to where economics stood on the following:
      Political economy or economics (name)
      State of classical economists (founding fathers, hence paternity)
      Ambiguity and conflict in value theory
      Threat of Marxian economics and philosophy – socialism in general
      Status of status quo in general (defined largely in economic terms;
        economics associated with it)
      Identity of economics as a science: its central problem in two interrelated
        senses:
        Its own identity re supra
        Central problem of analysis
      Identity of economics as a science: methodological issues

The quest for identity
  Quest for status and safety
  Desire for scientific status
  Desire for social role of expert (man of knowledge): authoritative
  "Activist" as to economic role of government
Themes from the classical past:
  Simple Smithian theory of economic development: "capital theory"
  Labor theory of value, more or less modified
  Established, independent theory of rent; ambiguity and conflict over
    wages, interest, profit
  Say's Law, coupled with quantity theory of money
  Income distribution analysis tied up with structure and relations of
    social classes in production: broad economic categories
  Confusion over economic role of government
Themes from the Marxian challenge:
  Labor theory of value used to support theory of exploitative economy
  Dynamics of capitalism specified in terms of inherent contradictions
  Technologically impelled class structure as critical variable for study
    and policy
Themes from the historical tradition:
  Evolutionary and institutional nature of economy
  Empiricism elevated over extreme apriorism
  Activist economic role of government
Themes from the conservative revolutionaries of the 1870s:
  Narrowing of economic categories: economics as economics of pure
    exchange in market economy, with market abstracted from social
    and institutional structure
  Micro-economic analysis – value and resource allocation – conducted
    with marginal technique; logic of microeconomics
      attractive
  Subjective theory of value: value as function interpersonal relations
    only as to utility
  Static theory of general equilibrium
  Imputation theory of distribution leading to marginal productivity and
    opportunity costs theories

2. General Character of Neo-classical Economics and its Development
  Diverse nature of neo-classical economics: Analysis of
    Market
    Price mechanism

Resource allocation
Constrained-maximization decision making
Logic of choice

Production
Exchange
Consumption
Distribution
Formal price theory replacing value theory, founded on integration of
cost-of-production and utility theories
Economics as economics of market mechanism, largely devoid of
consideration of social structure and institutional content and change
Posits, among other things, wants as given, and smooth operation of
price mechanism
Transformation of economic theory from value to resource-allocation
theory
Continued hold of "value" concept
Shift from vertical to horizontal axis as center of attention in some
aspects; in others, relatively equal attention
Price structure as mechanism of resource allocation
Accelerated emphasis upon theory of firm
Emphasis upon partial, static equilibrium analysis
Development of economics of firm and household
Development of period analysis as conceptual device
Continued refinement of marginalism in sense of maximizing conditions
– unique determinate optimal equilibrium solutions
Theory of distribution developed on two levels:
Analysis of particular factors of production or functional-income
claimants and their remuneration
Generalized theories encompassing all factors of production:
opportunity cost and marginal productivity
Continuation and refinement of and integration with theory of general
equilibrium, latter always serving unifying role

SET II-5

CONCLUDING LECTURE, Fall 1990

1. Importance of philosophical preconceptions as well as economic practice,
for development of economic theory.

2. Importance of problem-of-order elements: freedom vs. control, continuity vs. change, and hierarchy vs. equality, for development and significance of economic thought.
3. Economic conceptualization and analysis as cultural expression.
4. Power and ideology as filtration devices.
5. Three functions of economics: knowledge, social control, and psychic balm.
6. Problem of "presentism."
   a. Truth/falsity
   b. Hermeneutic circle

Set II-6

Economics 816

CONCLUDING LECTURES: THE HISTORY OF ECONOMIC THOUGHT IN RETROSPECT

1. the problem of Whig history of economic thought
   a. identification
   b. history of economic thought as history of theory, esp. microeconomics
   c. "two traditions" and problem of scope of actual history of economics
      i. "economic theory" conventionally considered
      ii. "theory of economic system"
   d. three additional themes:
      i. economy as more than market
      ii. "theory" as more than resource allocation theory: theory of organization and control, etc.
      iii. theory of pure market mechanism vis-à-vis institutions and power structure which form and operate through them

2. history of economic thought as a branch of intellectual history
   a. conceit re pursuit of truth as legitimation technique re ideas and status (discipline as such and particular schools)
   b. technical economics as manifestations of ideas
   c. more to economics than technique: ideas and modes of thought
   d. aspects:
      * methodological individualism/methodological collectivism/institutional individualism
      * teleological/mechanistic/probabilistic/Darwinian
      * multiple rationalities: Diesing:
         a. technical: ends-means analysis

        b. economic: constrained maximization through exchange
        c. social: conflict resolution through integrative processes
        d. political: structure of decision making and participation
        e. legal: conflict stabilization through rule or norm making
      * role of received cognitive system, or paradigm
      * multiple roles of theory

3. matrix approach re:
    a. plural views of economy
    b. plural views of economics, what it is all about
    c. plural views of particular schools
    d. plural views of evolution/history of economic thought
    e. particular texts

4. relativism/absolutism (internalism/externalism) in history of economic thought

5. Hicks: economics as set of tools, not necessarily a definition of economic reality

6. multiplicity in history of economic thought

7. selective construction, appropriation and use of the past
    a. e.g. Smith, Ricardo, Marx, Pareto, Keynes
    b. privileging interpretations
    c. matrix approach to meaning

8. the question of precursor status
    a. Aristotle: nothing new to say, only new ways of saying what is already known
    b. complex question of precursor status

9. the problem of (relatively) openended interpretation (using and paraphrasing Cass Sunstein review of Stanley Fish, New Republic, 6 December 1993, 42–46, but also using ideas of my own hitherto published): with regard to particular texts, theories, and approaches to the world:
    a. in re: claim that there is no single necessarily correct interpretation and that, accordingly, there is no warrant for a single privileged interpretation
    b. could mean:
        i. that all of us make assumptions and have commitments and live in the world (trivial); or
        ii. that all views are equally valid and that we can never decide among them on the basis of good reasons (wrong); or

      iii. that we have the burden of making choices and that we do in fact
          chose; e.g. the privileging of one interpretation is itself an act of
          choice; the important thing is to recognize the fact of choice and
          consider the alternatives carefully

c. it is not only a political matter to change an interpretation; the adoption
  of the existing interpretation was itself a political matter; – meaning by
  "political" an act of choice
     i. politics is not intruding into a situation which was neutral and from
      which politics had hitherto been absent; now a new set of political
      positions compete with the old
     ii. no way of avoiding politics; every interpretation is a matter of a
       certain set of preconceptions and convictions, many of them
       unanalyzed; politicization is both inescapable and ubiquitous

d. further complicated by fact that general concepts must be and indeed are
  given selective, specific meanings

e. for some, recognition of contingency is liberating – for people who are
  comfortable with openendedness and ambiguity; for some, it is
  dismaying – people who want closure and determinacy
     i. recognition of contingency is arguably congruent with the facts of life
     ii. permits understanding that change is possible, and can be considered
      on basis of our interests and needs
       a. interpretation as tool
    iii. recognition that analysis is circular, tautological, question-begging,
      and endless manipulable is disturbing to many – including those who
      reject the human origins of human claims
       a. others feel that legitimation requires appearance of logical
         compulsion – where manipulation is really at work
     iv. some believe that no such careful consideration is possible, that
      people do what they do without deep reflection and there is no way to
      improve matters

f. charge that recognition of contingency offers little that is useful
     i. re reaction to claim that public utility pricing does not merely give
      effect to rights but creates rights
     ii. importance of consideration of interpretations as so many tools:
       a. pragmatism: meaning to be reckoned in terms of consequences
       b. must still be concerned with questions of fact, value and interpretation
    iii. enables/compels deliberative rather than deliberative consideration,
      including direct comparisons
    iv. focuses on fact and importance of processes of working things out

     a. emphasis on human role in creating meaning and truth means more, rather than less, serious work

       i. "reality" of social construction of economy and of knowledge of economy

         a. role of pretense in legitimation

         b. can emphasize ubiquity of political interpretation and positioning while refraining from affirming a singular interpretation

           i. reliance on matrix analysis

   v. importance of self-referentiality, or self-reflexivity: apply contingency analysis to approach emphasizing contingency

     a. even if we all believe, in contingency interpretation,

       i. it is only one interpretation, and

       ii. it, too, must be worked out, as above

         a. how it is worked out is influenced by decisional structure and process

        ∗ i.e. do not treat it as having an extra-human ground, that is, as a philosophical realist position

g. in sum, multiplicity of possible interpretation requires, rather than denying, choice.

REVIEW ESSAYS

Hodgson's THE EVOLUTION OF INSTITUTIONAL ECONOMICS

WIE ES EIGENTLICH GEWESEN IST?

Bradley W. Bateman

A review essay on Geoffrey Hodgson's *The Evolution of Institutional Economics: Agency, Structure and Darwinism in American Institutionalism.* London: Routledge, 2004.

In the last decade, there has been a marked increase of interest in the history of American economics during the late 19th and early 20th century. This is a notable turn from the decades following the Second World War when it seemed that everything important in the history of economic thought up to 1940 was British (or written in Britain) and everything important after 1940 was American. Those post-War decades were, of course, a distorted time; the history of economic thought waned tremendously then in both the top flight journals and in graduate school curricula.[1] The focus in the profession was on the consolidation and advancement of mathematical modeling, focused even more narrowly for several decades on general equilibrium modeling. In that rarefied atmosphere, there was little patience among mainstream economists for careful historical work; and the history of economic thought, where it survived, was largely collapsed into a retrospective teleology about how the discipline got to its current cutting-edge brilliance. Hence, the stilted focus in the 1960s and 1970s on Smith, Ricardo, Marx, Marshall, Pigou, and Keynes.

A Research Annual
Research in the History of Economic Thought and Methodology, Volume 23-A, 137–165
Copyright © 2005 by Elsevier Ltd.
All rights of reproduction in any form reserved
ISSN: 0743-4154/doi:10.1016/S0743-4154(05)23005-5

These great theorists *are* central to the discipline's history, of course, but the focus on them during much of the second half of the 20th century was often solely in terms of trying to explicate their work from the perspective of what we have learned since they wrote. All that seemed important in their work was whether they had foreshadowed more contemporary work.

Mainstream economics has become much more eclectic in the last fifteen years, dropping its intense focus on general equilibrium, for instance, and adopting a plethora of theoretical approaches such as experimental economics and behavioral economics, many of which draw from frontier work in other disciplines, such as psychology.[2] At the same time, the history of economic thought has become a much more vital sub-discipline; the amount of work in original source material has increased tremendously and the quality of scholarship has likewise increased noticeably. Like their colleagues who specialize in economic theory, historians of economic thought have turned to the work in other disciplines (e.g. history and literary analysis) to sharpen their own skills and expand their outlooks.

The acquisition of these new skills, together with the loosening of the research program of mainstream economists, has combined to help feed the rising interest in the history of American economics.[3] On the one hand, historians of economics are anxious to explore new, untapped source material, and from Richard T. Ely to Irving Fisher and Walton Hamilton, there is a gold mine of primary documents and archival material. On the other hand, as the mainstream has opened up to alternative approaches, there seems to be more room now to think critically about the origins and nature of economic theory. From this point of view, American economists at the turn of the last century are a rich vein to tap for forming a critical perspective on the discipline; they represent a set of diverse talents who experimented not only with marginalism, but also with historical, ethical, mathematical, and institutional approaches to economic theorizing.

Unfortunately, the sharpening of skills and the increased quality of the work in the field has not caused a rapprochement between historians of economic thought and the mainstream of the discipline. Despite the fact that the work of historians of economics is significantly better, other economists continue to be largely uninterested in historical reasoning of any kind, much less intellectual history. They are willing to experiment with new psychological and game theoretical models, but the importance of history still seems to lie beyond their grasp.

A NEW DIRECTION IN HISTORY AND THEORY?

Geoffrey Hodgson would like to change all this with his *Evolution of Institutional Economics: Agency, Structure, and Darwinism in American Institutionalism*

(2004). Hodgson writes as both an economic theorist and an historian of economic thought, and he argues that in the history of Institutional Economics in America resides a valuable legacy upon which contemporary theorists can build. In truth, Hodgson's book must be read together with his recent *How Economics Forgot History; The Problem of Historical Specificity in Social Science* (2001), where he has argued for the importance of historical reasoning to economists.

The crux of Hodgson's argument about the legacy of Institutionalism is that at the turn of the last century Thorstein Veblen developed an important, but overlooked, body of work that attempted to build an economics based on Darwin's breakthrough work in the *Origin of Species* (1859). Hodgson's hypothesis is complex and multi-layered, but at its heart is the argument that Darwin insists on the importance of causality in historical time and that this same focus must be built upon in any economic theory worth pursuing. Hodgson argues that, in essence, Darwin is not only right about the evolution of species, but that his theory of selection is also at work in the historical trajectory of society.[4] Thus, society is actually (not metaphorically) evolving, and social science must encompass this truth in its basic theoretical structures.

Hodgson's argument is impressive on many levels. For instance, he is able to isolate the early influences on Veblen's work, philosophers (e.g. George Henry Lewes), psychologists (e.g. William James), and sociologists (e.g. Lester Ward) who were working in the same directions and who helped to form his theoretical apparatus. These parts of Hodgson's work give us a new, richer Veblen, whose accomplishments are placed in a context of contemporaneous advances. Likewise, Hodgson is impressive for his willingness to point out the weaknesses in Veblen's work. After recognizing the instinct of workmanship as the site of Veblen's theory of how social evolution takes place, Hodgson devotes a clear-eyed chapter (Chap. 9, The Instinct of Workmanship and the Pecuniary Culture) to why Veblen's theory is ultimately unsatisfactory. Hodgson's argument is not that Veblen got it *all* right, only that he saw the right direction and points the way to the ontology and methods that must inform any successful economics. The problem, as Hodgson sees it, is that Institutional Economics turned away from Veblen's approach to economic theory after 1918 and adopted a method and ontology that precluded the pursuit of a Darwinian economics.

Hodgson then performs an equally remarkable feat in working back through the early decades of the 20th century and uncovering the people in various disciplines who were then developing the ideas that had the potential to make Veblen's theory more robust and workable. The villains in Hodgson's story are behaviorist psychologists and logical positivists; the neglected heroes are the handful of philosophers and psychologists who were then developing the theory of emergent properties. Hodgson argues that a correct understanding of emergent properties

provides the basis for building a successful Darwinian economics and that had
Veblen's heirs only embraced the concept of emergent properties, they would have
had the tools to successfully triumph over the neoclassicism that eventually swept
the boards after 1945.

Thus, Hodgson has written a history with a purpose. By uncovering Veblen's
original intent, exposing his weaknesses, and pointing out a way to correct his
errors, Hodgson has attempted to show contemporary economic theorists how to
go forward in more fruitful and realistic manner. He offers a means for developing
a theory of how to model the effects on agents of the social institutions that they
inhabit and how they, in turn, affect and shape those institutions.[5]

WIE ES EIGENTLICH GEWESEN IST?

In many ways, Hodgson's book represents a virtuoso performance. It presents
a new and important interpretation of Veblen's work. Like Tiziano Raffaelli's
(2003) recent work on Alfred Marshall, Hodgson's book provides us with the
philosophical background of the economics of a major figure in the history of
economic thought. Understanding Veblen as a part of the emerging pragmatism
at the turn of the last century is an undoubted aid in getting the whole picture of
American economics in better focus.

But despite this triumph in his interpretation of Veblen, and despite his immense
and erudite knowledge of contemporary (21st century) philosophy of science,
Hodgson did not convince me that any successful economic theory must be based
on Darwinism. I do not disagree with Hodgson that economics is poorer for its
long neglect of history. Nor do I disagree with him that economic theory has
suffered for its neglect of institutions. And I agree completely with Hodgson
that a convincing and robust economics should be able to explain the interplay
between agents and social structures. But despite these agreements, I am unable
to see anything compelling about Darwinism as a solution to these problems in
mainstream economics.

Hodgson anticipates antipathy to the Darwinian part of his argument, and he
spends some considerable effort in the book trying to counter what he believes are
the reasons that people cannot see the importance of Darwinism to good social
theory. Like a good historian, Hodgson looks to particular historical moments to
explain Darwinism's demise as an element in American social theorizing. Among
other things, he points to the connection frequently made between Darwinism
and the Nazi's mass murders, the association of Darwinism with eugenics, and
the pall cast by Richard Hofstadter's famous *Social Darwinism in American
Thought, 1860–1915* (1944). Hodgson is right that these three things have caused

people to misunderstand what Darwinism really is and that the true connection of Darwinism to the Holocaust, to eugenics, and to American social thought is often confused in the public mind.

But even granting that Hodgson is right about the frequent misuse and misunderstanding of Darwinism, I remain unconvinced that it is the necessary basis for understanding human society. Rather than argue with Hodgson on philosophical grounds about Darwinism, I would like to explain my skepticism in terms of my somewhat different understanding of the history that Hodgson has told in his book. There are actually very few places where I think that Hodgson has misstated an historical fact, but there are many places where we interpret the history of Institutionalism differently. In fact, in many cases, we see exactly the same fact in quite different lights.

The key to Hodgson's approach to social science, of course, also gives him the key to historical explanation, for if the correct theory of current social activity is an evolutionary, Darwinian theory, then the processes that are driving current social life also explain the past unfolding of history. Like his American heroes who went to Germany in the 19th century to study, Hodgson wants to write history *wie es eigentlich gewesen*, as it actually was. As Hodgson (2001, p. 37) says, "The central task of science is to advance the understanding of how the world actually works." He believes that ultimately he can know the one true way that things happened; indeed, he must be able to know the one true way they happened so that the Darwinian unfolding can be exactly described. A process of selection is not open to different interpretations. We have to be able to know exactly what is being selected, exactly what conditions are acting on the material that is being selected, and, so, exactly what the causal path of the unfolding is. Hodgson (2001, Chap. 2) makes some allowance that there may be diversity of opinion among scientists, and he counsels pluralism in funding because of this, but ultimately, he says, the object of the scientific process must be to get down to the actual elements in a Darwinian evolution. When it comes to selection, there cannot be two different legitimate explanations; either you know what is being selected and can describe the process by which it is selected, or you are getting closer to that position.

Typically in my own work in intellectual history, I advocate strongly one interpretation of how the ideas I am studying came into being, influenced the world, and were themselves changed in their use. Likewise, I usually argue strongly that there are other competing stories that do not gibe with the facts as well as my interpretation. But I also know that in intellectual history (as in all historical narrative) more than one legitimate interpretation can simultaneously exist. I am not confident that historical narrative can ever successfully be reduced to just one story, as the understanding of biological evolution can be whittled down to just one story. To phrase my skepticism in the language of Hodgson's (2001) heroes, when I read his interpretation of what happened to Veblens's ideas, I wonder, "*Wie es eigentlich gewesen ist*?" (Was it actually that way?)

PUTTING ON THE LAB COATS

To make my point, it is probably just as well to start with how differently we see the reasons for the demise of Darwinism in American thought. While I do not disagree with Hodgson that the reasons he gives for Darwinism's demise have, in fact, had an adverse effect, I see other important reasons that he does not consider.

For instance, I would argue that initially it was Darwinism's association in the popular mind with liberal, progressive causes, rather than its association with eugenics or Nazism that originally undercut its effectiveness in American social science. There are many extant criticisms of Hofstadter's book, chief among them that the people he casts as Social Darwinists were not really Darwinian, but rather Lamarckian. Another criticism is that the people Hofstadter defined as Social Darwinians were either not very numerous or not very influential. But the fact of there being only a handful of the true "Social Darwinists," or "Social Lamarckians" for that matter, does not mean that Darwinism was not important in American society. In fact, quite the opposite is true. Darwinism pervaded American society at the end of the 19th century and the beginning of the 20th.

The Darwin that these progressive reformers revered may not bear a very close resemblance to the "true" Darwin, but they were nonetheless marching under a banner that they publicly described as Darwinism. When *Origin of Species* originally appeared, the United States was just entering the Civil War, so the initial reaction was delayed until the War was over. But the conservative religious reaction against Darwin, natural selection, and evolution was muted and did not last long. Instead, American Christians largely absorbed Darwin (as they understood him) and looked for ways to accommodate Darwin's arguments with Christian scripture. Indeed, it was the Higher Criticism developed by German theologians, not Darwin's work, that was seen as the real threat to Christian faith in the last decades of the 19th century.[6] Many of the people who most ardently embraced Darwin were liberal Protestant Christians, and many of the men who helped found the American Economic Association were in the vanguard of this movement.

These liberal Christians, in turn, became the backbone of the Progressive movement in the first decade of the 20th century. Men like Richard T. Ely, Jesse Macy, and E. R. A. Seligman founded the A. E. A. in the belief that they could be active agents in the progressive evolution of American society.[7] They got their first real toehold in the Progressive movement, and they spoke openly then about their work in the context of Darwin's ideas.[8]

But the Progressive movement took a turn in the second decade of the 20th century.[9] Many Americans became disillusioned with the unfulfilled promise of a moral evolution in American society, and so became restless with this Christian focus on "building a new Kingdom on this earth." At the same time, the increasingly pluralistic nature of American society began to become reflected in the people who were attracted to progressive reform. Thus, during the second decade of the new century, non-Christians such as Walter Lippmann moved to the forefront of the movement and American Progressivism began to simultaneously take on a more secular tone and to focus more on efficiency (as, for instance in its focus on Frederick Taylor's work).

But for better or worse, this change was not enough to save Progressivism from collapse after the First World War. In the public mind, Woodrow Wilson and the War were associated very strongly with the nationalism and the progressive, democratic rhetoric that had been used to justify entry into the War. The turn after 1912 to efficiency and to secularized arguments like Lippmann's and Herbert Croly's were not enough to save the progressive project from the sharp turn against idealism and moralism following the War. The turn was hard and fast as America sought a "return to normalcy" in the 1920s.

The consequences of this loss of public faith in the Progressive movement were devastating not only to Progressives in political office but to the entire structure of American social science. Everyone who writes about American social science (save for economists, it seems) talks about the sudden and radical realignments in American social science after the First World War.[10] The movement that followed from this disillusionment is usually referred to as scientism, and as Dorothy Ross (1991, p. 397) says, scientism was "an effort to make the achievement of science an end in itself and thereby to find order amid flux." To fully grasp the nature of what was going on, one must remember that throughout the Progressive Era (defined loosely as 1900–1918) most American social science remained firmly tied to Christianity and the idea of moral improvement. For instance, the early empirical work that Ely and Commons were closely associated with, the social survey movement, was very much an evangelical, Christian enterprise.[11]

Thus, when the atrocity of War was finally driven home and as Americans watched the victorious European nations act vindictively and hatefully against the defeated Germans, the entire public faith in Progressivism took a terrible beating.[12] The naiveté of the dream of moral improvement was all too apparent and the complicity of many progressives in demonizing the Germans during the debate about the country's entry into the War was a raw wound.

In this atmosphere, the moralizing social sciences felt they had but one strategy. In a period of only a few years, American social scientists cut their ties to their moralizing Christian roots and attempted to scientize themselves. In other words, they pulled on their white lab coats and tried to re-invent themselves as objective empirical investigators who did not bring any political agenda to their work. This latter effort was, of course, largely a rouse; most prominent American social scientists were still committed to some type of reform, but the time was not propitious to say that publicly. Now they wanted to be seen as scientists who approached things in an unbiased way, looking for the facts. If any reforms emerged from their work, they would have to be scientifically grounded.

The name for this movement in American economics was Institutionalism. All American economists pulled in their horns after the First World War, but the most innovative and scientistic economists were the Institutionalists. They wanted to secularize economics and to give it a new empirical, scientific basis. This was the project of Walton Hamilton and Wesley Mitchell, for instance.

NAILING JELLY TO THE WALL

But the crisis of Progressivism was also a crisis for historicism. Just as people turned away from the idea of moral improvement, they turned away from the idea that there was single historical narrative unfolding that could be captured in an account that explained things *wie es eigentlich gewesen*. The idea that people had understood to be progressive Darwinism, that history was unfolding toward a better future, simply did not hold water any more. For our purposes, and theirs, it does not matter that "true" Darwinism is not about a progressive or teleological evolution. For most people, lay and professional alike, Darwinism was associated with the progressive ideal of the previous two decades and it was now a discredited idea. But note that Darwinism was discredited not because of its mistaken association with conservative, reactionary, or eugenic ideas. Instead, it was discredited because of its association with Progressivism.

This was a difficult time to be a social scientist in certain senses, but an exciting time in others. The times called for a new kind of social science and many people answered the call. In this sense, the Institutionalists' story can be seen as a pioneering story. But it is their story and not Veblen's story. Veblen had been a teacher to some of these men, and his work inspired some of them, but he is not the central figure in the story. He is much more a kind of distant figurehead for them.[13] At a time when social science was under careful scrutiny, it is difficult to imagine anyone who would have wanted to bring in an acerbic, satirical person who had been unable to hold a regular position for most of his life and to make that person the acknowledged leader of their movement.[14] Theirs was a different project with different ends than Veblen's. Most Institutionalists respected Veblen, but they wanted to do things, such as launch large scale empirical projects, that were not really a part of what Veblen had advocated.[15] And Veblen's impressive array of intellectual influences did not help in this regard, either.

About all this Hodgson seems, well, incredulous. He acknowledges at some points that Veblen was not the real founder of Institutionalism and that the founders did not really acknowledge the movement as "his." But Hodgson's narrative repeatedly returns to an unbelieving exasperation that the Institutionalists trafficked in behavioralism and empiricism, and neglected not only Veblen but also the contemporaneous hints about emergent properties. A large part of Hodgson's point seems to be that Institutionalists were badly mistaken to not understand that they should have been deeply devoted to Veblen's ideas.

It must be granted that Veblen had a much better and more sophisticated understanding of Darwin than most of his contemporaries; and it must also be acknowledged that Darwinism now has a much different (genetic and ontological) basis than it did in the 1920s. But none of that explains why the Institutionalists should have followed Veblen's lead and tried to build a Darwinian economic science. In fact, Hodgson's own admission that Veblen was wrong in some of his most central ideas should help us to see why the Institutionalists were looking in a different direction. It would have been nice, perhaps, had they had the nearly superhuman courage and strength to resist the tide against Darwinian influences in social science in the 1920s, but Veblen's work does not seem to have given them much reason for having undertaken such a Herculean effort.

But more to the point, the story of Institutionalism is a richer, more multi-valenced story than the one that Hodgson wants to tell. The Institutionalists were subject to both concept and circumstance. They would not have been the Institutionalists if they had not been taking part in the shift to scientism in American social science following the First World War. Had they merely been disciples of Veblen, trying to build on and develop his legacy, they would be different people than who they actually were.

For my money, the story of institutionalism that Malcolm Rutherford (e.g. 1997, 1999, 2000, 2002) has been slowly developing over the last decade shows Institutionalism in much clearer light than does Hodgson's story. Veblen is given a role in this story, but not the central role. In Rutherford's hands, Institutionalism becomes something more than Veblen and Commons writ large and starts to become a story of many people with many motives, trying to build a secularized economics, based on empirical work that goes someplace other than the simple world of marginalist laissez-faire arguments. This is not the canned story of Institutionalism that was told in the decades after the Second World War, but it looks much closer to the truth than the old story. Rutherford is not yet finished telling his story, so we do not yet know what lessons might be learned from it. But if anything like Rutherford's story is correct, it is hard to imagine that the lesson from understanding Institutionalism is that all economics needs to have a Darwinian basis.

But, of course, Rutherford could be wrong. Likewise, I could be wrong in arguing that it was much more the association of Darwinism with liberal, progressive causes than its association with conservative ones that led to its demise and discrediting in American social science in the 1920s. After all, as Isaiah Berlin (1979, p. 156) has argued, writing intellectual history is like trying to nail jelly fish to the wall. Intellectual history is so overdetermined and so complex that one should always be wary when one thinks that one has got it all explained.

This is why I remain unconvinced that the history of ideas follows some Darwinian process of selection. It just does not seem that simple to me. The story of the birth and death of ideas does not have obvious, clear analogs for the genes that are selected in the evolutionary process going on around us at this moment.

NOTES

1. As Gayer (2002) points out, the history of economic thought still has not recovered in graduate school curricula.

2. For a general discussion of how general equilibrium theorizing rose, and fell, in mainstream economics in the postwar period, see the survey essay by S. Abu Taurab Rizvi (2003).

3. See, for instance, the essays by Mary Morgan (1994), Malcolm Rutherford (1997), Bradley Bateman (1998, 2001), and Thomas Leonard (2003).

4. There is not room in this essay to carefully reconstruct Hodgson's definition of what Darwinism is and is not. His argument is an important construction building on recent work in both biology and the philosophy of science.

5. It is one of the real mysteries of Hodgson's book why he does not embrace, or even mention, Amartya Sen's *Development as Freedom* (1999), a book that is built around the argument that good economic theory must be able to simultaneously address agency, structure, and their interplay. This is a mystery because Hodgson seems to have read and woven a remarkable amount into his argument.

6. Ferenc Szasz (1982) has explained the relative roles of Darwinism and the Higher Criticism in the late nineteenth century. As he shows, Darwinism and evangelical Christianity did not become seen as irredeemably opposed until after the Scopes Trial in 1925.

7. See, for instance Bateman (1998). It should be noted that Seligman was not a liberal Christian, but rather an ethical culturist, a group that had non-theistic ideas that were otherwise quite similar to the ideas of liberal Christianity as regards the necessity of social reform.

8. Everett (1946) discusses both the liberal Christianity and the Darwinian link for three of these figures.

9. Perhaps the best treatment of the transition of the progressive impulse from Christianity to a more secular basis is David Danbom (1987). See also Bateman (2001).

10. See Ross (1991) and Bateman (2001).

11. See Bateman (2001) for a discussion of the overtly Christian character of the social survey movement.

12. Steven Diner (1998) contains one of the most frank assessments of how the Progressives themselves felt the implosion of their movement.

13. Hodgson (2004) calls Veblen "an available figurehead," but he was not *the* figurehead of the movement and played something more like a distant role than an immediate one for most Institutionalists.

14. Hodgson is at great pains to minimize Veblen's sarcastic wit and his patchy employment record. But while it may be true that Veblen's virtues as a theorist are sometimes obscured by his personal problems and his biting social satire, one cannot overlook the very real effect that these things actually had on his career and the way that he was seen in his own time.

15. Hodgson puts these attempts to create a movement that went in different directions than Veblen's work down to a failure of their part to understand Veblen's work, and/or his importance. Instead, I would say that they point to the fact that they had other ambitions and did not see their movement as Veblen's own.

ACKNOWLEDGMENT

I wish to thank Sig Barber for help with an early draft of this essay.

REFERENCES

Bateman, B. (1998). Clearing the ground: The demise of the Social Gospel and the rise of Neoclassicism in American economics. In: M. Morgan & M. Rutherford (Eds), *From Interwar Pluralism to Postwar Neoclassicism* (pp. 29–52). Durham, NC: Duke University Press.

Bateman, B. (2001). Make a righteous number: Social surveys, the men and religion forward movement, and quantification in American economics. In: M. Morgan & J. Klein (Eds), *The Age of Economic Measurement* (pp. 57–85). Durham, NC: Duke University Press.

Berlin, I. (1979). *Concepts and categories: Philosophical essays.* New York: Penguin.

Danbom, D. (1987). *The world of hope: Progressives and the struggle for an ethical public life.* Philadelphia, PA: Temple University Press.

Diner, S. (1998). *A very different age: Americans in the progressive era.* New York: Hill & Wang.

Everett, J. (1946). *Religion in economics: A study of John Bates Clark, Richard T. Ely, and Simon Patten.* New York: King's Crown Press.

Gayer, T. (2002). Graduate studies in the history of economic thought. In: E. R. Weintraub (Ed.), *The Future of the History of Economics* (pp. 35–61). Durham, NC: Duke University Press.

Hodgson, G. (2001). *How economics forgot history: The problem of historical specificity in social science.* London: Routledge.

Leonard, T. (2003). 'A certain rude honesty': John Bates Clark as a pioneering neoclassical economist. *History of Political Economy, 35,* 521–558.

Morgan, M. (1994). Marketplace morals and the American economists: The case of John Bates Clark. In: N. De Marchi & M. Morgan (Eds), *Higgling: Transactors and Their Markets in the History of Economics*. Durham, NC: Duke University Press.

Raffaelli, T. (2003). *Marshall's Evolutionary Economics*. London: Routledge.

Rizvi, S. Abu Taurab (2003). Postwar Neoclassical microeconomics. In: W. J. Samuels, J. B. Davis & J. E. Biddle (Eds), *A Companion to the History of Economic Thought*. Oxford: Blackwell.

Ross, D. (1991). *The origins of American social science*. Cambridge: Cambridge University Press.

Rutherford, M. (1997). American institutionalism and the history of economics. *Journal of the History of Economic Thought, 19*, 178–195.

Rutherford, M. (1999). Institituionalism as 'scientific economics'. In: R. E. Backhouse & J. Creedy (Eds), *From Classical Economics to the Theory of the Firm: Essays in Honour of Dennis O'Brien* (pp. 223–242). Cheltenham: Edward Elgar.

Rutherford, M. (2000). Understanding institutional economics, 1918–1929. *Journal of the History of Economic Thought, 22*, 277–308.

Rutherford, M. (2002). Morris A. Copeland: A case study in the history of institutional economics. *Journal of the History of Economic Thought, 24*, 261–290.

Sen, A. (1999). *Development as freedom*. New York: Alfred Knopf.

Szasz, F. (1982). *The divided mind of protestant America*. Tuscaloosa, AL: University of Alabama Press.

REVITALIZING INSTITUTIONAL ECONOMICS: CAN WE GET THERE FROM HERE?

Daniel W. Bromley

A review essay on Geoffrey M. Hodgson, *The Evolution of Institutional Economics: Agency, Structure, and Darwinism in American Institutionalism*. New York: Routledge, 2004.

THE DECLINE OF INSTITUTIONAL ECONOMICS

It is not in doubt that institutional economics was, for a period (1914–1945), the essence of American economics. After World War II, institutional economics was shouldered aside by a different epistemological program engaged in by those with little interest in the institutional foundations of economic systems, but with a deep and abiding nomological interest in possessive individualism and how to model it with great elegance, if not necessarily to good effect. Of course many economists have lately come to imagine that they are now studying institutions when they construct models of evolutionary games, or when they engage undergraduates in experiments designed to elicit the emergence of norms of redistribution. Such activities (and their deduced theoretical insights) bear the same relation to the institutional foundations of economic systems as one gets by pondering Bernard Mandeville's charming allegory about bees.

Things are now looking up. The collapse of the Soviet Union has rekindled interest in how to constitute the institutional foundations of a *new* market economy. Several economists have been awarded the Bank of Sweden Prize in Economic Sciences in Memory of Alfred Nobel for work that bears some relation to institutions. And the "new" institutional economists have finally mustered up enough self-confidence to denounce the "old" institutional economists as assiduous collectors of facts, but as folks without a theory and – apparently more damning – as "anti-theoretical." Indeed, it is not clear to many of these new institutional economists that the old folks were actually economists. Perhaps they were sociologists. Maybe even German-type historians.

Against this backdrop, Geoffrey Hodgson has offered a detailed account of all of the twists and turns and accidents of history (and mal-directed libidinous thrusting) behind the routing of institutional economics from the halls of the academy. Indeed, adhering to one of his core ontological commitments that every effect has a cause, Hodgson offers not one but as many as ten or eleven causes of the decline of institutional economics (the *effect*). These causes are, approximately: (1) the dissolution of the original philosophical and psychological presumptions of institutionalism; (2) the widespread rejection of biological or (Darwinian) ideas from the social sciences; (3) reaction against the rise of Nazism in Europe; (4) the Depression and the incompetence of governments who had, evidently, been advised by some institutionalists; (5) the "theoretical deficit" of the institutionalists despite their constructive suggestions under the New Deal; (6) the rise of formalistic microeconomic theory; (7) the logistical demands of World War II that played to the strengths of the new breed of mathematically agile constrained maximizers coming out of the academy; (8) McCarthyism (in the U.S.) that terrorized anyone who might ask questions of a systems nature – such questions immediately being sufficient to be thought a communist sympathizer; (9) the absence of a "systematic theory"; and (10) a lack of "consensus on fundamentals." These various causes seem plausible enough, but I would add one more.

As we ponder the reasons why institutionalism lost market share after World War II, it seems necessary to look more closely at the demand side of the market. After all, even if the economics profession had made all of the right conceptual and empirical moves, no amount of clear thinking – and epistemological correctness – could have prevented a shift in the product mix if the demand for the product from Economics, Inc. had shifted. Hodgson notes that institutional tendencies originally leapt across the Atlantic at the end of the 19th century because the American economy was the subject of a construction project that had largely been completed in Europe. Just as the Industrial Revolution had become a spent force in England, the American Civil War ended and America was ready to become a serious economic player. From 1870 until the start of World War I, American economic change resembled what we see today in China – only more so. The institutional foundations of frontier capitalism were unformed and inchoate. As Matthew Arnold might put it, the economic situation in America materialized the upper class, vulgarized the middle class, and brutalized the lower class. Small wonder that institutional economists were seen to be useful.

World War II was transformative. The strength and reach of the American economy was validated by our ability to fight major battles on several fronts, and from that point forward there was no need for deep and reflective thought of systemic issues. The concern became not how to construct an economy that could produce wealth – a puzzle that had animated Adam Smith and many others – but rather how to refine and lock the extant system in place so that its capacity to produce stuff would never be jeopardized. The Soviet implosion in 1990–1992 was seen as a profound object lesson – do not get into a tournament for the production of stuff (in this case war-fighting stuff) with an unleashed capitalist state. Of what possible use are institutional economists if capitalism and what the right-wing is pleased to call "free markets" are now seen as signaling the end of economic history?

Therefore, to Hodgson's many causes of the decline of institutionalism, I must add the fact that, by 1945 there ceased to be a market for institutionalist insights. It is hard to sell what people do not seek. As an academic enterprise, Economics, Inc. must offer up what buyers wish to hear.

So far my quibble with Hodgson has been of a niggling sort. It is only important because my addition to his list points to a fundamental necessity if the next 50 years is to be more congenial to institutionalist approaches than we have seen over the past 50 years. My following concerns are more fundamental.

HODGSON ON INSTITUTIONS

Hodgson asserts that "We may define institutions broadly as durable systems of established and embedded social rules that structure social interactions" (p. 14). While this is a good start, on page 428 (Note 3) things go awry. He tells us of private correspondence with Douglass North in which the two of them have reached agreement that "organizations are also institutions." Unfortunately, it seems to me quite impossible to build a theory of institutions and of institutional change if one imagines that institutions are *social rules* AND the Catholic Church or the Bank of England. These organizations – all organizations – are *defined by* (are constituted by) the social rules that create them and that continue to tell us what they are, and what they do. If North and Hodgson wish to believe that rules and organizations are analytically equivalent then they must believe that driving rules (institutions) in a country (or a state in the U.S.) are not analytically different from the legislatures and highway departments that promulgate and enforce those rules. Doing so requires that different institutional arrangements about driving – on which side of the road it is best implemented, whether or not one must wear a seat belt, the maximum allowable speed, the meaning of "reasonable and prudent," whether motorcyclists must wear a helmet, the permissible blood-alcohol content – can be analyzed and explained as if each of them (or the aggregate of them) was nothing but the transportation department.

Apparently sensing a problem, we see that "Organizations are *special* institutions that involve: (a) criteria to establish their boundaries and to distinguish their members from non-members; (b) principles of sovereignty concerning who is in charge; and (c) chains of command delineating responsibilities within the organization" (p. 425, emphasis added). Why the adjective "special" is called for here gives us a hint that Hodgson is not quite comfortable with his own position that institutions are identical to organizations. What, after all, are criteria to establish organizational boundaries and to distinguish members from non-members of organizations if not institutions (rules)? What are principles of sovereignty concerning who is in charge, and chains of command delineating responsibilities within the organization if not *institutions* (rules)? One is either a member of a firm or the Catholic Church or one is not a member. Institutions (rules) central to – indeed constitutive of – the firm or the Catholic Church reveal that to us and to them. One cannot be in doubt about who is in charge of the Catholic Church or who is the C.E.O. of a corporation. Institutions (rules) central to the firm or the Catholic Church reveal that to us and to them. One cannot be in doubt about chains of command delineating responsibilities within the organization. Institutions (rules) central to the firm or the Catholic Church reveal that to us and to those bound by those institutions (rules). Quite simply, organizations are not – and cannot be – institutions. *Organizations are constellations of institutions.* Institutions come in three forms: (1) norms and conventions; (2) working rules; and (3) entitlement structures (Bromley, 1989).

I am unable to make sense of the proposition from Hodgson (and North) that organizations are established and embedded social rules. Organizations function *according to* established and embedded social rules, but this does not make organizations into (or nothing but) rules. There is another difficulty with Hodgson's treatment of institutions as they pertain to individuals. Specifically, he says that

> The idea that institutions <u>can be</u> reconstitutive of individuals is arguably the most fundamental characteristic of institutional economics. Obviously, institutions themselves differ, in time and in space. However, individuals themselves are *also likely* to be radically affected by these differences. Different institutions can act as more than constraints on behaviours: they *may actually* change the character and beliefs of the individual (p. 257, emphasis added).

This passage leads us to suppose that Hodgson regards individuals as completely autonomous (pre-institutionalized) entities who may or may not be affected by institutions. As above, he says: "... institutions *can be* reconstitutive of individuals ...," "... individuals are also *likely* to be radically affected by these differences," and "They (institutions) *may actually* change the character and beliefs of the individual." I do not understand this tentative construction. Of course institutions ("durable systems of established and embedded social rules that structure social interactions") affect individuals – how could individuals <u>not</u> be affected by those things that structure social interactions? Young children are socialized and schooled consistent with a particular constellation of institutional arrangements defining which books (which sacred texts) shall be read, which stories are repeated, which histories are studied and ratified, which practices must be followed, and which beliefs are advanced as "normal." None of us can possibly escape being formed and constituted by the institutional environment within which we are embedded. We are products of the institutions that have defined our fields of belief and our fields of action. Commons referred to this as the "instituted personality." If institutions did not make a difference in our lives they would not be institutions. Institutions are facts and events precisely because they are the end products of prior collective action. Institutions are also causes – and we are the effects. Since Hodgson likes causes that have causes, yesterday's institutionally constituted individuals brought about (caused) the institutional arrangements that in turn constituted (caused) us. We are the products (events) of yesterday's "social welfare function," to be economistic about it.

So the idea of "uncaused" individuals is quite impossible. Just as Wittgenstein rejected the idea of a *private language*, institutionalism rejects the idea of a *private being*. Because humans are social animals (even if many of us act in anti-social ways), the private (isolated and autonomous) sapient being is a logical contradiction. We are who we have been constituted to be by the institutions (the norms, the rules, and the entitlement regimes) that define for us what we come to believe is our *reality*. And our idiosyncratic "reality" becomes correct and right and normal because it is the only reality we have been socialized to apprehend.

Hodgson is troubled here: "We require an explanation of how individual intentions or preferences may change. Without such an account, a danger is that structural constraints are called upon to do the main work of explaining human behavior. As a result, the disconnection of agency and structure may end up explaining the individual solely by reference to structure, thus conflating the individual into the structure..." (p. 38). I have difficulty becoming alarmed that what Hodgson calls "structural constraints" will be called upon to do the main work of explaining human behavior. Perhaps his alarm comes from the fact that Hodgson (as with North) appears to see institutions as "structural *constraints*." However, to view institutions as constraints is one sided and incomplete; *institutions both liberate and constrain individual action*. Recall from Commons that formal institutions (working rules) indicate what: "Individuals ***must*** or ***must not*** do (*duty*), what they ***may*** do without interference from other individuals (*privilege*), what they ***can*** do with the aid of the collective power (*right*), and what they ***cannot*** expect the collective power to do in their behalf (*no right*)" Comons (1968, p. 6). If I am protected by a right then all others are bound by a correlated duty – for the simple reason that rights are incoherent in the absence of duties on others. Do we not suppose that the behavior of those with rights differs in interesting ways from those with duties? If institutions make no difference in behavior then one is hard pressed to explain why the courts spend so much of their time engaging individuals locked in battle over who, exactly, has which rights. The Coase Theorem was profoundly wrong on this score. It matters very much indeed who has rights and who does not. Therefore, why should we be alarmed that institutions – rules that define for us not only fields of action, but also socialize us into particular beliefs about what is normal, correct, and right – might bear some important role in explaining individual behavior?

I could gain an agreeable income stream by converting my single-family dwelling into student housing. I am unable to do so by local zoning rules. And my neighbors who prefer single-family quietude are enormously liberated by my inability. Prevailing institutions seem to bear some role in the absence of 8 rent-paying students in my house. One only needs to look at other neighborhoods with different zoning rules to see very different behavior among the house-owning class. Again, what is so unsettling about institutions – social norms, working rules, entitlements – doing some (much?) of the explaining of certain human behavior? Are not these working rules known (knowable) entities more instrumental to choice and action than the elusive idea of "preferences?" Indeed, the circularity of revealed choice "theory" reveals nothing quite so much as the perverse admission that preferences are the plausible *effects* of choice and action, not the <u>cause</u>. So much for rational choice theory.

HODGSON ON CAUSE, CAUSALITY, AND CAUSATION

In addition to Darwinian/Veblenian evolution, a dominant leitmotif of this impressive work is Hodgson's ontological commitment (a frequent phrase here) to the idea that *every event must have a cause*. Hodgson believes that when one finds a cause then one has found an *explanation* or a *reason* for something. He denounces critical realism on the grounds that "... there is no adequate explanation of the causes of reasons or beliefs" (p. 370). He is apparently attracted to Darwin on the belief that:

> It is part and parcel of Darwin's underlying philosophy that all intention has itself to be explained by a causal process. This causal explanation has to show how the capacity to form intentions has itself gradually evolved in the human species, and also how individual intentions are formed in the psyche. For Darwin, natural selection is part of these causal explanations. There can be no first and 'uncaused cause' .... From a Darwinian philosophical perspective, all outcomes have to be explained in a linked causal process ... Everything must submit to a causal explanation in scientific terms (p. 55).

Hodgson insists that every event (every effect) has a cause, and since there are, apparently, no uncaused causes, every event has a cause, which in turn has a cause, which in turn has a cause, which in turn .... Consider the following event (fact): the surprising death of a newborn child. Doctors inform the grieving parents that the child was born with a defective heart and that this is the cause of – the reason for – the death. This information will be duly entered on the death certificate. The defective heart explains the death. Or does it?

The defective heart may well be the efficient (mechanical) cause of this tragic death. But since, *pace* Hodgson, there are no uncaused causes, we must now ponder the cause of the defective heart. Was there a genetic (Darwinian evolutionary) cause that might explain this death? After all, the parents are no doubt asking why *their* child was born with this malady – what did *they do* to deserve this horrible injustice? Parents will not necessarily find probabilities of defective hearts compelling as an explanation for the death of *their* child. They might still wonder why. Depending on the mental predisposition of the parents – their habits of mind informed by their constellation of norms (which are institutions) – two candidate "causes" arise: (1) it was God's will; or (2) it was simply fate. These alternative thoughts constitute plausible "explanations." Of course many modernists will be appalled at the thought that these constitute reasons or explanations as opposed to "superstitions." Only their modernist conceit stands in the way of clarity in this matter. But Hodgson's "scientific imperative" of getting behind (explaining) all causes (and all human motivations and intentions) now impels us to search for reasons why some people choose to find comfort in fate, while others find comfort in faith. I think we are now outside of economics, and being there I find no compelling reasons to pursue this matter further. People have their reasons; fair enough.

But let us get back to the explanation of random events – a child born with a defective heart. Random events may or may not have causes, but they do not have explanations or reasons. Instead, random events have *justifications* of the form "the odds of a fatal defective heart in a newborn whose parents and grandparents fit a particular profile are x." This is not an explanation any more than is the assertion that ruminants are quite likely ($p \approx 1$) to have cloven hooves. It is a statistical regularity. The eminent philosopher Charles Sanders Peirce insisted that: ". . . each act of causation involves an efficient component, a final component, and a chance component. While each event is brought about by a previous event (the efficient cause), it is also part of a continuous sequence that is marked by a definite tendency (final cause), and it involves an aspect of irreducible novelty (objective chance)" (Hulswit, 2002, p. 215).

HODGSON ON A REVITALIZED INSTITUTIONAL ECONOMICS

After almost 450 pages of exegetical excursions it is surprising to find but $5\frac{1}{2}$ pages of "Conclusion and Beginning." Perhaps one should be able to distill the precise and comprehensive outline of Hodgson's vision for the future from all that came before this brief closing statement. But it may not be easy for some to get the complete picture. Indeed, he admits:

> If the reader has studied *How Economics Forgot History* as well as this present volume, he or she will have traversed almost 800 pages and about 400,000 words to come to this point. It is a long story, relating how economics has lost many of its past insights and even disavowed its own past. It has aspects of a Greek tragedy. But expectations may also be raised after such a long journey, for sustenance and riches at its end. But our expedition has been into the past, and we have merely returned to the present day. Hopefully we have become enriched by this experience, but the greater and more difficult expedition stretches into the uncertain future. The past has provisioned us for this passage. This final chapter is an exhortation to begin the journey, with a few meager thoughts on some of the problems ahead (p. 447).

First, Hodgson seeks a breakdown in the disciplinary boundaries among the social sciences – a laudable goal that has been with us for a number of years. Second, he asks us to look to biology for inspiration and method – but particularly the "methodology and approach of Darwin." He insists that much of what we want to say has already been said before, and he argues that ". . . the Darwinian movement within the sciences has now built up such a huge momentum that it is unstoppable"

(p. 450). Some of us may be excused for wishing that this were not so, only partly because we are agnostic toward all "unstoppable" tendencies and movements. Their very "unstoppability" is quite sufficient grounds for fearing them. I confess to some anxiety when I hear talk of *evolutionary causality* and *evolutionary explanations*. The problem with evolutionary explanations is that they have the unhappy tendency to confuse essence with accident – the naturalistic fallacy. Hodgson has failed to close the sale on behalf of these apparently irresistible concepts.

Hodgson is certainly correct when he worries that "Matters become even more complicated when we bring the human mind into the picture, along with the mysteries of consciousness and intentionality and the causal explanations of their emergence" (p. 451). But that takes us ever deeper into sorting out the individual – a tempting but dubious goal for institutional economics. In attempting to summarize a mere 452 (never mind 800) pages here, I have an uneasy sense that Hodgson has made it too hard. Of course the elaborate history is important, and an excursion into Darwin and Veblen and the other 78 "Dramatis personae principes" is useful. But if Hodgson believes that a science that does not seek universal causes for all facts (and events, and causes) is being "untrue" to its own mission I would like to see reasons advanced for that claim. And perhaps it is true that the way forward is lighted by layered ontologies and emergent properties. But somehow I worry that those who really wish to be inspired by the prospects of a revitalized institutional economics will find these seeds to be of meager fruit indeed. The belief in a pure (pre-institutionalized) individual seems inconsistent with what we know about the on-going construction project called the human mind. The reliance on Darwinian processes conjures up images of quasi-mechanism – and mystery and chance. And the talk of emergent properties adds to the mystery.

Does a viable and pertinent institutional economics need to be mysterious? Can't we find good seed all around us in the many rich empirical and conceptual studies that populate ALL of the journals in economics – not just the 4–5 anointed ones that carry the revelations of the High Church fathers (and a very few High Church mothers)? While I am not opposed to drawing selectively on those who wrote several hundred years ago, I worry about accounts that suggest they have said it all before, and urge that we can get to the future by going (almost) exclusively through our past.

Despite these reservations, let me be clear that Hodgson is a scholar of unrivaled creativity, commitment, and energy. He has done more than practically anyone to keep evolutionary and institutional economics alive in Europe, and to a certain extent in North America. His output is prodigious. He is a *dramatis personae principe* in his own right. The many favorable comments about the book (appearing both inside and on the cover) attest to Hodgson's intellect, his dedication, and his wide and impressive following. I agree with much of what the others have already said. And yet I wish for a short and compelling account from Geoff that will tell us – in say 20 pages or less – exactly what we need to do to reinvigorate institutional economics. I may not agree with it, but at least I would be clear about his vision for the future.

REFERENCES

Bromley, D. W. (1989). *Economic interests and institutions: The conceptual foundations of public policy*. Oxford: Blackwell.
Comons, J. R. (1968). *Legal foundations of capitalism*. Madison, WI: University of Wisconsin Press.
Hodgson, G. M. (2004). *The evolution of institutional economics*. London: Routledge.
Hulswit, M. (2002). *From cause to causation: A Peircean perspective*. Dordrecht: Kluwer.

EVOLUTION RECONSIDERED: *THE EVOLUTION OF INSTITUTIONAL ECONOMICS* BY GEOFFREY HODGSON

William Waller

A review essay on Geoffrey M. Hodgson, *The Evolution of Institutional Economics: Agency, Structure, and Darwinism in American Institutionalism*. New York: Routledge, 2004.

Geoffrey Hodgson's book is a crucial contribution to the future of both evolutionary and institutional economics. Hodgson demonstrates conclusively that institutional economics has not always remained evolutionary and has declined, at least partially, as a consequence. But the real contribution of the book is the recapturing of the evolutionary philosophy underlying Veblen's evolutionary economics and updating it for the purpose of reinvigorating institutional economics.

Hodgson presents a complex argument built on a foundation of extraordinary scholarship and careful exegesis. He builds his case for reconsidering evolutionary

157

theorizing in institutional economics so carefully and thoroughly that any summary of the argument must necessarily be extensive.

He begins with an exploration of the relationship between agency and structure in social theorizing. Here he begins his case for a layered ontology that rejects both methodological individualism and methodological collectivism as sufficient modes of causal explanation. Next he argues that causal explanations based on either biological reductionism or complete evasions of biology are both flawed – again supporting layered ontology. Layered ontology is crucial to the "Principle of Determinacy" which states that every event has a cause which Hodgson argues is central to Darwinism.

The second section of the book is a detailed exposition of Darwinian evolutionary theory. This section begins with a rejection of the coherence of "Social Darwinism" as a meaningful label for the inchoate misuses of Darwin's theory in social theorizing. Then Hodgson proceeds with his discussion of Darwinian evolutionary theory.

The first crucial element of Darwinism was embodied in Darwin's commitment to causal explanation. Darwin was committed to the notion that very complex biological developments could be explained in terms of successive step-by-step alterations. Hodgson writes that the philosophical position that emerged from Darwinism's central tenet was: ". . . every event is determined in accordance with laws by something else, and in turn the outcome becomes a beginning for the next link in the causal chain. Furthermore, these laws of change are matters for scientific investigation" (p. 90).

Next the Darwinian concept of variation is presented. The mechanism for change is the environmental selection of elements that are a function of the ubiquity of variation. Variation in Darwin is an ontological concept where ". . . the understanding of the essence of something involve[s] its placement in a population of similar but not identical entities" (p. 91). Hodgson continues: "For Darwin, the essence of any type included its potential to exhibit or create variation. Accordingly, an understanding of an item must also consider the *population* of similar entities in which that variation is present or possible" (p. 91).

From this foundation Hodgson notes that the Darwinian position that consciousness and intention – the foundation of agency and individual action – are themselves the outcome of evolutionary processes. Thus under the principle of determinacy these aspects of human behavior are to be explained causally like all other behavior, not merely assumed. Hodgson describes this as a minimal core strategy necessary for the philosophical foundations of institutional economics (p. 92).

Hodgson then presents "the seven philosophical pillars of Darwinism" (p. 95) which are the basis of his exploration and critique of institutional economics.

He begins: "Darwinism is associated with the ideas of variation, inheritance and selection. Moreover, underlying this theory of evolution are seven philosophical principles that are even more fundamental to Darwinism" (p. 95).

The Seven Principles are:

(1) The Principle of Determinacy.
(2) Emergent Materialism.
(3) Population Thinking.
(4) The Doctrine of Continuity.
(5) Cumulative Causal Explanation.
(6) The Principle of Evolutionary Explanation.
(7) The Principle of Consistency of the Sciences.

After introducing these principles Hodgson then explores early attempts to explicate concepts of emergence and multi-level evolution. Of particular interests are his discussions of the contributions of George Henry Lewes to the concept of emergence and David George Ritchie to multi-level evolution.

The next section of the book deals with Veblen's evolutionary theory. This section contains, in my opinion, the most complete exegesis on Veblen's evolutionary theorizing to date. The research is exhaustive, complete, and carefully crafted into a compelling argument that all institutional economists and all scholars interested in evolutionary social science must consider. In this section Hodgson establishes that Veblen rejected biological reductionism. He shows that Veblen believed that biology and social phenomena were both components of human behavior. Thus Veblen embraced a multi-level theory of evolution but did so without an explicit or well-developed concept of emergent properties (p. 139).

Additionally Hodgson shows that Veblen thought evolutionary principles operated on the evolution of customs and institutions (p. 141). He quotes Veblen's passage to that effect in *The Theory of the Leisure Class* (Veblen, 1899, p. 188) and concludes ". . . Veblen became the second writer after the *Origin of the Species* to apply with some rigour Darwin's principle of selection to the evolution of customs and institutions." Hodgson continues: "The decisive implication was that Darwinism could be applied to human society without necessarily reducing explanations of social phenomena entirely to individual psychology or biology. Once we consider the natural selection of institutions, and in turn treat institutions as emergent properties in the social realm, then that road is opened. Regrettably, however, Veblen did not go far enough down this route" (pp. 141, 142).

In Chap. 7 Hodgson explores the Darwinian mind of Veblen. In this context he looks at several important contemporaneous issues and topics within social theory and how Veblen's thought relates to each of these issues and topics.

First, he establishes Veblen's rejection of positivism. Hodgson notes that Veblen "appropriately identified the 'preconception of causation' as necessary for 'the actual work of scientific enquiry.' Veblen (1908, p. 398) elaborated: Causal sequence . . . is of course a matter of metaphysical imputation. It is not a fact of observation, and cannot be asserted of the facts of observation except as a trait imputed to them. It is so imputed, by scientists and others, as a matter of logical necessity, as a basis of systematic knowledge of the facts of observation" (p. 148).

Hodgson then explores Veblen's views on Darwinism and Lamarckism. Hodgson shows that Veblen preferred Darwin's approach because of his "more adequate causal explanations of process." He also notes that Veblen did not take a position on the possibility of the inheritance of acquired characteristics (p. 149). Hodgson elaborates that Veblen's adoption of Darwin's concept of causation necessarily included the concept of cumulative causation and the rejection of teleological reasoning (p. 150).

Following this analysis comes what are possibly the most important observations regarding Veblen's philosophy and the relationship between agency and social structure. First, he takes up Veblen's views on the relationship between mind, matter, and human intentionality. Human intentionality for Veblen, as with Darwin, was itself an outcome of evolutionary processes, therefore was subject to causal explanation. However, the absence of a conceptualization of emergence left this position underdeveloped (p. 157). Second, Hodgson takes up Veblen's principle of evolutionary explanation. He describes it thus: "because the human agent was a subject of an evolutionary process, he or she could not be taken as fixed or given. A causal account of the interaction between the individual and social structure had to be provided. This causal account should not stop with the individual, but it should also attempt to explain the origin of psychological purposes and preferences" (p. 157). Third, Hodgson demonstrates that Veblen believed that individual behavior was constituted from a combination of biological instinct, habits, and reason. Moreover, biological instincts and habits are primary causes, necessary components for the capacity to reason to emerge. Hodgson notes: "Humans do act for reasons – but reasons and beliefs themselves are caused, and have to be explained. It is proposed here that reasoning itself is based on habits and instincts, and it cannot be sustained with out them. Furthermore, consistent with the evolutionary doctrine of continuity, instincts and the capacities to form habits, developed through a process of natural selection that extends way back into our pre-human past" (p. 175).

Hodgson then proceeds with his presentation of Veblen's evolutionary institutionalism, summarized in his discussion of the following six propositions Veblenian institutionalism shares with other modern social theory including critical realism:

(1) The dependence of social structures upon individuals.
(2) The rejection of methodological individualism.
(3) The dependence of individuals upon social structure.
(4) The rejection of methodological collectivism (p. 179).
(5) The temporal priority of society over any one individual (p. 181).
(6) Reconstitutive downward causation (p. 188).

Within the framework of his exegesis of Veblen's evolutionary philosophy Hodgson sketches Veblen's extension of Darwinian evolutionary theory to the evolution of institutions. He does this by focusing on the mechanisms of variation, inheritance and selection (p. 188). This section clarified for me a misunderstanding of Hodgson's earlier writings. Hodgson is critically examining how Veblen's theory acknowledges and accounts for these three components of Darwinian evolutionary theory. He is not constructing analogues from Darwin's biological evolutionary arguments to Veblen's social evolutionary arguments. Thus difference between earlier versions of Hodgson argument and the position take by Jennings and Waller (1998) was based at least on my misunderstanding of Hodgson's purpose.[1]

Hodgson shows that: "The difference between natural and social evolution was in the units of selection and in the details of the evolutionary processes, not in the exclusion of variation, inheritance or selection from the social sphere" (p. 191). Beyond this, Veblen's theory remained underdeveloped. From here Hodgson goes on to discuss Veblen's interest in the instinct of workmanship and pecuniary culture. Hodgson suggests replacing the instinct of workmanship with "an institutionalized propensity to provision for human needs" which is itself an outcome of evolutionary processes. He sees this as broadly consistent with the instrumental value principle of later institutionalists (p. 201).

Hodgson goes on to critique Veblen's distinction between pecuniary and industrial motivations as overstated. He also critiques Veblen's notion that exposure to the machine process and matter-of-fact knowledge leads to changes in human motivation and understanding as vague and over-reaching.

Chapter 11 discusses the missed connection between Veblen's social theory and concepts of layered ontology, emergent properties, and the significance of both for a theory of social evolution. He concludes this chapter with a list of "The elements of Veblenian institutionalism on emergentist foundations" which includes ". . . the following six negative positions:

(1) A rejection of positivism and empiricism.
(2) A rejection of regularity determinism.
(3) A rejection of biological reductionism as unviable.
(4) A rejection of methodological individualism as unviable.
(5) A rejection of methodological collectivism as unviable.

(6) A rejection of evolution as a teleological or necessarily optimizing process.
(7) Veblen's institutionalism also adopted the following doctrines or principles.
(8) The principle of universal causation or determinacy.
(9) The Darwinian doctrine of causality.
(10) The Darwinian principle of cumulative causal explanation.
(11) The extension of Darwinian principles to socio-economic evolution.
(12) The principle of evolutionary explanation.
(13) The principle of consistency of the sciences.
(14) The temporal and ontological primacy of instincts and habits over reason.
(15) The dependence of social structures upon individuals.
(16) The dependence of individuals upon social structures.
(17) The temporal priority of society over any one individual.
(18) The possibility of reconstitutive downward causation.
(19) Institutions as units of evolutionary selection.
(20) Institutions as repositories of social knowledge.

The following important and connected elements were unclear, underdeveloped or absent in Veblen's works . . ..

(1) Population thinking, as a Darwinian ontological commitment.
(2) An irreducible and layered ontology, including physical, vital, mental and social levels.
(3) Emergent properties, associated with complexity of structure and causal interactions between dissimilar components.
(4) Emergent properties as a source of novelty in evolution.
(5) Consciousness and intentionality as irreducible emergent properties of the nervous system, its components and their interactions.
(6) Human social interaction as involving extensive intersubjective interpretations of intention and meaning, leading to particular emergent properties of human society.
(7) The possibility of spontaneous order or emergent self-organization in social and other systems.
(8) The existence of important emergent properties at the level of social and macroeconomic structures" (pp. 246, 247).

In Chap. 12 Hodgson discusses the launching of the institutional economics movement or school of thought in the early twentieth century. The focus of the institutionalist movement on the problem of social control is highlighted. Moreover, the loss of Veblen's connection to biology, the rejection of instinct in his psychology, the flirtation with behaviorism, and the reinterpretation of evolution as merely the recognition of the pervasiveness of change all came together to undermine the philosophical foundations of institutionalism, thereby weakening the intellectual foundations of the school just as its focus on policy relevance and cultural analysis brought it to the forefront of the American economics profession. Only for institutionalism to soon be eclipsed by the neoclassical-Keynesian synthesis.

In part four of the book Hodgson discusses the work of later institutional economists including John R. Commons, Wesley Clair Mitchell, Frank Knight and Clarence E. Ayres. Additionally he discusses the Ayresian dichotomy in detail and the decline in institutionalism after World War II. In each of these chapters these other institutionalists' main ideas and contributions are sketched. The point of these chapters, while acknowledging and celebrating the contributions of these important institutional economists, is not a thorough explication of their positive contributions. It is, rather, to show how far they have moved from Veblen's evolutionary framework of analysis. In this regard the book does not really discuss the evolution of institutional economics as much as it carefully explores the evolution of evolution in the evolution of evolutionary economics – but that would be an awful book title. This is the one section that would not suffice if this book were used as a text in a course on institutional economics. But it would be a reasonable introduction to the contributions of these other institutionalists, to be supplemented with some of their own work.

Though Hodgson is critical of the abandonment of Veblen's evolutionary philosophy by later institutionalists, he is mindful of the reasons for it. Indeed, the reasons are some of the very principles of Veblen's own philosophical position. Most especially the role of the principle of consistency of the sciences is responsible for some of the missteps. Institutional economists were not the first to call into question the use of biology in the social sciences, they did not originate positivism and extreme empiricism, nor were they the first to call instinct psychology into question, nor were they the first to adopt some form or another of behaviorism. All of these changes in the intellectual environment were considered advances to be incorporated into scientific work. Indeed, this points to an impediment that will remain even in a reconstructed evolutionary institutional economics. Consistency among the sciences and social theory will be difficult to achieve when the theories of underlying ontological levels are in flux.

Hodgson's discussion of a potential revival of Veblenian institutionalism begins with a discussion of changes in the intellectual landscape that favor a reconstruction. He notes that behaviorism is in decline and that evolutionary psychologists and biologists have a renewed interest in the exploration of instincts. He notes the decline of positivism and the revival of pragmatism. And he notes interest in complexity and the re-emergence of emergence in philosophy. He also notes the poor condition of the neoclassical microfoundations project and other

reconsiderations of mainstream neoclassical economic theorizing. While all of
these observations of changes in the intellectual environment are correct, it is also
the case that these changes are recent and provide little in terms of substantive
support to the theoretical core of such an institutionalism. For example, while
other scientists have begun working out the character of human instincts, there is
not at this point any consensus on what the instincts might be, how they manifest
themselves, or their evolutionary origins. Similarly, while revival of pragmatism
and re-emergence of emergence in philosophy are important, these positive trends
have certainly not filtered down to the day-to-day work of scientific practitioners
or most social theorists. Moreover, the poor state of the neoclassical economics
project would be a surprise to most neoclassical economic practitioners since they
have been taught to assiduously avoid considering such philosophical discussions.
Alas, methodology and philosophy are a specialist, if not an elite, discourse in
economics.

Hodgson's Chap. 20 "On individuals and institutions" provides a very positive
discussion on how an evolutionary economics should proceed. He incorporates
some contemporary work of the new institutionalists and shows how the
incorporation of an evolutionary economics can build on elements of these new
discussions emerging from mainstream theory. He includes a nice demonstration
of modeling habit and the evolution of institutionalized behavior.

As stated at the beginning of this essay Hodgson presents a compelling
case for original institutional economists to reconsider the current status of
their evolutionary theorizing. Moreover he identifies how to reinvigorate both
the evolutionary character of institutional economics and the institutional
research program generally. Moreover, his presentation also shows the "new
institutionalists" how their work fits into a genuinely evolutionary institutional
economics.

The book's audience is clearly the above-mentioned group of economists,
namely original and "new" institutionalists with both categories being broadly
and eclectically construed. The nature of Hodgson's argument is such that all
parties discussed are evaluated in terms of both their positive contributions and
their errors and omissions. Throughout the book when critiquing Veblen, and for
that matter anyone else, Hodgson is extremely careful and generous in noting the
original authors' own caveats, uncertainties, and reservations concerning their own
ideas.

Ironically, in a footnote Hodgson professes not to understand what is radical
about radical institutionalism (p. 396, n. 12). In William Dugger's (1989) edited
volume of that title Dugger describes the use of the term "radical" in two senses.
The first is radical in the sense of going to the root. The second sense is in terms of
exploring the progressive policy implications of institutional economics – which

Hodgson recognizes in radical institutionalism. The irony is that in returning to the Darwinian evolutionary roots of Veblen's philosophy Hodgson himself has pushed the "radical" element of the radical institutionalists' agenda in the first sense forward more than any single author to date.

NOTE

1. Hodgson has made repeated attempts to explain these differences to me; alas I required the full exposition of the current volume to understand him.

REFERENCES

Dugger, W. (1989). *Radical institutionalism: Contemporary voices*. Westport, CT: Greenwood Press.

Jennings, A., & Waller, W. (1998, Summer). The place of biological science in Veblen's economics. *History of Political Economy, 30*(2), 189–217.

Hodgson, G. (2004). *The evolution of institutional economics: Agency, structure, and Darwinism in American institutionalism*. New York: Routledge.

Veblen, T. (1899). *The theory of the leisure class: An economic study in the evolution of institutions*. New York: Macmillan.

Hunt's CRITICAL HISTORY OF ECONOMIC THOUGHT

J. E. King

A review essay on E. K. Hunt, *History of Economic Thought: A Critical Perspective*, updated second edition. Armonk, NY and London: M. E. Sharpe, 2002. xxii+543 pp. ISBN 0-7656-0606-2 (hard cover); 0-7656-0607-0 (paper).

As Kay Hunt writes in the preface, "This book . . . is very different from any other history of thought now in print" (p. xvii). It is written from an explicitly Marxian viewpoint and is consistently – and vehemently – anti-utilitarian. Hunt begins with a definition of capitalism (pp. 3–8) and ends with "comments on the social perspective underlying the present book" (pp. 514–520), in which he denounces utilitarian psychology and ethics as a conservative ideology for capitalism. No social theory, he argues, can possibly be value-free. His own ethical position is derived from Veblen, Marx and Maslow. There exists a hierarchy of human needs, and they are rarely satisfied under capitalism, which encourages us to treat other people as means, not ends, and thereby promotes alienation and social fragmentation. "I believe," Hunt concludes, "with Veblen and Marx, that capitalism is not the highest stage of human development and that if human beings ever assert their collective humanity against the irrationality of capitalism, they will open a vista of passionate possibilities hardly dreamed of during the reign of capitalism" (p. 520).

In between, he surveys the history of economic thought from Mercantilism to the present day: "I have selected ideas that I believe were important in their time and continue to have importance today" (p. xix). He emphasizes two central issues: whether capitalism is harmonious or conflict-ridden, and whether it is

A Research Annual
Research in the History of Economic Thought and Methodology, Volume 23-A, 167–171
Copyright © 2005 by Elsevier Ltd.
All rights of reproduction in any form reserved
ISSN: 0743-4154/doi:10.1016/S0743-4154(05)23006-7

stable or unstable. Since he recognizes "that social theories and social-historical processes are reciprocally interconnected" (p. xvii), Hunt is very careful to place the economic ideas that he discusses firmly in their historical context. Thus Chapter 1 is devoted to the history (and pre-history) of early capitalism, and throughout the book there are lengthy and generally very helpful accounts of the economic, political and social environment from which economic thought emerged. Chapter 2 deals, much too briefly, with economics before Adam Smith, while the next three chapters focus on Smith, Malthus and Ricardo. This is standard fare. Chapters 6 and 7, however, are unusual; the first presents the economics of Bentham, Say and Senior as leading exponents of "rationalistic subjectivism," and the second promotes William Thompson and Thomas Hodgskin as authors of "the political economy of the poor." In Chapter 8, the "pure" utilitarian Frédéric Bastiat is compared with the "eclectic" utilitarian John Stuart Mill, and Chapter 9 offers an unusually clear summary of Karl Marx's political economy. This is followed by two chapters on the birth of neoclassical economics, concentrating first on Jevons, Menger and Walras (Chapter 10) and then on Marshall, Clark and Böhm-Bawerk (Chapter 11). Hunt returns to heterodox economists in Chapter 12, which is on Veblen, and Chapter 13, with a sympathetic discussion of the writings of Hobson, Luxemburg and Lenin on imperialism. Chronology gives way to criticism in Chapter 14, which bears the title "Consummation, consecration, and destruction of the invisible hand: neoclassical welfare economics." Keynes and Sraffa are the subjects of Chapters 15 and 16, and the final three chapters deal with "contemporary economics," in its mainstream, Post Keynesian and institutionalist, and Marxian versions, respectively.

There are some very real strengths in Hunt's approach to the history of economic thought. First and foremost, he writes exceptionally clearly both on writers with who he feels great empathy and on those he believes to be fundamentally mistaken. I cannot recall having read a better summary of Marx's economics than that found in Chapter 9; it is quite devoid of any Hegelian flourishes, and none the worse for that. The twenty pages dedicated to Walras are equally lucid, and surprisingly favourable:

> Walras's theoretical framework for his general equilibrium model was and still remains significant. If we drop his highly unrealistic faith in the automaticity of the market, his system of market interrelationships shows just how difficult it would be for a capitalist market system ever to achieve a full-employment general equilibrium. The theory can also show how, once a crisis starts, it spreads to all sectors of the economy and becomes a general crisis or depression. Walras's general-equilibrium framework is the best theoretical context within which to analyze the anarchy of the market. Many underconsumption theorists would have avoided innumerable logical and theoretical inadequacies had they formulated their theories within some framework akin to Walras's general-equilibrium theory. Therefore, Walras's theory of general equilibrium must be judged one of the most significant theoretical achievements in the history of economic

ideas. The theory can be easily extricated both from Walras's naïve faith in the automaticity of the market and from his conservative, utilitarian ideology with which he justified competitive, laissez-faire capitalism (pp. 278–279).

This passage is quite typical of the book, which is throughout a pleasure to read.

Second, and especially in the earlier chapters, Hunt allows his protagonists to speak for themselves. Rather than attempting to deal with every economist of any significance, he selects a small number of prominent writers and quotes extensively from their work. This serves as a complement to rational reconstruction, not as a substitute for it. In Chapter 5, for example, lengthy extracts from Ricardo's *Principles* are interspersed with diagrams illustrating his theories of rent, distribution and the determination of relative prices with different compositions of capital, along with numerical examples explaining Ricardian price theory and the principle of comparative advantage. The chapter concludes, like several others, with a critical assessment of its subject's views on social harmony and class conflict. The reader will take away from these thirty pages a very clear impression of Ricardo's ideas and their difficulties, together with some respect for his literary abilities.

Third, there is a very welcome balance in Hunt's treatment of mainstream and non-mainstream thought. As already noted, he gives roughly equal space to neoclassical economists and to their critics. In dealing with the latter, he is by no means a one-eyed Marxist. After pointing to the problems with Veblen's analysis of wages, profits and capitalist crisis, Hunt concludes that

There were, however, areas in which Veblen's analysis was decidedly superior to Marx's . . . Veblen's analysis of the power of patriotic fervor and emulative consumption, which conditioned workers to accept these self-defeating attitudes, was extraordinarily perceptive and insightful. It remains to this day one of the most powerful and accurate explanations of why workers not only endure exploitation and alienation, but very frequently support the very institutions, laws, governments, and general social mores that create and perpetuate this exploitation and degradation (pp. 343–344).

Similarly, in the two concluding chapters on contemporary critics of economic orthodoxy, Hunt pays more attention to Clarence E. Ayres (pp. 478–484) than to Paul Baran and Paul Sweezy (pp. 520–524), and he devotes as many pages to Sraffian price theory (pp. 489–495) as to the revival and development of the labour theory of value (pp. 498–504). His is an open, tolerant and eclectic view of the history of heterodox economic thought.

There are also, inevitably, some weaknesses. First, the early focus on "great men" leads to some unfortunate omissions. Sismondi and Bray might well have been included in the chapter on pre-Marxian socialism, for example, and Rudolf Hilferding should certainly have made an appearance in the discussion of imperialism. There is no reference in Chapter 6 to James Mill, who is often credited – if that is the right word – with originating Say's Law. And I was particularly disappointed to see so little mention of Joan Robinson, and only the barest of references to Michal Kalecki. Other readers will have their own lists of complaints about overlooked heroes.

For a writer with an avowedly political focus and strong political motivation, Hunt is not as careful as he might have been in his political judgements. Crucial definitions come very late in the day:

> From the late nineteenth century to the present, there has been a split in the neoclassical intellectual tradition between a liberal wing and a conservative wing. These terms are sometimes confusing because the nineteenth century doctrine of laissez faire was then known as 'liberalism' whereas today the more extreme advocates of laissez faire are now called conservative and the neoclassical economists who temper their analysis and advocate government intervention to correct 'market imperfections' or 'market failures' are now called liberals (p. 457).

I am not sure that this is still true, even in the United States (where "liberal" seems these days to be used mainly as a term of abuse), and it will not prove very helpful to overseas readers. Eyebrows will undoubtedly be raised at Hunt's description of Keynes as "one of the most brilliant conservative economists of this [sic] century" (p. 404), and of Nikolai Bukharin as a "conservative Communist" (p. 447). Disappointingly, Hunt offers no discussion of neoliberalism (or neoconservatism).

There is a third and much more serious problem, which concerns his treatment of twentieth-century economic thought, above all its neoclassical wing. There is simply not enough of it. The critique of orthodox welfare economics in Chapter 14 is vigorous and convincing, but it is not written as history of economic thought. Hunt admits as much: "in this chapter we will rarely refer to the writings of any significant economic theorist. This is because neoclassical welfare economics is essentially an elaboration, with relatively minor modifications, of the analysis of Walras, and no particular theorist added so significantly to Walras's version of this theory as to merit individual treatment" (p. 375).

This "principle of insignificant elaboration" seems to have guided Hunt's discussion of post-Walrasian economic theory more generally. Chapter 17, entitled "Contemporary economics I: the bifurcation of orthodoxy," is one of the least satisfactory in the entire book. It begins rather incongruously with an outline of the Bolshevik revolution, Soviet industrialization and the Great Depression. It then moves on to a brief assessment of the ideas of W. Arthur Lewis and a rather more substantial analysis of Paul Samuelson, concluding with a critical account of the Austrian and Chicago schools, which Hunt regards as being very similar. Precisely what the "bifurcation" is remains unclear, and the gaps are all too apparent. There is nothing on imperfect competition, on the formalist revolution in economic theory after 1945, on Arrow-Debreu, on game theory, on New Classical macroeconomics, on the relentless search for "microfoundations," on the rise and rise of econometrics – on most of the developments, that is to say, that characterized neoclassical economics in the second half of the last century. Nor is Hunt's treatment of heterodox economics after Lenin very much better. Sraffa gets his due, or perhaps rather more than his due, but institutionalists will be surprised at the omission of Galbraith and Hodgson, while Post Keynesians will barely recognize their thriving school in the brief and somewhat distorted sketch on pp. 484–489. Unaccountably, Hunt relegates Paul Davidson and Hyman Minsky to a single, five-line bibliographical footnote (on p. 495, where he also manages to spell Jan Kregel's name wrongly, twice, and in two different ways).

The problems with these concluding chapters highlight one final weakness. In what is claimed to be an "updated second edition," there is not much evidence of any systematic updating. Compared with the first (1979) edition, only Chapter 18 on Post Keynesian and institutional economics is new, and this is one of the weakest. Relatively little seems to have been changed elsewhere, though the separate chapter devoted to the labour theory of value has disappeared. The (rather sparse) footnote references at the end of each chapter rarely cite sources later than 1978, and the (equally limited) suggestions for further reading at the end of the book culminate in a number of Edward Elgar collections published in 1988–1990. An opportunity has been missed here.

On balance, while the strengths of *History of Economic Thought* do outweigh the weaknesses, it is really two books. One is a genuinely first-class text covering the period 1776 to 1916, and the other is a very patchy and uneven sequel.

Hoover's CAUSALITY IN MACROECONOMICS[☆]

Julian Reiss

A review essay on Kevin Hoover, *Causality in Macroeconomics*, Cambridge: Cambridge University Press, 2001.

INTRODUCTION

In the 19th century, John Stuart Mill argued that economics could not be an inductive science because it lacks that which is the essence of inductive science, *viz.* the experiment. Since there is no experiment, economic claims cannot be established inductively but must instead be justified deductively on the basis of antecedently accepted theoretical claims about human behaviour.

By and large, economic method and methodology have followed Mill's reasoning up to this day. A large number of economic claims are established on the basis of models, which themselves are constructed from the building blocks of *a priori* economic principles, such as the principles of human rationality. This is, of course, not to say that empirical work has no place in economics. But the role it plays is one of testing the deductive implications of economic theory against data. Unlike inductive sciences, the scientific procedure in economics *ends* with an empirical investigation; it never *originates* in it. Let us call Mill's stance the "received view" of economic method.

Work on this paper was conducted under the AHRB project *Causality: Metaphysics and Methods*. I am very grateful to the Arts and Humanities Research Board for funding.

A Research Annual
Research in the History of Economic Thought and Methodology, Volume 23-A, 173–182
© 2005 Published by Elsevier Ltd.
ISSN: 0743-4154/doi:10.1016/S0743-4154(05)23007-9

The received view has been challenged if not explicitly, certainly implicitly, by a number of developments in economic method over the past few years. One of these new currents is the advancement of methods of causal inference in the special sciences and, in particular, in economics. Methods such as the Bayes'-nets approach of Peter Spirtes, Clark Glymour and Richard Scheines (Spirtes et al., 2001) and Judea Pearl and his associates (Pearl, 2000), and invariance accounts such as David Hendry's (Hendry, forthcoming) or James Heckman's counterfactual approach to causal inference (Heckman, 2000, 2001) challenge the received view because they make claims about causal relations in economics that are relatively theory free and certainly free of *a priori* assumptions about human behaviour. This essays looks at one contribution to this literature in more detail, that is, Kevin Hoover's *Causality in Macroeconomics*. Before engaging with Hoover's study, I will provide some background by reviewing Mill's argument against causal inference in political economy.

MILL ON CAUSAL INFERENCE IN THE MORAL SCIENCES

Mill thought that causal inference in political economy, and in the moral sciences in general, is an impossibility because of the lack of experiment (Mill, 1994 [1836], p. 58):

> There is a property common to almost all the moral sciences, and by which they are distinguished from many of the physical; that is, that it is seldom in our power to make experiments in them [. . .].

> The consequence of this unavoidable defect in the materials of the induction is, that we can rarely obtain what Bacon has quaintly, but not unaptly, termed an *experimentum crucis* [. . .].

It is important to note that what Mill calls an "*experimentum crucis*" is neither Francis Bacon's "crucial instance" (despite Mill's insinuation) nor a "crucial experiment" as it has come to be known in the philosophy of science. Bacon's "crucial instance" refers to a situation (experimental or non-experimental) whose observation decides between two competing causal hypotheses (Bacon, 1620 [1994], book II, aphorism 36. See also Hacking's discussion (Hacking, 1983, ch. 15)). This decision could not, however, be decisive for Bacon. By contrast, the term "crucial experiment" of modern philosophy of science tends to be used to refer to a situation that gives conclusive evidence in favour or against a scientific hypothesis.[1]

In contrast to both of these, Mill refers to a pair of situations in which either his method of agreement or his method of difference is applicable. Recall that the method of agreement compares two situations which are different with respect to all factors except the putative cause C of some effect of interest E. If in both situations C is followed by E, then C is a cause of E. The method of difference compares two situations which are identical with respect to all factors except that in one C is absent while in the other C is present. If E is present when C is present and absent when C is absent, then C is a cause of E. Mill thinks that we will never find such pairs of situations in political economy (Mill, 1994 [1836], p. 59):

> How, for example, can we obtain a crucial experiment on the effect of a restrictive commercial policy upon national wealth? We must find two nations in every other respect, or at least possessed, in a degree exactly equal, of everything which conduces to national opulence, and adopting exactly the same policy in all their other affairs, but differing in this only, that one of them adopts a system of commercial restrictions, and the other adopts free trade. This would be a decisive experiment, similar to those which we can almost always obtain in experimental physics. Doubtless this would be the most conclusive evidence of all if we could get it. But let any one consider how infinitely numerous and various are the circumstances which either directly or indirectly do or may influence the amount of the national wealth, and then ask himself what are the probabilities that in the longest revolution of ages two nations will be found, which agree, and can be shown to agree, in all those circumstances except one?

It is in fact two circumstances that make the application of Mill's methods difficult or impossible in economics: the number and variety of causal factors responsible for a phenomenon and our inability to control factors.

On this basis, Mill argues in favour of what he calls the "method *a priori.*" Deductions are to be made from the known laws of human nature. The results of this process Mill calls "truths in the abstract" – they are truths only of situations free of "disturbing causes." Disturbing causes, in turn, are those causes that may have effects on the phenomenon of interest which are (originally) not accounted for by the method *a priori*. If we are lucky, however, the laws of the disturbing causes get to be known and thus can be brought under the theory – such as friction in physics (Mill, 1994 [1836], p. 60). In that case, the results of moral science have the same precision as those of any other science.

It must be noted that Mill's expression "method *a priori*" is slightly misleading. This is because the basic building blocks of political economy, the "laws of human nature" are not known *a priori* in a strict sense, i.e. prior to *all* experience. Rather, they are established independently of any particular inquiry at hand (an inquiry such as whether free trade contributes positively to national wealth) and by different methods. These methods are mainly introspection and casual observation. We know that humans tend to desire wealth and avoid labour by observing ourselves and others. *These truths*, then, are established inductively. It is only truths about market or aggregate phenomena that escape the inductive method.

Let us summarise the received view in the following theses:

(1) *Complexity and Inaccessibility.* Aggregate phenomena are brought about by a very large number of causal factors, which in general cannot be controlled by intentional human action (for ethical, economic, practical or other reasons).
(2) *Inapplicability of Methods of Causal Inference.* Because of (1), methods of causal inference cannot be applied to aggregate phenomena.
(3) *Method* A Priori. Because of (2), economics must resort to the method *a priori*, that is, it establishes claims deductively on the basis of antecedently accepted principles about human nature. These claims can then be tested against aggregate data.

HOOVER ON CAUSAL INFERENCE

Already the title of his book *Causality in Macroeconomics* suggests that Hoover intends to contest the received view. Hoover's aim is to present a distinct method of causal inference that pays respect to the particularities of macroeconomics. In this section I analyse his approach in order to pave the ground for an assessment of the question of what is left of the received view if Hoover succeeds.

To take a closer look at Hoover's approach to causal inference in macroeconomics, let us exploit the above three theses. Hoover's stance on the three claims will provide valuable information about the relation of his view to the received view. As will be apparent, Hoover generally accepts each claim with a qualification. That is, he accepts it as a general claim but points out that there are situations in which it does not apply, and which in turn can be very useful for causal inference.

Complexity

That market phenomena are complex is a topic discussed at greater length by Hoover. He believes that economics is characterised by what he calls the "Cournot problem": "There are too many individuals (firms and consumers) and too many goods to be handled by direct modelling" (Hoover, 2001, p. 110). But in Hoover's view, this is just a problem for the methodological individualist, not for the macroeconomist *per se*. This is due to the fact that macroeconomic aggregates supervene on microeconomic states of affairs and that they may bear locally stable causal relationships among them.

To see why this is so, recall that the relationship of supervenience (between a set of "micro" and a set of "macro" properties) is a many-to-one relationship. That is, the same micro state implies necessarily the same macro state but not the other way around. If this is so, it is entirely possible that two different countries share the same causal structure at the aggregate level while they differ greatly in the micro properties on which the aggregate level supervenes. Thus it may be the case that macroeconomic causal structures are comparatively simple (e.g. involving only a small number of variables and their relations) although the structures on which they supervene are very complex.

Inaccessibility

With respect to our ability to control economic phenomena, Hoover, too, agrees with Mill as far as the general problem is concerned but he points out that there are exceptions. It is our background knowledge that is responsible for the exceptions. Because we sometimes knowledge that a structural break (an "intervention" in Hoover's terminology) has occurred, we do not always need intentional control of the putative cause variable (Hoover, 2001, p. 143):

> Other sciences [than physical sciences], including economics, often cannot intervene so deliberately in the processes they wish to observe. There is, nevertheless, often institutional or historical information that suggests that interventions occurred of particular types at particular times. There would be very little doubt, for instance, that a statistical relationship among Federal Reserve policy instruments and the stock of money that was stable up to 6 October 1979 and changed to a new, but also stable, relationship after 6 October 1979 reflected a change in monetary policy . . . at that date. We would be convinced by such extra-statistical information as the minutes of the Federal Open Market Committee and the public announcements of the Federal Reserve Board, which signaled an intentional intervention in the money-supply process.

As a general rule, intervention is difficult in economics, in particular for the "experimenter" – the economist. However, background knowledge allows him or her to interpret certain events as interventions (and to test hypotheses to that effect by means of statistical tests). Because Hoover accepts the two parts of the first thesis of the received view only with qualifications, he need not accept thesis two, which follows from the first. And indeed, the majority of the book is concerned with the development of a method of causal inference, which does not shy away from the particularities of macroeconomics. Let us look at the method in more detail.

Causal Inference

Central to Hoover's approach to causal inference is the idea of "invariance under intervention." If, say, a relationship between two factors C and E remains stable after an intervention which changes aspects of the process that generates C, then the relationship is causal. Importantly, this invariance should be mirrored in the statistics that describe the processes C and E. Consider one of Hoover's examples. Does government spending (G) cause taxes (T) or vice versa? In case G causes T, if an intervention obtains that changes aspects of the distribution of G such as its mean, its variance or its higher moments, then the marginal distribution of T and the conditional distribution of G on T should co-vary but the conditional distribution T given G should remain stable (and the other way around for the case T causes G).

The intuition behind this test for causality is fairly straightforward. Imagine a correlation were merely accidental such as the famous correlation between Venetian sea levels and British bread prices (for a discussion, see Sober, 2001; Hoover, 2003). In this case, one would not expect the process generating sea levels to be disturbed by an intervention that inflates bread prices, say. On the other hand, facing a genuinely causal connection such as that between smoking and lung cancer (say), breaking the cause process by, for example, increasing its mean should affect the effect process likewise. However, when the cause variable is held fixed, nothing should be expected to happen.[2] The test also appears to be able to distinguish causes from correlative effects. A ban on smoking is expected to reduce lung cancer occurrences. A ban on yellow teeth isn't.

But we must add a number of cautions. First, "invariance under intervention" is not, strictly speaking, necessary for causality. Although intuitions about this issue will differ, it is conceivable that there are relations that are genuinely causal but very fragile – they change or disappear under interventions. Hoover's test is a test for a specific kind of causal relations, *viz.*, *autonomous* relations. As one knows from the history of econometrics, this kind of relation is of immense importance for economics (and economic policy in particular) but it may not be the only kind of genuinely causal relation.

Second, "invariance under intervention" may not be sufficient for causality either. This is in part due to the particular sense in which Hoover understands the term. Consider his outline of the general research strategy for causal inference (applied to his example regarding taxes and spending) (Hoover, 2001, p. 194):

> First, if it is possible to determine from historical and institutional knowledge periods in which there are no important interventions in either the tax or the spending processes, regression equations corresponding to each of the conditional and marginal distributions...can be estimated and should show stable coefficients. Second, if we can then identify periods in which there are interventions clearly associated with the spending process and periods in which there are interventions clearly associated with the tax process, we can check the patterns of relative stability of the alternative partitions, and, thereby, determine which causal ordering (if any) is consistent with the data.

Reconsider the sea levels and bread prices. Let us assume that we have stable periods with satisfactory regression equations and also a period in which there is an intervention on bread prices. Let us also assume that the patterns of relative stability display the order "bread prices cause sea levels." What has gone wrong? A number of things may be responsible. There may be a cause of sea levels that – accidentally – acted just at the same time as our intervention. Or, our intervention and the sea levels may have a cause in common. This case may be particularly relevant for economic inquiries. Suppose that the government fixes spending in response to the observation of a cause of taxes other than spending such as "economic conditions." In this case the co-occurrence of breaks would not be informative of a causal relation between spending and taxes. Moreover, our intervention may cause the putative effect either directly or via a route different from the route via the putative cause. Unfortunately, Hoover's formal apparatus does not exclude any of these possibilities.

Further, certain interventions might break the causal laws responsible for both variables altogether. In this case, no pattern of relative stability will be particularly informative. Again, Hoover explicitly allows for interventions of this kind and hence a test based on such an intervention may yield a wrong result. (Hoover does take into account most of the above caveats in his practical applications of Chapters 9 and 10. Hence my criticism concerns the presentation and theoretical discussion of his method rather than the application.)

The gap in Hoover's presentation can, however, be fixed. I suggest the following adaptation of James Woodward's definition of an "intervention" as a definition of a "Hoover-intervention" (where *H-I* is the Hoover-intervention, *X* the purported cause, *Y* the purported effect and *Z* a cause of the intervention) (cf. Woodward, 1997, p. S30):

Definition Hoover-Intervention (on X with respect to Y)

(1) *H-I* changes a moment or moments of the distribution of *X* from what it would have been in the absence of the intervention and this change in *X* is entirely due to *H-I*.

(2) *H-I* changes the distribution of *Y*, if at all, only through changing the distribution of *X* and not directly or through some other route. That is, *H-I* does not directly change *Y*'s distribution and does not change the distribution of any causes of change of *Y*'s distribution that are distinct from *X* except, of course, for those causes of *Y*, if any, that are built into the $H\text{-}I \rightarrow X \rightarrow Y$ connection itself; that is, except for: (a) any causes of *Y* that are effects of *X* (i.e. variables that are causally between *X* and *Y*); and (b) any causes of *Y* that are between *H-I* and *X* and have no effect on *Y* independently of *X*. Moreover, a similar point holds for any cause *Z* of *H-I* itself – i.e. *Z* must change the

distribution of Y, if at all, only through affecting the distribution of X and not through some other route.

(3) H-I is not correlated with other causes of Y besides X (either via a common cause of I and Y or for some other reason) except for those falling under (2a) and (2b) above.

(4) H-I does not change the causal relationships between Y and its other causes besides X.

Further, I suggest to accept the following as a sufficient condition for a causal relationship.

If the conditional distribution of Y given X remains (approximately) unchanged when, as a result of a Hoover-intervention on X (with respect to Y) the marginal distribution of Y changes, then the relationship between X and Y is causal.

The reason not to take this as a *definition* of causality is that, in my view, there may be causal relationships that are non-autonomous or non-invariant under intervention. Alternatively, we may define a new concept of "Hoover-causality" and take the above clause as necessary and sufficient.

HOOVER'S APPROACH AND THE RECEIVED VIEW

As a consequence of the above discussion, we see that the big issue between Hoover and Mill (and his deductivist followers) turns on the point of whether or not there are interventions of the kind Hoover requires numerous enough to conduct causal inference with appreciable significance. This is surely an empirical question. We can neither deny that that there are interventions of the right kind on an *a priori* basis (which would be an implication of the received view) nor can we claim that they just wait there for us to be picked up in passing.

In favour of the received view, we must admit that the demands for knowledge Hoover's approach requires are indeed very high. Consider Table 1, which summarises the structural breaks in the U.S. government spending and taxes processes and associated them with a likely intervention:

If any of these interventions is to count as a Hoover-intervention, we need to know not only that it changed the distribution of the putative cause-variable (which is what Hoover mainly tests for) but also whether it does not change the distribution of the putative effect-variable either directly or via some other route, that it does not share causes with the putative effect and that it does not destroy the causal laws involved. Large-scale events such as hot or cold wars, are however notoriously difficult to assess in all their relations with other variables. Who is to bet on whether the expectation of a war does not cause both taxes and spending, which in

Table 1.   Summary of Structural Breaks.

Expenditures		Receipts	
Conditional	Marginal	Marginal	Interventions
		1951.1	Korean War tax bills
1953.1	1953.1		Effective end of Korean War
		1954.1	Korean War taxes removed
		1964.2	Tax cut
1965.1	1965		Vietnam War buildup
		1968	Tax surcharge
		1969.2	Surcharge removed, major tax act
		1981.2	Reagan tax cut
	1982.4		Reagan military buildup

Source: Hoover, 2001, Table 1, p. 240.

turn may lead to an arms race that only waits for a trigger to result in an actual war? Far be it from me to suggest that anything of this kind invalidates Hoover's results; but one must concede to the received view that it may be enormously difficult to identify Hoover-interventions.

In Hoover's favour, we should note that the complexity of the social world can also come to an advantage of the researcher due the wealth and variety of social data. If a tax and spending change due to a war is not a good intervention, there may be other interventions, e.g. due to a policy change that has occurred for reasons that are completely exogenous with respect to one of the two processes. If the U.S. history does not have any interventions of the right kind, it is still possible that histories of other countries do. Further, if the period envisaged is too eventful, the may be the case that some other period is calmer. It is important to see that only meticulous historical and institutional analysis can yield information of the kind required to identify a Hoover-intervention. There is no way *a priori* to determine whether they are typical, exceptional or infinitely rare.

Thus I want to conclude with an optimistic note. The combination of econometric technique and institutional and historical analysis characteristic of Kevin Hoover's approach to causal inference in macroeconomics has never been attempted as a research programme. It is well possible that it fails because the demands it makes regarding background knowledge are extraordinary indeed. But there is no reason to reject it from scratch because there are no plausible grounds for claiming there are no Hoover-interventions. And the potential gains for his method are high: well-founded inductive causal inference without the necessity of "economic theory." If he succeeds, he might well turn economic methodology on its head.

NOTES

1. See for example Lakatos's criticism that there exists no crucial experiment – in this sense (Lakatos, 1978, Ch. 10).

2. If an intervention suddenly reduces the mean of the smoking process (e.g. by a ban on advertisement or on smoking itself), we expect the marginal process of lung cancer to drop, too, but not the process of cancer given smoking. A ban on smoking is not expected to change the incidence of cancer of people that smoke 20 cigarettes a day.

REFERENCES

Bacon, F. (1994 [1620]). *Novum organum* (edited by P. Urbach & J. Gibson). Chicago and La Salle (Ill.): Open Court.

Hacking, I. (1983). *Representing and intervening*. Cambridge: Cambridge University Press.

Heckman, J. (2000). Causal parameters and policy analysis in economics: A twentieth century retrospective. *Quarterly Journal of Economics*, *115*(1), 45–97.

Heckman, J. (2001). *Econometrics counterfactuals and causal models*. Keynote address: International Statistical Institute, Seoul, South Korea.

Hendry, D. (forthcoming). *Causality in econometrics. Causality: Metaphysics and methods*. Technical Reports. CPNSS, LSE, London.

Hoover, K. (2003). Nonstationary time series, cointegration, and the principle of the common cause. *British Journal for the Philosophy of Science*, *54*(4), 527–551.

Lakatos, I. (1978). *Mathematics, science and epistemology: Philosophical Papers* (Vol. 2). Cambridge: Cambridge University Press.

Mill, J. S. (1994 [1836]). *Essays on some unsettled questions of political economy*. London: Parker. In: D. Hausman (Ed.), *The Philosophy of Economics* (1994). Cambridge: Cambridge University Press.

Pearl, J. (2000). *Causation: Models, reasoning and inference*. Cambridge: Cambridge University Press.

Sober, E. (2001). Venetian sea levels, british bread prices, and the principle of the common cause. *British Journal for the Philosophy of Science*, *52*(2), 331–346.

Spirtes, P., Glymour, C., & Scheines, R. (2001). *Causation, prediction and search*. Cambridge, MA: MIT Press.

Woodward, J. (1997). Explanation, invariance and intervention. *Philosophy of Science*, Supplement to *64*(4), S26–S41.

Maes's ECONOMIC THOUGHT AND THE MAKING OF EUROPEAN MONETARY UNION

Robert W. Dimand

A review essay on Ivo Maes, *Economic Thought and the Making of European Monetary Union: Selected Essays of Ivo Maes*, with forewords by Guy Quaden and A. W. Coats, Cheltenham, U.K., and Northampton, MA: Edward Elgar Publishing. ISBN 1 84064 800 7, hardcover, 2002.

European economic integration, leading to the Single Market and at the start of 1999 to the replacement of eleven national currencies by the euro, remains tumultuous, with France and Germany exempting themselves in November 2003 from the budget deficit limits of the Economic Growth and Stability Pact (the Maastricht Treaty), which had been binding on less politically powerful countries such as Portugal. Ivo Maes is ideally suited to provide insight and perspective on the economic thought underlying these developments. As Deputy Head of the Research Department of the National Bank of Belgium and formerly an administrator (that is, a generalist rather than a specialist economist) with the Commission of the European Communities, he is a central bank insider whose book carries a foreword by Guy Quaden, Governor of the National Bank of Belgium, and concludes with a long essay written with Jan Smets, Director of the Research Department of the National Bank of Belgium and Commissioner-General for the Euro, and Jan Michielsen, formerly Head of the Foreign and Financial Market Departments of the National Bank of Belgium. In Part 3, Maes, Smets, and Michielsen argue

A Research Annual
Research in the History of Economic Thought and Methodology, Volume 23-A, 183–186
Copyright © 2005 by Elsevier Ltd.
All rights of reproduction in any form reserved
ISSN: 0743-4154/doi:10.1016/S0743-4154(05)23008-0

that Belgium played a leading role in shaping the Economic and Monetary Union (EMU) and especially in promoting Franco-German agreement. At the same time, Maes can view the monetary authorities as an academic outsider, a professor at the University of Leuven and at the ICHEC business school in Brussels, a sometime visiting professor at Texas Lutheran College and Duke University, and a respected historian of economics. His Brussels vantage point, in a city and country particularly closely engaged in the evolution of the European Community but not in one of the major powers within the Community, also contributes to an enlightening perspective. There has been a torrent of books on the politics and economics of the euro (e.g. Padoa-Schioppa, 1994), as well as specialist periodicals such as the *Journal of Common Market Studies*, but Maes stands out by considering the process as an historian of economics.

Six of the seven essays in this volume have previously been published in English. The last and longest was published in full in Dutch, but only in an abridged version in English. The essays retain their separate bibliographies, and cross-reference the other essays as the original articles, rather than as chapters in the same book. The essays benefit from being reprinted together. Indeed, they may be considered as three long essays, two of which were first published in sections. The three essays in Part 1 comprise a narrative history of the evolving theory of economic integration. The first paper covers the pioneering debates about trade-creating and trade-diverting customs unions among Jacob Viner, James Meade, and Jan Tinbergen in the 1950s, and the second paper the relevance for European monetary integration of the debate over optimum currency areas among Robert Mundell, Ronald McKinnon, and Peter Kenen in the 1960s. The third essay examines the theoretical debates surrounding the unsuccessful efforts in the 1970s to create a European monetary union, starting with the Wenner Report of October 1970, which envisioned monetary union by 1980. The path to European monetary integration was complex, and it is very helpful to have Maes's annexes presenting the relevant chronology (pp. 44, 45, 79, 104, 126, 192, 193) and the intricate structure of the twenty-three Directorates-General of the Commission (p. 77) and of Directorate-General II – Economic and Financial Affairs (pp. 78, 86, 127). Readers, especially those outside Europe, will wish to bookmark the chronological annexes.

The three articles reprinted in Part 2 also fit together as a single, longer essay: an overview article on economic thought in the European Community institutions (especially D-G II), followed by an article on macroeconomic thought in the European Community institutions in the 1970s and an article on macroeconomic thought in those institutions in the first half of the 1980s. Part 2 will be of particular interest to historians of economics, as it examines developments that are much less widely known than the theorizing about customs unions and optimum currency areas.

The development of macroeconomics in D-G II is a story of negotiation and interaction among differing national interests and styles of thought, among competing intellectual schools, and between academic researchers and policy-oriented public servants. D-G II was headed by a succession of Italian directors-general and subject to a succession of French commissioners (except when the president of the Commission happened to be French), with the director for monetary affairs drawn from France, although Germany was the principal source of D-G II economists, followed by Belgium. Similarly, D-G IV (Competition), primarily staffed by lawyers rather than economists, had German directors-general, and D-G VI (Agriculture) had French directors-general. Economics at the Commission emphasizes policy, empirical studies, loyal team membership, and the primacy of higher-level political decisions rather than individual originality, with economists frustrated by the need to provide economic arguments to justify, to give a particularly glaring example, the Common Agricultural Policy, source of the butter mountain and wine lake of unsaleable surpluses. The worldwide trend towards internationalization or Americanization of the discipline of economics is reflected by the increasing use of English, especially since the United Kingdom joined the European Community, and of mathematics and quantification, accelerated while Tommaso Padoa-Schioppa, a student and coauthor of Franco Modigliani of MIT, was Director-General of D-G II from 1979 to 1983. Maes presents the results of a survey of D-G II economists, with replies from 74 of D-G II's 130 university-trained staff, showing that those younger than forty are more likely to have studied in North America (Maes, pp. 54, 55).

In terms of substance, economics in D-G II was shaped by the tension between the market-oriented German Ordo-liberalism, which was inspired by Ludwig Erhard, and French indicative planning (Maes, pp. 60, 116). The French Planning Office drew on an activist, interventionist tradition stretching back to Colbert and provided the Continental bridgehead for Keynesianism, taking up Edmond Malinvaud's distinction between classical unemployment (due to real wages being too high) and Keynesian unemployment (due to insufficient effective demand). Germany responded to the 1973 OPEC oil price increase as an inflationary shock, but France treated it as a recessionary shock, leading to a divergence of inflation rates that took France out of the European "snake" of exchange rates. The European states cooperated in a short-lived Concerted Action Plan of demand expansion in 1978, while the Keynesian Social Democrat Karl Schiller was German Finance Minister (Maes, pp. 101, 109), but the French demand expansion of 1981–1983, at the start of the Mitterand presidency, was a unilateral move that shook the European Monetary System and ended with a realignment of exchange rates. French indicative planners saw monetary integration as a means of reducing exchange rate fluctuations, preserving substantial national policy independence, while German Ordo-liberals saw monetary integration as the coping-stone for a broad program of liberalization of factor and trade flows and policy convergence (Maes, pp. 83, 137, 150). North American monetarism influenced German Ordo-liberalism through the Konstanz Seminars, which were founded by Karl Brunner in 1970 and regularly attended by H. Schlesinger of the Bundesbank, which adopted money supply targeting in December 1974 (Maes, pp. 94, 95).

Tommaso Padoa-Schioppa emerges from Maes's account as a crucial player, who raised the level of economic analysis in D-G II. Despite the scepticism of some commissioners and their cabinets, Padoa-Schioppa introduced individually-signed publication by D-G II researchers and, to obtain objective outside advice, funded the establishment by the Centre for European Policy Studies in Brussels of the CEPS Macroeconomic Policy Group, the so-called Dornbusch Group. The Dornbusch Group, consisting primarily of European economists such as Rudiger Dornbusch, Olivier Blanchard, and Willem Buiter, who had trained and taught at leading United States universities, made a "sophisticated Keynesian" case for reducing unemployment by expanding temporarily at a rate faster than the long-run sustainable growth rate, while D-G II placed more emphasis on classical unemployment (Maes, pp. 111, 117–120). While heading D-G II, Padoa-Schioppa became acquainted with Jacques Delors, then chair of the economic and monetary committee of the European Parliament. After Padoa-Schioppa had returned to the Research Department of the Bank of Italy and Delors had become President of the European Commission, Delors invited Padoa-Schioppa to chair a study group on the economic implications of the internal Single Market. Padoa-Schioppa (1987) concluded that, once capital movements within Europe were unrestricted, exchange rate stability would be inconsistent with autonomous national monetary policies, and persuaded Delors to call for monetary union in the Delors Report of April 1989 (Maes, pp. 63, 64, 68; Padoa-Schioppa, 1994). The Exchange Rate Mechanism (ERM) crumbled in September 1992, when George Soros gained fortune and fame betting against the Bank of England. Only a single currency would be safe from speculative attack. Maes has written a valuable and readable book, proving the value of having historians of economics write about contemporary macroeconomic policy debates. The essays gain from being republished together. The slight flavor in Part 3 of special pleading for the centrality of Belgium's role is a small price for these insights into the origins of the EMU and the development of modern European macroeconomic thought.

REFERENCES

Padoa-Schioppa, T. (1987). *Efficiency, stability, equity*. Oxford: Oxford University Press.
Padoa-Schioppa, T. (1994). *The road to monetary union in Europe*. Oxford: Clarendon Press.

Sakamoto and Tanaka's THE RISE OF POLITICAL ECONOMY IN THE SCOTTISH ENLIGHTENMENT

Willie Henderson

A Review essay on Tatsuya Sakamoto and Hideo Tanaka (Eds), *The Rise of Political Economy in the Scottish Enlightenment*, London: Routledge, 2003 pp. xii+215. ISBN 041529648X £60.00.

This volume is composed of thirteen short but concentrated essays and an introduction on the rise of political economy in the Scottish Enlightenment, each written by a distinguished Japanese scholar. Although the contributors are engaged in international scholarly activities, the volume devotes one chapter to "Adam Smith in Japan" and elsewhere draws attention to scholarly interpretations of Smith in the "West." Both suggest that the perspective, whilst linked directly to international scholarly discussion through modern works consulted and themes identified in earlier literature (the edited volume by Hont and Ignatieff (1983) being cited, amongst others, as historically significant for the development of the approach set out in the collection), carries insights that arise out of earlier but sustained Japanese interest in the notion of social and cultural modernization and reform. It is perhaps also in this context that they hit on the centrality of the issue of "manners," shorthand for morals, values, political behaviour, economic motivation and so on. Tatsuya Sakamoto makes this notion of "manners" explicit in his interesting chapter on Hume (p. 92) and Shoji Tanaka makes central the formation of free individuals liberated from feudalism and "religious delusions" (p. 134).

A Research Annual
Research in the History of Economic Thought and Methodology, Volume 23-A, 187–193
© 2005 Published by Elsevier Ltd.
ISSN: 0743-4154/doi:10.1016/S0743-4154(05)23009-2

The term "Scottish Enlightenment" is, of course, a product of historical analysis, and so a way of referring to a complex of people, discussions and projects, intellectual and practical, that were manifest in Scotland after the Union. It can be an unhelpful term, and some in Scotland and elsewhere, are willing to contest both it and the periodization and segmentation of history that the term inevitably carries with it. "When did it start?" "What was its focus?" "When did it finish?" Such are the questions that gather round an idea of an intellectual movement. So we get, conventionally, the (Scots-Irish) "father" of the Scottish Enlightenment, Francis Hutcheson, the "Golden Age" with Smith, and "the final stage" as represented by Dugald Stewart (Hisashi Shinohara, Chap. 12). Thoughts active in the world through intellectual effort are not as neatly organized, I hold, as such labels suggest. Locke, Newton and even Bacon, set a prior context for intellectual discussion in Glasgow, as did the continental analysis of "natural law," Mandeville's infamous poem on human motivation and manners, and other aspects of European thought. Echoes of the socio-cultural concerns of Adam Smith reverberate through the 19th century. Dugald Stewart influenced Walter Scott (who wrote novels around contrasting systems of "manners") and Carlyle. Carlyle influenced Ruskin who also read and criticised Smith, and who had a bigger intellectual debt to the 18th century than he was prepared to admit (Henderson, 2000). Scholarship on John Ruskin is also significant in Japan. It is interesting, in the context that I have just outlined, that Shoji Tanaka sees Smith developing an understanding that "the corruption of moral sentiments resulting from the blind pursuit of wealth is an immanent problem of human nature not reducible to institutional problems" (p. 144). Tanaka sees this tension as "the essential dilemma of modern enlightenment thought that has remained unchanged to this day" (p. 147).

The volume sometimes gives the impression that the "Scottish Enlightenment" is something tangible and well defined: "This book seeks to provide a comprehensive view of the rise and progress of political economy in eighteenth-century Scotland with special emphasis upon its internal connections with the Scottish Enlightenment" (Sakamoto & Tanaka, p. 1). Placing "manners" as the centre focuses on long-term cultural change and processes that periodization cannot always handle. The contributors are, however, aware of different concerns and views held by the wide-range of writers – wider here than normally included within more conventional discussion of the rise of political economy – identified as grappling with cultural and economic reform, issues that pre-date the conventional demarcation of the Enlightenment in Scotland. They are also aware of the need to integrate Scottish historical thinking into the ways in which economists discuss the Scottish Enlightenment (see the very interesting chapters by Kimihiro Koyanagi on Henry Home and William Robertson, by Shoji Tanaka on Hume, Home and

Smith, and by Hideo Tanaka on John Millar) as well as the contributions of Dugald Stewart (see the chapter by Hisashi Shinohara).

The rise of political economy in Hume, Steuart and Smith is set within a particular context, reforming and economic discussion in Scotland prior to and after the Union. Adequate reflection takes place on the differing views, problems and analyses within the set of individuals taken to exemplify Enlightenment and pre-Enlightenment thinking in moral and cultural terms. The combination of perceived, comparative economic backwardness, the discovery of the continued cultural significance of history and the contextualization of human nature in "customs and manners" and the institutional constraints that they place on what is economically possible and the analysis of such possible interactions, are not limited in time. The Japanese interest in Smith in the twentieth century, in the account given by Hiroshi Mizuta, testifies to this. Enlightenment philosophy seems to require, I suppose, an *ancien régime*, in some form, in order to come fully to life, and time to reflect on its modernising messages. Marx was, in Japan, at first, more significant, and in context at first, a more obvious choice for consideration, than Smith.[1] The unexplored potential here is for connections between 18th century political economy and the cultural discussion in modern-day literature on economic development.

This volume is striving towards an account of the "shaping of political economy" within the concerns for "morals, values and politics" as discussed within "Enlightenment" and Scottish "pre-Enlightenment" texts and contexts. The volume explores a wide range of texts on the understanding that common themes of the literature examined are "the national need to civilize Scotland in all conceivable human and material terms" and the intention of promoting "moral, political and economic improvements of the nation" (p. 3). Hume is included as one of the *dramatis personae*, though it is worth pointing out that many of Hume's concerns were either universal or focused on English (or at least British) issues rather than on specifically Scottish ones. This is explicitly recognised in Ikuo Omori's chapter. The focus on the nature of "commercial civilisation" readily encompasses Hume, even if his context, like that of Smith is broader. For much of his working life, Hume was a frustrated intellectual outsider and it is really only with the success of his *Political Discourses* that he starts coming in from the cold. A point to be made here is that specific Scottish concerns such as the need for economic progress, were made general concerns by Hume and by those he influenced. The work of the "Scottish Triangle" (Hume, Steuart and Smith) is both set within the context and contributes to the context.

The main focus is therefore the "way in which economic discourses were man-ifesting themselves in eighteenth-century Scotland" (p. 2). "Economic" is taken in a broad social sense of socio-economic and hence includes moral and political behavior. So the volume includes detailed reference to (the anti-Unionist) Andrew

Fletcher (by Shigemi Muramatsu), Sir John Clerk, Patrick Lindsay, Thomas Melvill and others (by Gentaro Seki), writers who reflected upon issues relating to the Union and to socio-economic development. Agricultural improvement by reform of the land tenure system, smaller-scale land holdings and shifting funds from other sectors in agriculture, attracted Fletcher (Shigemi Muramatsu, pp. 13, 14). Fletcher also absorbed Petty's notion about the disruptive international effects of the formation of a national trading economy and the detrimental effects on "manners" of the concentration of wealth (potentially consumed as "luxury") and power. To cope with international tensions, Fletcher proposed an international constitution after the model of the "Achaean League" (p. 18) and so raises the ancient-modern issue that became a feature of the Hume-Wallace debate on population and other aspects of the ancient-modern divide (treated in separate chapters by Yoshio Nagai and Yasuo Amoh). According to Muramatsu, Fletcher put the issue of how "to maintain 'good manners' and realize peace among nations in a commercial civilization" firmly on the agenda. The manners theme is pursued by Gentaro Seki who sees the policy debate in the 1720s and 1730s (as developed by Clerk, Lindsay and Melvill) as "grappling with the problem of shaping adequate economic agents" (p. 36) capable of taking on new legal, commercial and manufacturing roles. Hutcheson, in contrast, in a contribution by Toshiaki Ogose, is depicted as having primarily theoretical and conceptual interests ("the Modern Order Problem") rather than details of economic life and policy (p. 39). Hume and Smith are depicted as taking up issues of conflict between Hutcheson idealisations and contingent reality.

Such writers exercised views and opinions that Hume, according to Phillipson, seems to have been familiar with. Justification for their inclusion can therefore be found in the wider literature. This pre- and post-Union debate was "sustained and sophisticated" especially on the issues of constitution, commerce and culture (Phillipson, 1989, p. 30). Hume's concerns in the *Political Discourses* were with the appropriate ways of "pursuing virtue and happiness in a modern polity" in a context of commercialization (Phillipson, 1989, p. 9). Though Muramatsu does not explicitly say so, Hume's essays on trade analyse the issue of "unfounded jealousy" and challenge the manners and assumptions of his contemporaries. It could also be added that Hume's concerns, and Smith's too, with challenging "superstition and enthusiasm," (a detrimental set of "manners") in Smith's case through the development of education that secured, in the context of the division of labor, the humanity of working people, are also relevant.[2]

Tatsuya Sakamoto in a chapter entitled "Hume's political economy as a system of manners" explores Hume's economics writing from this point of view. Sakamoto points towards Adam Smith rather than back towards the issues raised by the earlier contributors but the links between commercial and economic progress and "manners" (though Smith usually links "customs and manners" together in a double phrase that stresses legal as well as social contexts) are clearly specified. J-B Say, according to Whatmore, developed a political economy within the context of Republican as opposed to Monarchical manners, so the issues that Sakamoto's paper raises have wider connotations that go beyond the development of political economy in the Scottish Enlightenment (Whatmore, 2000). With the refinement of the practical arts, according to Hume, comes new knowledge. Knowledge is spread by trade, re-contextualizes human nature and so alters "manners." Production refines knowledge and enhances "industrious manners" and consumption refines taste and manners (Sakamoto, p. 98). I would add that the Anglo-Irish writer Maria Edgeworth picked up the significance of the link between a specific economic context, that of rent and landlordism, (from her reading of Adam Smith) and "manners" in her comedy of manners, *Castle Rackrent* (1800), a work that influenced Walter Scott and his portrayals of the contrasting socio-economic cultures of Scotland. The volumes insistence on the centrality of the associated themes will help strengthen the case for *Castle Rackrent* as a Smithian economic novel. Indeed the socio-economic novels of the 19th century may well have their origins in Edgeworth and hence a direct intellectual home in Smith and Hume.

Evidence from the *Wealth of Nations* is used to support Sakamoto's argument about Hume's concerns and achievements. Smith points to Hume, according to Sakamoto, as the "only writer" who understood the role that urban trade played in the development of liberty. Sakamoto's conclusion, that, "it is almost clear that manners as the fundamental motivating force for economic development and civilization is logically identical with the knowledge-producing pattern of economic development" (p. 99) is both interesting and bold.

Ikuo Omori's chapter is another key contribution assessing the "shaping of political economy." Omori makes the link with the earlier Scottish literature explicit, and holds that "political economy was born in mid-eighteenth century Scotland as a result of the attempt by members of the 'Triangle' to show the compatibility between wealth and virtue in a free and civilized society" (p. 104). The theme of "manners" continues in Steuart's notions of "the sprit of a people" and of "freedom in the industrious man" and the formation of "manners" in the context of Smith's notion of propensities in human nature "to better our condition" (p. 115). The role of the legislator is examined in the context of the development of monetary theory in as much as monetary theory is used to ground Steuart's notion of effectual demand (p. 111). The question of managing the emerging commercial economy is raised in thinking through the implications of Steuart's view and that of Smith on the role of the legislator. Smith's "invisible hand" is contrasted with "artful" hand of the statesman in Steuart, though the interpretation of both Steuart and Smith in this respect is carefully nouanced. Steuart is seen as being concerned with the "gradual introduction of social reforms into a free society" (p. 113) and Smith as more accommodating of interventions than is usually supposed. Omori, in this respect, reaches the conclusion that the "gulf between" the two writers "may not be as wide as is often assumed" (p. 115). Steuart is seen as developing a demand-side theory of economics in monetary terms and Smith as developing "a supply-side economics in real terms" (p. 116). The following chapter by Keiichi Watanabe examines how Smith understood British society "from the viewpoint of taxation" (p. 119).

This is an interesting volume and a demanding read. The reader has to do a fair amount of work in negotiating this book, given its intellectual range and density of treatment. The "Editors' Introduction," whilst helpful, could have been more robust in pulling the themes together. Some writers, for example, make the internal links, backwards and forwards very clear, others leave them implicit. It has not been possible in a short span, to review all aspects of the material presented. Books are normally reviewed from a particular perspective. I am interested in the cultural significance of the *Wealth of Nations* so I found myself sympathetic to the arguments that were being presented. The notion of "manners" in the sense developed in the volume and the associated notion of "polite knowledge" (not really developed in the volume though mentioned in passing) helps with tracing the embedded cultural context and helps to further the understanding of aspects of the work of J-B. Say (as developed in Whatmore's analysis of significance of Republican, as opposed to Monarchical, manners in Say's political economy) in relation to those of Smith and Hume and the other literature referred to. The volume will help me to sort out ideas about readership and the relationship between Hume's target readers and those of Smith, although this is not an issue for the contributors. It helps challenge aspects of periodization. Even if periodization is not an explicit issue in the papers presented, it is implicit it its references to the pre- and post-Union debates. By highlighting behaviours in a commercialized economy, it also helps (indirectly) in thinking about Smith and his impact on the socio-economic novel. This is a topic that is less well explored than (say) Marx's impact, but a topic that is of some significance. It is not explored in the volume but reflecting on this topic, was an unexpected outcome of my reading. This collection can be read, therefore, with interest by a range of social and cultural historians whilst remaining of interest to historians of economic thought. It follows through themes such as "wealth and virtue" and "classical republican traditions" that have been touched upon by writers in other contexts and focuses and nouances the discussion on the development of political economy. Readers will find in this collection a challenging set of arguments that place the development of political economy in a new context.

NOTES

1. One unexpected benefit that I gained from reading this chapter was the information that Yukichi Fukuzama translated Millicent Garrett Fawcett's *Political Economy for Beginners* (1870) into Japanese and so helped in propagating "the name of Adam Smith as a liberal economist" (Mizuta, p. 196). This is useful to me in another context.

2. In cultural terms the "Adam Smith doctrine" as developed by Dugald Stewart and his followers from Smith's belief, set out in the *Wealth of Nations*, in the need for education to counteract the detrimental effects of the division of labour, to help developing minds avoid "superstition and enthusiasm" and to maintain a coherent society in the context of potential fragmentation caused by the division of labour, continues to influence education in Scotland and in the United States of America.

REFERENCES

Fawcett, M. G. (1870). *Political economy for beginners*. London: Macmillan.

Henderson, W. (2000). *John Ruskin's political economy*. London: Routledge.

Hont, I., & Ignatieff, M. (1983). *Wealth and virtue: The shaping of political economy in the Scottish enlightenment*. Cambridge: Cambridge University Press.

Phillipson, N. (1989). *Hume*. London: George Weidenfeld & Nicolson.

Whatmore, R. (2000). *Republicanism and the French Revolution: An intellectual history of Jean-Baptiste say's political economy*. Oxford: Oxford University Press.

Wood's MEDIEVAL ECONOMIC THOUGHT

Willie Henderson

A review essay on Diana Wood, *Medieval Economic Thought*, Cambridge: Cambridge University Press. 2002. pp. xii+274. £45.00. ISBN 0521452600 and £14.99. 0521458935.

The economic thinking of the Medieval period is not always treated in histories of economic thought. Its inclusion or omission depends on the decisions of authors with respect to the purposes and audiences that their histories intend to serve. Where the focus is the evolution of modern-day economics in terms of the development of economic analysis, it may be reasonable to predict that early economics or as some would have it "proto-economics" or Schumpeter's "rudimentary economic analysis" (Schumpeter, 1986, p. 53) would have no place in history texts. In as much as there is no identification of "the economy" separate from households, it is possible to hold that there is no genuine economic theory. Such a tidy solution is not found, however, in the development of actual histories of economic thought. John Kells Ingram started with "Ancient Times" and then moved to "The Middle Ages" (Ingram, 1910). Erich Roll also starts early and works forward from there (Roll, 1939). Gide and Rist started with "The Physiocrats" (Gide & Rist, 1909), and Mercantilism in the early modern period is another possible starting point. Some fairly robust and well-established texts, concerned with substantive issues in the development of thought and analysis, include ancient and Medieval economic thinking. Gordon's work on *Economic Analysis before Adam Smith* (1975) includes very early sources. Long-established texts such as those of Schumpeter (which views Aristotle as having enough systematic knowledge to qualify as economically

A Research Annual
Research in the History of Economic Thought and Methodology, Volume 23-A, 195–202
© 2005 Published by Elsevier Ltd.
ISSN: 0743-4154/doi:10.1016/S0743-4154(05)23010-9

interesting) and of Ekelund and Hébert, for example, include "Scholastic Economic Analysis" (Ekelund & Hébert, 1997, p. 25). But there are caveats:

> Writers like Plato, Aristotle and St. Thomas Aquinas lived in nonmarket societies in which individual economic decisions were taken by tradition and command rather than by individual, unconstrained economic agents. Consequently the lasting influence on western social thought of these early writers lies not so much in their insights into the operation of market forces, but rather in their preconceptions regarding the nature of social laws (Ekelund & Hébert, 1997, p. 9).

Such generalisations, useful as starting points, are likely to need both hedging and nuancing since Medieval economic life did change. Wood insists on the changing nature of economic life and the intellectual adjustments that change requires. Wood, for example, places her discussion of "property" in a "growing sense of individual rights and possession" and on "conflicting legal ideas on property" (p. 19). The transition from poverty as something to be chosen as recommended by St. Francis to the notion that "a copious body of misers is the essential foundation of the State," held by a fifteenth-century merchant Prince, also nicely highlights the transitions (p. 207).

Classical thinking is mentioned in the above passage with Medieval thinking and there is ample justification for this, well-rehearsed by Schumpeter. Aquinas harnessed Aristotle to the service of Scholastic scholarship in partnership with Christian thinking and his synthesis endured (Schumpeter, 1986, pp. 88–89). Schumpeter and Ekelund and Hébert make the point that there is interest in studying Medieval economic thinking, such as it was, because the discussion of social laws and natural justice are required to make sense of later arguments concerning the way or ways in which the natural law tradition influenced the evolution of thinking about economics. If we are to understand (say) the evolution of political economy in the eighteenth century we need to understand something about the notion of natural law and justice and hence something of Medieval and Classical social thinking. Similar points are made in other texts, particularly the need to think through issues of economic justice and what constitutes appropriate motivation for a fully-developed human life (Landreth & Colander, 1994, p. 31). Medema and Samuels' recently published "Reader" provides extracts from Aristotle and Aquinas, implicitly recognising the close relationship between the two on a number of issues. Whilst Medema and Samuels also recognise the lack of "theoretical or empirical economics" in early texts, and the "subordination of economic thinking to theology" they hold that such texts exhibit a number of general problems such as "the nature and place of private property in the social structure" (Medema & Samuels, 2003, p. 1). This was a problem that also exercised the Enlightenment as political economy started to take shape as a subject so there are continuities. Wood notes that Locke also observed that "God had given the earth to man in common" (p. 41).

For historians of economic thought, there are choices to be made and justifications to be offered. Diana Wood is not an historian of economic thought and is careful to declare her credentials in the Preface, which she does in the following way:

> The third assumption was that it should be feasible for someone like myself with no training in economics, but with experience in teaching medieval economic and social history (the two being inseparable) and the history of political ideas to write about medieval economic thought (Wood, 2002, p. ix).

This she offers without "judgement" though she is frank enough to tell us that her other assumptions, made as a basis of developing the book, turned out to be mistaken. There was more written on Medieval economic thought than she had assumed and she was unable to write about economic thought without looking at economic practice. Wood was faced with a huge intellectual and rhetorical challenge and writes, later in the same passage, of the efforts made to balance "theory and practice" whilst "desperately trying to keep the book to a manageable length." It is easy to warm to a writer that can communicate honestly and effectively with the reader from the first page. Wood's interests are, of course, in the period and in the thinking in its own right.

Wood is writing for "teachers and students," mainly, students and teachers of Medieval history, and her interest is based around the rich tapestry of medieval thought and thinkers of the period roughly from the twelfth to the fifteenth century. Her work is a work of synthesis rather than of fundamental research, but both its length and its organisational structure suggest that Wood has managed the balancing act well. The work consists of eight substantive chapters organised thematically around what she has identified as significant themes: "Private property vs. communal rights"; "Wealth, beggary and sufficiency"; "What is money?"; "Sovereign concerns: weights, measures, and coinage"; "The mercantile system"; "The just price and the just wage"; "The nature of usury: the usurer as winner"; "The theory of interest: the usurer as loser." There is an introduction and concluding section, both very useful in understanding the overall significance of Medieval thinking and Wood's achievements in making the thought accessible to modern-day readers. In common with history of thought texts, she makes it clear, in an elegant phrase, that Medieval thinking about economics is embedded in religious and social contexts "imbued with questions of ethics and morality, with the motives rather than the mechanics of economic life" (p. 1).

This is a range of topics that goes significantly beyond what would normally be included in the highly summarised versions of medieval thinking found in a (comprehensive) history of economics text that includes the topic. It should be clear that Schumpeter's coverage, though based on "only a few representative names," manages to cover a surprising range of topics (Schumpeter, 1986, p. 94). Of the huge list of the main *dramatis personae*, supplied by Wood in an Appendix, Schumpeter mentions, according to the "Index of Authors," eight (Schumpeter, 1986, pp. 1209–1229). These eight are: Aquinas, Albert the Great, Aegidius Collonna (referred to in Wood as "Giles of Rome" or "Aegidius Romanus"), John Buridan, Duns Scotus, St. Antonine (referred to in Wood as "Antoninus"), Mattheo Palmieri and Nicholas Oresme. Of course, Schumpter knew of many other sources and recognises them in various footnotes. Ekelund and Hébert mention in their "Name Index," five, three in common with Schumpeter (Aquinas, Buridan, Oresme) and in addition Gerald Odonis and Henry of Friemar. Ekelund and Hébert mention the synthesis achieved by John Crell (c. 1590–1633) and I can find no reference to him in Wood. He is essentially outside of her timeframe. Another difference, already mentioned, is that whereas Wood develops themes to embed the topics in a wider context and in a range of texts, Ekelund and Hébert work through summarisations of the contribution of significant individuals to a particular topic.

If Wood supplies the set of relevant main writers then any encyclopaedic history of economic thought text is likely to be exemplifying them from a sub-set. Ekeland and Hébert justify their selection in terms of five that "stand out in the tradition of Aristotelian value theory" (p. 25). Aristotle is one of the classical authors who is held in the modern world to have achieved a level of economics understanding that goes beyond common sense, Xenophon, though contested, is another. Equally Scholasticism is grounded upon Aristotle, whom Aquinas calls "the philosopher," so a double incentive exists to choose in this way. Wood approaches the subject through themes rather than through individual scholars or discussants. What is useful from my point of view as a teacher of economic thought in a History of Ideas programme, is the range of textual exemplifications that Wood provides to illustrate key aspects of thought in a range of social contexts. Wood draws her evidence from sources that come from the works of Medieval scholars, from vernacular poems that rehearsed moral and economic problems and from legal discussion and manorial rolls. A number of poems are resorted to for exemplification of themes, in particular, *"The Libelle of Englische Polyce"* (an anonymous poem written sometime around 1436–1438 promoting the argument for a policy of protection and control of the sea routes) (pp. 123–125) and the engaging debate between "Wynnere and Wastoure" (an "alliterative poem in Middle English") (p. 223). Given the nature of economic concerns in embedded economic life, it is hardly surprising that the available secular literature should develop some such themes. Economic themes developed in literature in later periods, beyond the scope of Wood's work, include examples such as Moore's *Utopia* (reflections upon the Tudor economy) and Mandeville's *Fable of the* Bees (reflections on economic manners and behaviours in the early 18th century). *"The Libelle of Englische Polyce"* is known in history of economic thought writings but I doubt if the same is true, to the same extent, for "*Wynnere and Wastoure*."

Chapter 1, "Private Property vs. Communal Rights: The conflict of Two Laws," is useful in order to illustrate Wood's approach, as is Chapter 3 "What is money."

The problem of private property is set up as a conflict of two laws, the "divine-natural law" and "human law." The moral conflict over property is easy to specify. It is a means of sustaining life and of sharing. It can also become the object of avarice and a means to power and exploitation. Divine law supported communal property, human law sanctioned unequal possession. The two laws were in conflict and an intellectual problem to be faced was their reconciliation. This was attempted first by Augustine, who made God the indirect source of human law and then by Medieval scholars such as Rufinus and later Aquinas. Rufinus produced a three-fold classification of divine law in which two categories were fixed (basically right and wrong acts biblically defined) and a third category based on "demonstrations." The latter included ideas about possessions and his ideas were used later to suggest that circumstances alter cases and hence the possibility of some accommodation between the strict divine law and human law. Aquinas sees human law as an extension by "right reason" (reason being an aspect of human nature that is close to divine nature) of the natural law. If "right reason" shows that institutional arrangements are for the "common good" then the two laws can be reconciled by addition. Aquinas needs to show "right reason" for the existence of private property. He does this by using Aristotle's arguments to demonstrate that life will be better conducted when there is private rather than communal property. Aquinas also linked the existence of private property to individual human effort. John of Paris and Fortescue both extended this notion. Wood sees both as anticipating "John Locke's idea that man by joining the labour of his body to something made it his property" (p. 25). In this way, private property could be reconciled for those who could not choose to live without possession. For those who did so choose, a number of patterns were elaborated including the monastic life, absolute poverty in the manner of St. Francis and Christian stewardship (property held in trust by one generation of pilgrims for the next). Those who held private property were to be constrained to share. A practical solution to the question of taxation evolved in England where private property by consent could be taxed for the common good.

In Chapter 3, Medieval notions of money are explored in terms of the conflict between two ideas of money essentially derived from two different works by Aristotle. These are that money is both artificial (and useless) and that money, as it was made of precious metal, was something of intrinsic value. Money emerges in Aristotle's *Ethics* as a means of reconciling different values in exchange and does so not "by nature but by law" (p. 72). It is created and can be rendered worthless by law. But in the context of *Politics*, Aristotle is concerned with the development of the household and exchange based on demand. Households grow to wish for exchanges based upon direct exchange through barter. Given the existence of money, it is possible that households move beyond this to seek after money as an end in itself and hence move from a natural to an unnatural way of working and living. The introduction of money is the foundation of Locke's views on the corruption of human nature (p. 82).

The Medieval word inherited a problem created by Aristotle i.e. the need to "define the nature" as well as the function of money (p. 72). The distinction between nature and need is nicely presented by a reference to Aquinas who seems that goods are measured "by need, according to nature, and by money, according to convention" (p. 74). Such an approach maintains the unnatural notion of money. Money is only useful as a measure of other things in the process of "ordinary transactions" (p. 75). Aquinas's view had implications for the discussion of usury, for what was significant were the things exchanged or borrowed and not the money. The important thing was the restoration of an equivalent in terms of physical commodities and to avoid charging for the use of the underlying goods as well. Medieval thinkers, in the Aristotelian tradition, such as Henry of Friemar, worked-up a comprehensive list of its properties including convenient size, dependability, durability and so on. Time belonged to God and two later chapters work on the way in which a theory of interest gradually emerged from the notion of sinful usury. This only happened as a result of the extension of the monetized economy and the further intellectual challenges that the extension posed.

Treatment of money as a commodity, and hence as something whose value could fluctuate, was largely forced on scholastic scholars by significant changes in economic circumstances, and metalists such as John Buridan and Nicholas Oresme, tried to think through some issues. Oresme looked to money as a way of exchanging over time. Whilst exchanges over time were considered, a possible and related discussion of savings and accumulation remained limited. The functions of money and its importance as a sign (and hence to issues of sovereignty) were the most significant outcomes of the Medieval discussion. Control of coinage, weights and measures was necessary "for preserving the government of any lordship, since they are used in the payment of tributes, since their use decreases quarrels and protects fidelity in purchases and sales, and finally, since they, like coins, are instruments of human life and, even more than coinage, imitate natural action . . ." (Ptolemy of Lucca, p. 89). Divine authority, derived from Plato's concept of universals, and from Christ's statement in Matthew's gospel, "Render to Caesar the things that are Caesar's" justified actions. Claiming the means of control did not mean that control was effective.

This is a work that places medieval thinking in the context of Aristotelian thought as well as of a series of intellectual and moral conflicts, in the world as it is, as compared with the world as it ought to be. Wood also justifies her interests in practice by referring to the origins of the early modern world and links with Locke's thinking or with the ethical issues involved in thinking about the balance between developed and developing countries in today's world. Such justifications are in line with statements made in comprehensive histories of thought texts. There is clearly, given the significance of the natural law tradition and its impact on Enlightenment thinking, a need to know something about its distant origins and Wood's work can provide a gentle introduction to making earlier ways of thinking credible.

Medieval thinking was both practical and idealistic, in that it worked towards "the mean," in other words, a balance between practical demands and ethical considerations. A final quote from Aquinas, displaying what I take to be an aspect of his Aristotelian credentials, makes the issues clear, on matters of justice, such as the just price, "We sometimes have to make the best estimate we can, with the result that giving or taking a little here or there does not upset the balance of justice" (p. 209).

Wood does not "claim to reach original or definitive conclusions" (p. 206) and it is not a book of primarily theoretical investigations. It is however an interesting, balanced and well-written read that embeds medieval thinking in intellectual and practical problems. Its span is wider that is normally found in histories of economic thought. It makes the concerns real and the intellectual and the spiritual and ethical struggles credible. It is accessible. Its focus is on Medieval thinking but there is enough on Aristotle to suggest origins and continuities and just enough looking forward to Locke and hence, by implication, to the development of political economy in the Enlightenment, to make it of interest to students and teachers of the history of economic thought. In this respect, however, Schumpeter, goes further by making very detailed links, though his primary focus is not Wood's. The main interest is that Wood's work is one of synthesis and as a result it provides access to a range of primary and secondary sources in an engaging way, capable of helping those new to Medieval thought understand it as valid intellectual endeavour, in a nuanced context.

REFERENCES

Ekelund, R. B., Jr., & Hébert, R. F. (1997). *A history of economic theory and method.* Singapore: McGraw-Hill, international edition.
Gide, C., & Rist, C. ([1909] 1960). *A history of economic doctrines.* London: George G. Harap, second edition, seventh impression.

Gordon, B. (1975). *Economic analysis before Adam Smith: Hesiod to Lessius*. New York: Harper Row & Macmillan.

Ingram, J. K. (1910). *A history of political economy*. London: Adam & Charles Black, second edition.

Landreth, H., & Colander, D. C. (1994). *History of economic thought*. Boston, MD: Houghton-Mifflin, third edition.

Medema, S. G., & Samuels, W. J. (2003). *The history of economic thought: A reader*. London: Routledge.

Roll, E. (1939). *A history of economic thought*. London: Faber & Faber, second edition.

Schumpeter, J. (1986). *History of economic analysis*. London: Routledge.

McCann's THE ELGAR DICTIONARY OF ECONOMIC QUOTATIONS

Warren J. Samuels

A review essay on Charles Robert McCann, Jr., Ed. *The Elgar Dictionary of Economic Quotations*, Northampton, MA: Edward Elgar, 2003, pp. xi, 315. $150.00.

Charles McCann believes that a Dictionary of Quotations is a repository of statements on which writers and debaters can rely for accuracy: Not only to avoid misstatement and erroneous attribution, but also misperception of original context. (What is an alternative motivation? To show the brilliance of economists? Or their facility with words?) Of course, one could search original sources but it is more efficient, time wise, to have a sourcebook of passages, perhaps especially one arranged overall alphabetically by author and for each author by topic.

I have several such books at home. I use them for McCann's purposes and for enjoyment and edification as well as restoration of memory. I once had on the door to my study a quotation, I believe from an Oxford librarian found in *The New Yorker*, that one can learn merely by sitting in a room lined with books. In my case, it is more being reminded. With Dictionaries of Quotations it is both learning and being reminded.

It goes without saying that misstatement and erroneous attribution are *mala en se*. How to avoid misperception of original context? McCann's solution is to avoid presenting merely pithy phrases. His procedure is to "include as much material as necessary for the reader to appreciate the argument presented, as well as the phrases which have come to such importance" (pp. vii, viii). The principal problem here is

A Research Annual
Research in the History of Economic Thought and Methodology, Volume 23-A, 203–208
Copyright © 2005 by Elsevier Ltd.
All rights of reproduction in any form reserved
ISSN: 0743-4154/doi:10.1016/S0743-4154(05)23011-0

the definition of scope of context. Is it the framework of, say, the paragraph in which the famous expression is found, the local framework? Or is it a larger framework, that of the larger argument, perhaps the chapter or article? The former can be accomplished by including some surrounding lines; the latter, by introductory editorial material, often taking more space than the quotation. McCann, providing a sourcebook rather than a teaching/learning device, sensibly follows the former route.

McCann knows that users and reviewers of his book will inevitably find at least three types of faults with it. One type of fault will deal with authorial coverage. Each reader will think of people who have been excluded and should not have been, and of others who should have been. The second type of fault has to do with the selection of quotations from any particular author. The third type of fault has to do with the relative number of selections from various authors. These are sort of generic faults; they go with the territory, as do much of what follows.

Writings on economic ideas can be classified as scholarly or scientific, popularizing, pieces in persuasion, journalistic, and/or works outside the author's principal area of recognized expertise. Numerous sources of quotations are hard to pigeonhole, though this, like the next problem, presents no difficulty for McCann.

A problem that McCann had to resolve is the inclusion of non-economists and the omission of some economists His justification for including non-economists is that he is concerned with ideas of interest to economists and others interested in economic topics, not solely ideas by economists in economic texts. Some non-economists have more entries than some economists.

A list of the names of entries under the letter "A" will help provide a sense of what the foregoing means. Using the short forms of names where possible, they are: Henry Aaron, Henry Carter Adams, George Akerlof, Johan Åkerman, Armen Alchian, R. G. D. Allen, St. Thomas Aquinas, G. C. Archibald, Aristotle, Kenneth Arrow, William Ashley, Edward Atkinson, Lyman Atwater, Clarence Ayres, and William Edmonstoune Aytoun (an Irish poet who opposed free trade). Obvious, but not necessarily objectionable, omissions include Jack Amariglio, P. W. S. Andrews, Philip Arestis, Thurman Arnold, Brian Arthur, Robert Aumann, and Robert Axelrod.

Female authors are represented elsewhere: Phyllis Deane, Millicent Fawcett, Emma Goldman, Rosa Luxemburg, Deirdre McCloskey, Edith Penrose, Ayn Rand, Joan Robinson, and Barbara Wooton. Only two are currently active.

It should already be evident that quotations are not limited to authors whose native language is English, though all quotations are in that language.

McCann also had to work out the topics serving to classify individual quotations. McCann's choices are straightforward, typically unsubtle, topics on which a variety of subtle points can be made. These include the following: banking, econometrics, entrepreneurship, exchange, innovation, interest, manufacturing, Marxism, methodology, trade, usury, wants, and wealth distribution as well as those listed in the next paragraph.

The topics with the most selections, as indicated by their number of lines in the Index include, alphabetically: Business, Capital, Capitalism, Communism, Community, Competition, Economics, Economists, Government, Justice, Labor, Laissez-faire, Law(s), Man, Market, Mathematics, Money, Political Economy, Poor, Poor Laws, Poverty, Private Property, Production, Property, Science, Socialism, Society, State, Tax(es), Taxation, Value(s), and Wealth. Did McCann overwork any topics? It is hard to say without negating his objective of providing a sourcebook useful to writers and speakers. Redundancy is a matter of interpreting subtle differences of nuance. Are any topics missing? There are many topics covered in one way or another but in a discipline – broadly or narrowly defined – laden with technical materials many, many are missing. To fault McCann is, again, to negate his purpose in compiling *these* quotations. Writers and speakers on technical topics should expect to find neither the topics nor technically specific quotations. I have no quarrel with this.

I suspect that McCann worked on several fronts simultaneously: making decisions on authors, particular quotes, and topicality, accumulating as he taught, read, and wrote. (He acknowledges help from colleagues.)

The alphabetical listing of names (with birth and death dates) runs from pp. 1–221. The list of references (sources of quotations) covers pp. 223–248. An extremely detailed and useful index covers pp. 249–315 (most entries are topics or points followed by name(s) and entry number; e.g. "pomp of life: Barbon 10"). Alas, there is no table of contents providing a list of the names of those quoted, though the reference list is a close substitute.

Some reviewers have a compulsion, at least a sense of duty, to find some fault with the book under review. I have no such desire or need. But I should point out a few personal plusses and minuses regarding inclusion and exclusion. I was pleased to see included William Stanley Jevons on all classes being trade unionists at heart. I missed John R. Hicks's admonition that no one theory can answer all of our questions and Frank William Taussig's declaration that it is better to have the money-hungry Napoleons of industry than the blood-thirsty Napoleons of history. Paul Samuelson's writings are a rich source, though he already has a page and one-third. Kenneth Boulding's various writings are another rich source, even given the page and one half or more already given him. Vilfredo Pareto has one and one-fifth of a page – and he, too, could have been given more space. Amartya Sen has no space at all.

But such judgments are beside the point, given McCann's rationale. My points reflect my thinking that certain omitted quotations would be worthwhile for people to know about. But he is intent on providing a sourcebook for quotations people more or less vaguely already "know" and want to find and use, perhaps in deploying argument by appeal to authority. And that is surely a legitimate objective – even though I suspect that many users will likely not already have known the quotation for which they were looking with which to add spice to a writing of their own.

Nonetheless, when I went through the collection I had several topics of personal interest to me particularly in mind – economics and economists, government, laissez-faire, and property-private property. On each topic I found that a reader would learn something of the variety of positions taken, that stereotypical or ideological examples do not represent the only positions on certain ideas, and the richness and complexity of economic ideas.

None of this represents history of economic thought, nor does McCann say it does. A collection of quotes, even with some attention to context, especially what I called local context above, does not make a history. It is more akin to a collection of sound bites taken from the conversation that is economics, ala Deirdre McCloskey. But if someone says that security of property is what makes property important and someone else says that neither property nor any other "principle" is absolute, an inquiring mind should be induced to look into the matter more deeply. However, for someone delving into this collection to find a quotation with which to spruce up a talk, or make a point by invoking an authority, such likely is irrelevant.

When one reads a book, one undertakes a long, continuing conversation, if only one-sided, with the author. Perhaps not ultimately one-sided: An author should anticipate some interests and questions of readers and make an effort to comply. In that sense, the conversation is somewhat two-sided; of course, we cannot communicate our nuances etc. to the author. When one reads a Dictionary of Quotations, no such long, continuing conversation can exist, however imaginary and one-sided it is. One is bombarded with statements of point of view; in no one case can one continue with the author, even in the foregoing limited sense. Of course, no one (other than reviewers) is likely to *read* a Dictionary of Quotations. It is like a conventional dictionary of words. One seeks a particular definition and if a wandering eye comes across an entry that elicits interest, we may pause and inquire. Unlike a good book, dictionaries have no story to tell. Aha, a Dictionary of Economic Quotations does tell a story, precisely because it is a dictionary of *economic* quotations. The story is an account of the *multiplicity* of views on every idea or topic that may be found. McCann may not have intended this result, but it follows inexorably from the nature of his subject.

Not only multiplicity but flagrant conflicts of views. Still restricting myself to the "A" listings, Armen Alchian on property must be juxtaposed at least to Henry Carter Adams on laissez-faire and to St. Thomas Aquinas and Aristotle on property.

Even more dramatic is the conflict between two successive quotations on page 3, the first from Kenneth Arrow (from 1974),

> An economist by training thinks of himself as the guardian of rationality, the ascriber of rationality to others, and the prescriber of rationality to the social world.

and the second from William Ashley (from 1907, here only the first third of McCann's quotation),

> When one looks back on a century of economics teaching and writing, the chief lesson should, I feel, be one of caution and modesty, and especially when we approach the burning issues of our own day.

Even though one can properly suspect that there is more to Arrow's and to Ashley's respective positions than is contained in these quotations, how delicious is their immediate juxtaposition.

Too bad the expected reader is looking only for intellectual support through invocation of an authority, perhaps "some academic scribbler of a few years back" (Keynes, of course, quoted here on p. 87), and not edification.

Which brings me to Gresham's law applied to economic ideas, with due regard to the fact that what are bad and what are good economic ideas is a matter of perspective and judgment. Several points: (1) The "expected reader" of the immediately preceding paragraph provides evidence for those who see economics in part as the handmaiden of those in (or would like to be in) power, who use economic ideas to advance their own agendas, as the coin of reelection campaigns, debasing the currency in the process. (2) Politics makes for both risk aversion and risk assumption, withdrawal and aggression (egoism), independent of the content of the ideas bandied about. (3) Stigler's statement (from 1959) that "In general there is no position . . . which cannot be reached by a competent use of respectable economic theory" is probably correct. But correct only within limits. One limit is that the statement is, in some hands, only a tautology depending on and giving effect to the meaning of "respectable." Another limit is how some ideas drive others out of circulation, and still another how some ideas thrive and others dry up, depending on their ostensible congruity or incongruity with the dominant ideology or, more narrowly, the dominant school of economics.

In this connection, I offer McCann a quotation for his second and expanded edition:

> There is *no established* economic usage for anything in economics.

This is Frank Knight, as recorded in F. Taylor Ostrander's notes from lectures in Knight's course on Economic Theory, Economics 301, University of Chicago, 1933–1934, published in volume 22B of this series. The statement is very close to that of Stigler, just quoted.

Alas, the price of *The Elgar Dictionary of Economic Quotations* is several times those Dictionaries of Quotations with which I am familiar. The difference in price is due to different market sizes and to different pricing policies. I find no quotations in McCann's collection dealing directly with this matter. Perhaps there should be. Which brings to mind the interesting quotations to be found in the correspondence between Alfred Marshall and his publisher, Macmillan, who on occasion felt compelled to lecture the leading professor of economics in England on the book market. But these statements may or may not satisfy McCann's stated purpose behind his collection.

The author is indebted to Ross Emmett for suggestions.

Busch's THE ECLIPSE OF MORALITY: SCIENCE, STATE AND MARKET

Glenn L. Johnson[*]

A review essay on Lawrence Busch, *The Eclipse of Morality: Science, State and Market*, Aldine DeGruyter, New York, NY, 2000.

Lawrence Busch's *The Eclipse of Morality: Science, State and Market* joins a number of other books and related efforts concerned with what is wrong with the modern world. Among these are Huston Smith's *Why Religion Matters* (2001), which is so relevant for Busch's work that this is almost a joint review of the two books.

Daniel Yergin's and Joseph Stanislaw's *Commanding Heights* (1998) (also presented in video form) and Hernando Desoto's *The Mystery of Capitalism* (2000) are also pertinent as are such books as those by Frederick Ferrré on postmodernism (1996 and 1998). At the opposite extreme of Ferré's highly academic works are the street-level activities of demonstrators at Seattle, Montreal, Geneva, Washington, and Berlin, the terrorist activities of religious extremists in the Middle East, Ireland and against the United States in many locations, not to mention the pro-Iraqi activists throughout the United States and the world. Also relevant is the outburst of publications by the biophysical scientists and theologians engaging in the current scientific/theological dialogue made profitable by tens and even hundreds of millions of dollars provided by Sir John Templeton. These and other efforts are noted here because they are all concerned with the shortcomings of this

*Professor Emeritus Johnson had completed a handwritten version of this article prior to his death on October 7, 2003. The manuscript was brought to publication by A. Allan Schmid with suggestions from Lawrence Busch and Warren Samuels.

A Research Annual
Research in the History of Economic Thought and Methodology, Volume 23-A, 209–227
© 2005 Published by Elsevier Ltd.
ISSN: 0743-4154/doi:10.1016/S0743-4154(05)23012-2

modern world and what can, could, or should be done to remedy them. They are all a part of the numerous modern/post-modern concerns now being widely discussed. Busch, himself, holds postmodernism at arms length (p. 7) and is apologetic for using a post-modernist term "decenters" (p. 140).

Busch anchors his work in his view of the consequences of such early or pre-modernists as Bacon, Hobbes and Adam Smith (hereinafter BHS). Busch's effort is post-modernist as he seeks ways of overcoming what he sees as the shortcomings of modernity growing out of the works of BHS.

It should be noted that the works of Yergin and Stanislaw, Huston Smith, Desoto and other current contributors collectively provide a better, more complete account than anyone of them alone including Busch. Thus, in this review of Busch's work, references to the works of other reputable contributors indicate how topics neglected in Busch's effort can be considered. Reciprocally, stressing Busch's substantial accomplishments calls attention to topics neglected by his contemporaries. This reviewer is grateful for all of their contributions to our ability to understand our modern world. This reviewer owes personal gratitude especially to Busch and to the editor of this journal. Reviewing Busch's effort has prompted this reviewer to expand his own long-term study of science (including the social ones), religion and society. Perhaps this reviewer will also help others explore the contributions Busch and his contemporaries are making to our understanding of the problems our modern world encounters in dealing with: (1) the technical changes the biophysical sciences are facilitating; (2) the changes the social sciences are helping generate in government, markets and other institutions; (3) impacts of the social sciences on human capacity and performance; and (4) how both the biophysical and social sciences impact the preservation of exhaustible natural resources and their replacement and/or augmentation with human-made resources. It will be seen later that this reviewer believes the collective contributions of the multi-disciplinary professions are as important or more important than those forming specialized disciplines including the humanities and theology as well as the science disciplines. In the last section of this review, it will be seen that religion has an important role to play in overcoming the moral shortcomings of our modern world while it is, at the same time, a source of such shortcomings.

Successive sections of this review:

(1) Compare Busch's positions on morality with those of other important contemporary authors, especially Huston Smith.
(2) Focus on both undue faith and undue fear of Busch's three leviathanic eclipsers of morality.
(3) Consider the neglect of the social sciences in the current science/religion dialogue and the mishandling of market theory by Busch and H. Smith.

(4) Concern the general neglect of multidisciplinary professions by both Busch and his contemporaries, including H. Smith.
(5) Consider the contributions theology can make along with other academic disciplines and multidisciplinary professions to the alleviation of immorality in modern society, including immorality attributable to religions.

BUSCH'S POSITION ON MORALITY IN THE MODERN WORLD RELATIVE TO THOSE OF SOME OF HIS CONTEMPORARIES, ESPECIALLY HUSTON SMITH

Busch focuses on what he regards as the three broad causes of immorality in the modern world: scientism, statism, and marketism. He views these three "isms" pejoratively and originating respectively with Francis Bacon, Thomas Hobbes and Adam Smith. Each is treated as a "leviathan" spewing immorality from its multiple heads in the form of *undue faith* in the *three different kinds of social order* they generate.

Though he argues against pejorative treatment of the terms science, state, and market (pp. 135–136), his title treats them pejoratively as sources of immorality! There is also a pejorative use of the words science, state, and markets on p. 135 where he argues against such usage! Rather closely related to Busch's book is Huston Smith's *Why Religion Matters*, which connects Busch to the extensive current literature on science and religion to help fill the social science gap in the dialogue. H. Smith's book leads us to a deeper, more meaningful definition of morality and immorality than the mere consequences of undue faith in the social orders generated by science, markets and state.

Huston Smith, a theologian, has only one leviathan – scientism, which he treats pejoratively, while I like Busch's treating science with respect. He views modern man as walking in a tunnel or darkness with a floor, a left (not political) wall, a ceiling, and a right (again, not political) wall. The floor is "scientism" which differs, for H. Smith, from science in that scientism is reserved for logically positivistic reductionist "scientists" who believe that disciplinary knowledge of reality is limited to answers to questions of What?, Where?, and When? about the material world bounded by space and time.

The light H. Smith hopes he sees at the end of his four-dimensional tunnel comes largely from certain biophysical scientists who H. Smith believes are themselves free from the metaphysical and epistemological shackles of scientism. The floor is seen as dominating the left wall, academia, to eclipse (using Busch's term) all knowledge of values, religion and, hence, morality. The ceiling of H. Smith's tunnel is the press dominated by an academia that is, in turn, dominated by scientism. The

right wall is the law or legal system; again (regarded by H. Smith) as dominated by
the scientism that dominates modern academia. The light Huston H. Smith hopes
he sees at the end of the tunnel of darkness, comes largely from what he regards as
reputable scientists (not scientism-ists) who have freed or are freeing themselves
from the reductionist shackles logical positivism places on science when regarded
as *the* rather than as only *one* philosophy of science (also see Ferré, 1996, 1998;
H. Smith, pp. 174–186). H. Smith finds that the Einstein/Pudolksky/Georgescu-
Roegan studies of physics, David Walsh's (1999) biology research reported in
his *The Third Millennium*, and the insights of the cognitive psychologist, Colin
McGinn (1999) presented in his book *The Mysterious Flame* indicate to H. Smith
that at least these three mainly biophysical scientists have or are overcoming the
reductionist shackles that logical positivism places on science. Were H. Smith more
familiar with the history of philosophers' value theory and/or economic thought
(the two histories being virtually identical), he would have probably included a
number of neo-classical and modern economists in his list of "scientists" free
of the reductionist shackles of logical positivism. Such names of neo-classical
and modern economists as Alfred Marshall (1946, orig. 1890), A.C., Pigou
(1932) John Hicks (1939), Vilfredo Pareto (Samuels, 1974), Melvin Reder (1947),
and Amartya Sen (1984) come to mind. Instead, H. Smith dismisses the social
sciences (including economics and Busch's sociology) on pp. 80–84 as unduly
reductionist, logically positivistic and, by implication, scientistic (pp. 84–86).
Similarly, H. Smith neglects the political science and political economy stressed
at his alma mater, The University of Chicago! H. Smith unwisely (pp. 84–86,
91, 131) draws on a misinformed sociologist, Robert Bellah, to substantiate
his belief that social scientists, in general, are reductionist modernists – and
scientistic. If this were true, why would Busch be concerned with the eclipse of
morality? Any why do the social sciences, economics and political science focus
so sharply on measuring and explaining extensive non-monetary and monetary
values (Samuels et al., 1997; Stigler, 1946), now conceived to be *relative* to time
and space (Georgescu-Roegan, 1971)? Here we see shades of Einstein, Podolsky,
and Georgescu-Roegan so approvingly quoted by H. Smith.

H. Smith's metaphysical hopes that physics, cognitive psychology (largely
biologic), and evolutionary biology are revealing dependency between knowledge
of realities of the material and non-material worlds to obliterate "scientism."
However, this reviewer finds that his own academically reputable colleagues,
a physicist (Peter Schroeder), a cognitive psychologist (Loren Harris) and an
evolutionary biologist (Robert Pennock) believe H. Smith's hopes to be poorly
grounded. H. Smith's criticism of scientism, however, survives examination
by this reviewer and his academic colleagues including those with theological
and philosophical expertise. It seems safe to conclude that H. Smith's view

of scientism's shortcomings is more substantial philosophically than Busch's definition of scientism as "undue faith in the social order science generates." However, both H. Smith and Busch fail to utilize knowledge of the downfall of reductionist logical positivism in philosophy that took place in the 1930s (Achinstein & Barker, 1969). Scientism as defined by H. Smith blindly persists even in present day society, in general, among a majority of top biophysical scientists and even among some social scientists, especially psychologists. H. Smith's concern about scientism as science constrained by the metaphysical and epistemological, empirically untested presuppositions of reductionist logical positivism seems much better grounded and significant than the undue faith in the order science generates that is the basis for Busch's scientism and one of his eclipsers of morality.

DO BOTH UNDUE FAITH AND UNDUE FEAR OF BUSCH'S LEVIATHAN ECLIPSE MORALITY?

Busch concentrates on the undue faith to the neglect of undue fear of the orders produced by his three leviathans as eclipsers of morality. Busch shares his concerns about undue faith in science with anti-HMO activists, anti-cloners, anti-nuclearists, all environmental activists – the list goes on. All are concerned about undue faith in science (scientism) as a dominating determinator of decisions to develop, create, adopt and use the technologies made possible by advances in the biophysical sciences. H. Smith joins Busch tangentially in this respect.

This reviewer finds that undue faith in science (Busch's scientism) is a source of incorrect (and hence at least somewhat immoral) decisions concerning the development and use of new technologies. However, Busch neglects the incorrect (and also somewhat immoral) decisions that originate in undue fear of technologies (such as those listed above) to the extent that such fears lead to unwise and, hence, somewhat immoral decisions about technology. Such deception is immoral in the sense that they unjustly deprive potential needy beneficiaries of the benefits of the technology involved. Immorality arises especially when the opposition to new technology is dishonest and self-seeking. Clearly, there is undue fear of, as well as undue faith in several basic technologies.

A broader-based understanding of science (as opposed to scientism) alleviates both undue fear and undue faith in science that leads to furtherance of morality. H. Smith's discussion of scientism and science is more complete than Busch's but both would benefit from more use of ideas from Ferré (1996, 1998) and Achinstein and Barker (1969) among many others. Relevant classical and neo-classical economists/philosophers and value theorists include Adam Smith, J. S. Mill, Alfred Marshall, A. C. Pigou, and John Hicks.

Science, fully understood and practiced, is not a likely source of immorality. Multi-disciplinary professions, using knowledge about values, precluded from scientism the metaphysical and epistemological "contrary to experience" presuppositions. Thus, technological professionals (physicians, engineers, agriculturalists, architects, bio-engineers and the like) are more compatible with science than scientism. Science fully understood is not a source of immorality. Neither H. Smith nor Busch deny this. They both respect science, yet neither is very specific about it. Later in this review, a deeper, more significant meaning of morality will be developed in the section on multi-disciplinary professions.

Undue faith in the order generated by governments is Busch's second misplaced leviathan. He uses the term *statism*. Busch views misplaced faith of statismists to be a major source of immorality in today's modern world. Reflection on experience indicates that Busch's concern is real. But similar reflection also reveals a reciprocal kind of immorality growing out of undue fear of the order generated by governments. Both those who fear that government can do no good and those who have undue faith that governments can do no evil are likely to reach erroneous decisions about governments that immorally impose unjust costs and confer benefits. Such eclipses of morality are reducible with a fuller understanding of how governments work. Such understanding is enhanced by supplementing knowledge from the *discipline* of political science with knowledge available from the *professions* of public administration. Still further, the interdependence of governmental and market activities is given particular attention in the additional "discipline" of political economy (Thompson, 1966). There appears to be no academic discipline concerned only with non-governmental non-market institutions that might be called, say, "non-market non-governmental institutional science of sociology, anthropology and institutional economics" and that might contribute some help in understanding how such institutions contribute to society without becoming embroiled in either undue fear or faith in the order they help establish. Non-market institutions will be considered again in the next sections on marketism. Market institutions operate subject to distributions of the rights and privileges established and maintained by non-market institutions. Busch's treatment of statism is far superior to that of H. Smith's treatment of the right wall of his tunnel of darkness, namely, the law. Smith unfortunately regards the law as dominated by his kind of scientism rather than as by Busch's statism, more or less independent of Busch's scientism.

John J. Mearsheimer (2002) addresses the relationship between what he terms "liberal talk" and realistic thinking. Busch's third leviathan is the market or marketism. Busch's view of market economics is similar to that of Huston Smith, both being inadequate. Busch is more concerned about undue faith in the order markets create in society then he is about those with undue fear of the order generated by markets. H. Smith also bemoans market order while displaying minimal knowledge of how markets operate both in practice and in theory. As is true for scientism and statism, marketism includes both opponents and advocates neither of whom understand well how markets work, including their interdependence with states and other non-governmental, non-market institutions.

The theory of markets is devoid of capacity to assert that markets either justify or deny that free voluntary exchanges among individuals or other decisions making units do the best that can be done for society. Much has happened in market and philosophical value theory since Adam Smith wrote his *Wealth of Nations*. Busch neglects the aforementioned works of Marshall, Pigou, Hicks, and Arrow. Busch (pp. 141, 142) cites Arrow (1951) in a way that indicates he does not understand that Arrow's second theorem does not suggest a "marketismic faith" in market order as maximizing welfare over all possible distributions of the ownership of property rights and privilege other than the existing one. Such justification depends upon the imposition of non-voluntary changes in resource ownership on market participants by non-market governmental or other non-governmental institutions. Reciprocally, market theory does not support anti-marketismic fears of the order markets create. Such support for or disapproval of the market order for any given distribution requires knowledge of values of a rigor that market theorists are now unwilling to presume can be possessed by economists. Busch and H. Smith, make reference to Arrow's Nobel Prize-winning Ph.D. Thesis. Busch's citation of it displays misunderstanding. Incidentally, pp. 128, 129 of Busch's book is devoted to "economism." Busch's "economism" is so close to his marketism that the difference is hardly discernable. Both must be classified on the "undue fear" side of marketism.

Busch considered religion as a possible fourth leviathan (pp. 133, 134). He examined various forms of Christian, Judaic, and Islamic fundamentalism as sources of undue faith in the particular kind of religious fundamentalism each endorses. Had Busch written after 9–11, 2001, he would likely have treated religion as a leviathan not only in NY, DC and PA, but in Ireland, the near east, and during the partition of India. H. Smith concentrates so much on the evils of scientism that he neglects the immorality of religious institutions, though he does consider the restrictive nature of Christian fundamentalism (pp. 209–212). Charles Kimball's commendable *When Religion Becomes Evil* (2002) looks particularly at what causes some components of the great faiths (Judaism, Islam and Christianity, both Catholic and Protestant) to become immoral. Kimball's book clearly treats religion as sometimes, even often, a fourth leviathan. As such it complements Busch's broader analysis. Busch's brief consideration of religion focuses on it as a possible solution for the immorality generated by his three -ismatic leviathans. He looked at fundamentalist rather than the main bodies of Christian, Judaic and Islamic thought and found little reason to expect them to overcome the immoralities originating with his other leviathans. As for Busch's other three leviathans, religious eclipses of morality involve both those who have *undue faith* in the order supposedly arising from a particular fundamentalism and those who *fear unduly* the order various religions and their associated fundamentalisms often strive to establish. There are religious conservatives and liberals, "rightist" and "leftist" advocates of autocratic and participatory religious governments and institutions, anti and pro free markets contenders, scientistic supporters and opposers as well as anti and pro groups *vis à vis* different faiths, denominations and sects. Had Busch fully treated religious fundamentalism (alternatively, extremism, radicalism, fanaticism and literalism) as a fourth leviathan, he would have probably ignored those who unduly fear religious fundamentalism while concentrating on undue fundamental religious faith much as is the case for his concern about undue faith in the orders generated by science, states and markets.

This section has stressed the existence of both *undue faith* and *undue fear* of Busch's three "ismic" leviathans and of religious fundamentalists and sects. Neither Busch nor H. Smith stress this symmetry. Busch does recognize that science, states and markets make substantial contributions to our modern world while H. Smith vouches for religion and for science as opposed to scientism. This reviewer holds that deep academic understandings are available to help circumvent the eclipses of morality originating in both undue faith and undue fear of the four kinds of order generated by science, states, markets and religions.

THE NEGLECT OF THE SOCIAL SCIENTISTS IN THE CURRENT SCIENCE/RELIGION DIALOGUES AND THE MISHANDLING OF MARKET THEORY BY BUSCH AND H. SMITH

For more than a decade, there has been an intense science-theology dialogue. Funds from the Sir John Templeton Foundation have fueled this dialogue. Busch's book does not reference this dialogue. H. Smith's does so (pp. 75–77, 201, 202) with focus on the Center for Theology and the Natural Sciences at Berkeley and on the Zygon Center at the Lutheran School of Theology at Chicago. More recently (October, 2001), Harvard joined the dialogue with a three-day international conference entitled "The Quest for Truth, Knowledge and Values in Science and Religion." H. Smith correctly deplores the scientism, as he defines scientism, of the Berkley/Chicago effort. Smith's scientism also characterizes the Harvard effort though to a lesser degree.

Templeton funding stresses the natural sciences to the neglect of the social. While H. Smith is dissatisfied with the scientism of the Templeton/Berkley/Chicago dialogues, he does not regret the omission of the social science that he regards (along with the sociologist Robert Bellah), as based on the scientistic assumptions of "positivistic, reductionistic relativism and determinism," (p. 84) and as being "the very ethos of modernity" (p. 85).

Most theologians are inadequately educated with respect to economics. Though the labor theory of value of classical economics had lost much of its credibility before Marx's time, Marx used the theory ideologically with great unfortunate impact on the 20th century world. Many theologians still react favorably to Marxian labor theory ideology, such as David Jenkins (2000), Samuel Gregg (2001), John Atherton (1992), and Samuel Brittan (1998). Somewhat similarly, some sociologists do likewise. In the current science/religion debate one group of theologians at the Acton Institute, with their journal, *Markets and Morality*, established in 1998, displays rather full comprehension of how free uncoerced exchange among individuals optimizes welfare within a given pattern of ownership. This gives them some justified faith in the order markets can establish. Unfortunately they seem to be, in Busch's terms, anti-statists who fear unduly what governments so. Thus, they fail to acknowledge the full meaning of Arrow's theorem and do not see that political entities (governments) may need to redistribute the ownership of rights and privileges to the disadvantaged such as women, racial minorities and the poverty stricken. Acton Institute personnel would and do advocate that individuals *voluntarily* redistribute ownership patterns in accordance with Christian (and Judaic and Islamic) teaching. However the Institute seems to have a fear – inconsistent with a full understanding of Arrow's theorem – that government can do no good. In Busch's terms they are marketistic. There is a need to go beyond the morality of single decision units to the redistributive morality of public decision made in politics, statesmanship, macro-economics, administration with respect to technical change, education humanistic advances, religious changes and indeed, reforms, revolutions and, yes, war.

The following is a quotation from an earlier work by this reviewer that draws meaningfully from Frank Knight's contributions to economic literature (Johnson 1986, pp. 77–79):

Among those in the early neoclassical period who greatly extended our understanding of the morality, immorality or lack of morality of markets in their broad sense was Frank Knight. In his book entitled *The Economic Organization* (1951, orig. 1933, pp. 59–66), Knight clarified how markets determine prices, income distribution, patterns of resource utilization, production and consumption and, less explicitly, savings and dissavings. In his *Ethics of Competition*, Knight also wrote (1936, p. 56) that '...income does not go to factors but to their owners, and can in no case have more ethical justification than has the fact of ownership. The ownership of personal or material productive capacity is based on a complex mixture of inheritance, luck and effort.... What is the ideal distribution form the standpoint of ... ethics may be disputed but of the three considerations named above certainly none but the effort can have ethical validity.' He also wrote (1936, p. 58), 'It (the market) distributes the produce of industry on the basis of power which is ethical only insofar as right and might are one. It (again the market) is a confessed failure in the field of promoting social progress, and its functions in this regard are being progressively taken over by other social agencies.' In another book entitled *Freedom and Reform*, Knight (1947, p. 67) noted that the savings and dissavings determined through time in a market characterized by nonequal initial endowments of income earning rights and privileges can be expected to lead to 'cumulative increase in inequality of ... power.' No wonder another of Knight's students refers to Knight as 'the radical economist and the conservative' (Patinkin, 1962, p. 798).

Whether we are concerned with decisions about the *technologies* and *resource* and changes that grows out of biophysical scientific advances, or the *institutional* and human changes that grow out of social science research, the social sciences are essential in understanding decisions about the creation, adoption and evaluation of the *four fundamental changes* that characterize progress in the modern world (North, 1966, p. 973). Such decisions are not understandable without scientific, as opposed to scientistic, social sciences.

Our scientific (social as well as biophysical) knowledge of our material and non-material sub worlds and all our institutions is all social in nature. We deprive ourselves unduly if we ignore the social sciences in our science/religion dialogue and when considering eclipses of morality.

Prescriptive and proscriptive knowledge is about "oughts" and "ought nots." Such knowledge is not based directly on experience. Instead it is derived by processing empirical knowledge about both the material world and values (goodness and badness) through decision processes. The sciences (biophysical and social) generate much empirical knowledge about values (goodness and badness), including conditions, situations and things essential for and of great usefulness in making both private and social decisions. The biophysical sciences are particularly good at generating knowledge about instrumental values, i.e. the goodness of proteins in the diets of children, animals and fowl. Such social sciences disciplines and sub disciplines as economics, political economy, institutional economics, sociology and anthropology, generate much knowledge about extrinsic or exchange values, non-monetary and monetary. They use experiences and logic to generate knowledge with which social systems (such as markets, governmental and non-governmental institutions) generate exchange values, with the decision processes they employ (Schmid, 1997 and Samuels, Medema & Schmid, 1997). When a science becomes scientistic the metaphysical and epistemological non-empirical presuppositions of logical positivism deprive that science of the empirical knowledge it is capable of generating about values (Moore (1956), C. I. Lewis (1955), and Achinstein and Barker (1969) among many others).

Every social science, and every biophysical science at one time or another, has partially sterilized itself by becoming scientistic. Among economists making such unfortunate attempts are Nevelle Keynes (1963), father of John Maynard Keynes, Harry Johnson (1975, pp. 149–152) and Milton Freidman (1953, 1962) all of whom seem to have compromised the social science of economics by trying to make it scientistic in the Huston Smith sense if not in the Busch sense.

H. Smith and Bellah, too, seem totally unaware of the common history of economic and philosophic value thought, including the labor theory of value, utilitarianism, and physicocratic (land and nature) theories of value. They are unaware of the significance of having Marshall (1946, orig. 1890) in England and Clark in the U.S. merge cost or supply side explanations of value with demand side (utility, needs, desire) explanations into a single interactive explanation of exchange (extrinsic) values, both monetary and non monetary. Such perceptions of quantitatively measurable values are hardly positivistic through, perhaps, somewhat reductionist. Since Marshall's and Clark's breakthrough, welfare economics, with its inherent attention to more intrinsic values, has developed through the thought and empirical work of A. C. Pigou (1962, orig. 1920), Pareto (see Hicks, 1939, pp. 1–43; Arrow, 1951, pp. 13, 36), Hicks (1939), Arrow (1951), Etzioni (1988), Sen (1984), Ayres, and many others including the empiricists who emerged from the pragmatic Wisconsin School of Institutional Economics and those scientists at the National Bureau of Economic Research who developed the U.S. national income accounts and other empirical measures of the value of conditions, situations and things.

Institutional economists are more pragmatically (Dewey, 1938) than positivistically oriented. They are concerned with the processes whereby market, political and other social institutions establish extrinsic values both non monetary and monetary (Samuels, Medema & Schmid, 1997).

Both institutional economists and political economists (keep in mind the *Journal of Political Economy*) are concerned about institutions and institutional changes that establish and maintain ownership of property and political rights and privileges without which market and democratic institution are unworkable. How the ownership of property rights and privileges is distributed determines what non-coerced exchanges are possible in free markets. Such distributions also empower their owners to become productive contributing members of society. The same institutions that establish such ownership patterns must also protect their owners from involuntary deprivation of those rights and privileges by others – otherwise the "evil side" of human nature will prompt people to engage in involuntary (unfree) deprivation of the ownership distributions. It is important to note that redistribution of the ownership of *political* rights and privileges typically involves the possibility of imposing (by some level of majority rule) individually unacceptable redistributions of property rights and privileges on producers, consumers and resource owners. A full understanding that the economics of non-coerced, mutually acceptable exchanges involves only a limited maximization of general welfare is crucial. Market maximizations apply *only* for the distribution of property rights and privileges that exists. They do not maximize across other possible distributions. The crucial point to note here is that the maximization of welfare that results from free, voluntary, mutually acceptable exchanges cannot be used as moral justification for either preserving or changing an existing distribution of ownership of rights and privileges. Neither marketists who have undue faith in the market nor market order can find justification for their fears or faiths. Market adjustments are morally justified in the theory but not redistributions of the rights and privileges within which a market operates. Justification of redistribution of such ownership patterns requires a greater morality than that of free markets. Except for his own contribution in the book being reviewed here, Busch confines his attention to the social sciences, mainly to marketism and statism, without covering economics, political science, or their blend, political economy in an adequate manner. Huston Smith's coverage of the social sciences is even less adequate. In a sense both authors join those engaging in the Templeton Foundation's inspired science/religion scientistic dialogue that neglects the social sciences. Scientistic neglect of the social sciences is not new as reflected by the exclusion of the social sciences from the American National Academy of Sciences and from the conception of science in modern thought.

THE GENERAL NEGLECT OF MULTIDISCIPLINARITY AND PROFESSIONS BY BUSCH AND HIS CONTEMPORARIES**

Busch, H. Smith, most participants in the ongoing science/religion dialogue, and many post-modernists do not grasp the importance of the multidisciplinary professionals as generators of value and prescriptive (or proscriptive) knowledge. Professionals (entrepreneurs, engineers, politicians, MD's, public administrators, business administrators, educators, farmers, parents, resource owners, agriculturalist, architects – the list goes on) make crucial decisions about the four driving forces for society: technical change, human development, institutional improvements, and resource preservation and enhancement.

In making such decisions professionals both draw on existing and create new knowledge. Part of the knowledge they use and *create* is "positivistic" knowledge about the material world. However they also find it necessary in making their decisions to use and create new knowledge about values (Johnson,

1986a, pp. 58–62) and (Johnson, 1997, pp. 271–282). The knowledge they develop about values as part of the real non-material world is based (like the knowledge developed about the material world created by disciplinary bio-physical scientists) on experience and logic. Prescriptive and proscriptive knowledge is an exception to this statement because such knowledge is obtained by processing experience-based knowledge through a decision rule that determines the prescription or proscription (Johnson, 1986a, b).

Large scale public and private professional decision making units often maintain bureaus and divisions designed to generate both value or positivistic knowledge for use in making prescriptive and proscriptive decisions about what "ought" or "ought not to be done" to solve the problems they face. Democratic *processes* generate such knowledge iteratively *and* interactively with their participants and produce much useful knowledge. Decision makers may also contract with disciplinary units of universities to generate needed information, a procedure that works well when the needed knowledge is specialized in one or a set of closely related disciplines. Another important source of both value and value free (relatively, at least) knowledge are the processes used in solving problems. These processes are governmental (particularly democratic ones; Busch, Ch. 6), administrative, and social. Such processes "harvest" knowledge based on real world experiences of both the material world and the immaterial world of values, institutions, cultures, religions, etc. The more interactive and iterative these processes are, the more effective they are in harvesting knowledge (Johnson, 1996).

A tragedy of modern thought is that scientism does not grant respect to professional activity as an important source of knowledge about values. The experiential origin of such knowledge of values makes it more important with respect to morality than the logical but much less than the experiential knowledge of values generated by such abstract disciplines as theology and philosophy.

The specialized discipline of economics under the leadership of Frank Knight (1941) took the lead in developing dynamic decision making theory. Empirical work on private decision making processes of farmers in the 1950s and 1960s and by non-agriculturalists (Johnson et al., 1961), including leaders in the Harvard School of Business Administration, revealed the essential multidisciplinary decision process. This multidisciplinarity is inherent when making dynamic decisions concerning problem involving technical, institutional, human and/or resource changes. This multidisciplinarity moves decision theory out of the specialized discipline of economics where it originated into the multidisciplinary professions, the subject of this section (Schmid, 1997, Ch. 2 and 3).

Busch rejects rational choice theory (pp. 141–143). Following the sociologist Robert Bellah, H. Smith rejects (pp. 84–88) the social sciences as scientistic based on the assumption of "positivism, reductionism, relationism and determinism."

Busch and H. Smith have failed to get out of the sub-specialization of the specialized descriptive work of economics into the multidisciplinarity of professionals whose complexity seems to overwhelm the simple method of combining experience and logic to produce descriptive knowledge of the material and/or non-material worlds. This is because the multidisciplinary professions are concerned with producing prescriptive and proscriptive knowledge about rightness and wrongness, the "oughts" and "ought nots."

Even a brief and superficial sketch of the multidisciplinarity of both private and public dynamic decision making makes it clear that the eclipsing of morality is far deeper than Busch's concern about undue faith in the social orders that science, markets, states and (even) religions establish. Decision makers can carelessly fail to acquire enough or may wastefully acquire too much of different kinds of knowledge needed to make accurate decisions, thereby imposing immoral unjust losses or conferring immoral gains on various members of society. Even greater immorality occurs when decision makers succumb to opportunities to use false information in the pursuit of their own interests. That highly immoral tendency is offset by laws put in place by governmental as well as non-governmental institutions to protect accepted distributions of the ownership of rights and privileges. Such laws and regulations exist in all societies, both secular and religious. Societies experiencing rapid technical, human, institutional, and resource changes often find their laws and regulations have become obsolete. Such obsolescences open up opportunities for dishonest self-seeking immoral persons. Included among such persons and groups are business executives, some of both pro- and anti-free trade activists, religious leaders, politicians, those exploiting undue fear of technological advance as well as those with undue faith in it. The same is true of both those who fear governments can do no good and of those who believe governments can do no evil. There also seems to be less self-seeking but dishonest highly immoral activity among those who promote excessive equality in the possession of property, voting rights and the likes. This reviewer, having taken the reader into much more immorality than Busch, is now ready to turn in the next sections to religion, a topic skirted by Busch and not adequately treated by H. Smith.

POTENTIAL CONTRIBUTIONS OF RELIGIONS IN OVERCOMING IMMORALITY ARISING FROM UNDUE FAITH AND FEARS OF SCIENCE, MARKETS, STATES AND RELIGIOUS FUNDAMENTALISM

Much of what seems to be meant by extreme immorality involves self-serving dishonesty on the part of both public and private decision makers.

Morality seems easier to understand as the opposite of its negative – immorality. On the positive side of morality most if not all of the major religions of the world ascribe morality to honesty, love of fellow humans and, often, of nature itself. Humans seem to find it difficult to be honest and concerned about others as well as themselves (including their kin and kith). When dishonest self-serving activities are observed, they are recognized as immoral more quickly than are honest acts of love towards others (and nature) recognized to be moral. Busch's book does not indicate clearly what he means by the morality eclipsed by undue scientism, marketism, statism, and even religious fundamentalism. This reviewer regards morality as the opposite of the gross immorality which arises from self-serving dishonesty. The second section of this review focused on both the undue faiths and fears of the orders generated by Busch's three (possibly four) leviathans. A deeper understanding of morality and immorality emerges when self-seeking dishonesty arises in seeking the benefits of the orders generated by Busch's three (four?) leviathans. The major religions endorse honesty and love of others (including nature) as moral.

It seems undeniable that human beings have a tendency towards self-serving dishonesty. Such dishonesty is destructive of science, markets, governments, other social institutions and, indeed, religions. The human tendency toward self-serving dishonesty is so pervasive that even religious orders often succumb to it. One function of governments, religions, other institutions and legal systems is to protect people, science, governments, social institutions and religious organizations from the corruptions, theft, authoritarianism (the list goes on) that follow self-serving dishonesty. Though religions and religious hierarchies are also plagued by self-serving dishonesty, the world's great religions all promote honesty and love of fellow humans and nature. It is such honesty and love that make it possible to concentrate on the benefits of science, markets, governments and other institutions including, indeed, the world's religions without being overcome by undue faith in or fear of the order that science, markets, governments and religion establish in society.

IN CONCLUSION

This reviewer concludes that Busch has made a substantial contribution to the current extensive science/religion dialogue that neglects the social sciences. In addition to science (scientism), Busch expands the dialogue to include economics (marketism). The breadth Busch adds, *vis-à-vis* the social sciences, is much needed and welcomed by this reviewer. Such famous participants in the science/religion dialogue as Huston Smith (2001), Polkinghorne (1998), Nancy Murray (1990), Ted Peters (2003), Phillip Heifner (1993), and Whitehead (1978) neglect the social sciences. Busch pushes the dialogue in a needed direction without seemingly participating in the dialogue.

Huston Smith focuses on traditional, modern and post-modern thought with stress on the adverse role played by logically positivistic reductionism in modern thinking. By joining mainline philosophy in the abandonment of reductionist logical positivism, Smith avoids the modern and post-modern problems he finds afflicting present-day thought. Both authors accept the contributions of science while decrying the evils of "scientism" – defined in different ways however. Busch, a social scientist, does not regard the social sciences as scientistic; instead he regards economics as marketistic and political science as statistic involving undue faith in the *orders* they establish. Busch does not elaborate on his own apparently undue *fear* of the orders they establish, to include undue *faith* in those orders. Both are widely shared in society. Nor does Busch point out how deep basic understandings of science, economics, political science and, indeed, religion render such fears and faiths inappropriate even if they do exist in society. Neither Busch nor H. Smith stress how scientism (in the Smith sense) has restricted the social sciences. The social sciences are precluded from the National Academy of Science (in the U.S. if not in all countries), and apparently from most divinity schools (judging from ignorance of the social sciences in theological circles) and from positions of "high respect" in the so-called "Great Knowledge-based" universities of the U.S. "Scientism" in the H. Smith sense rejects the possibility of objective knowledge of such non-material "things" as institutions, culture, goodness and badness, and religion. "Scientism" denigrates such knowledge as "emotions," "subjective" and even as "superstitions" and in doing so degrades both the social sciences and theology.***

Busch and H. Smith, like most academicians, do not ascribe appropriate significance to the professions and the professionals and "doers" of society. It is their decisions and actions vis-à-vis new technology, institutional change, human development and resources enhancement that have great moral or immoral importance. It is engineers, teachers, business administrators, parents, public administrators, farmers, medical doctors, nurses, architects, civil servants, militarist soldiers and psychiatrists, priests (or pastors, rabbis, and imams) who make and execute the decisions we judge as moral or immoral. Dishonest self-seeking (as opposed to honest beneficent) decisions are a common mark of great immorality whether prompted by undue fear or faith in science, markets or governments – or something else that encourages the dishonest self-seeking decision.

Neglect of academia's professional units and activities by its scientistic leaders deprives academia of the knowledge pertaining to both the material and non-material worlds that is generated by the professionals and "doers" in society. Professional experiences and thinking (logic) generates much knowledge of the non material world that ranks as to objectivity with that about the material world generated by the most specialized of the scientific bio-physical disciplines. The more iterative and interactive such processes are, the more efficient they are in harvesting knowledge (Johnson, 1996).

Several levels of morality and immorality were distinguished in the section above on multidisciplinary professions. These include the erroneous (and hence immoral) decisions caused of undue faith in the orders created by science, markets and government as stressed by Busch. They also include erroneous decisions based on undue fear of such orders that Busch does not clearly recognize. Public and private decisions are often erroneous and immoral because decision makers fail to obtain as much information as is worthwhile (economically advantageous). Such information includes obtaining the deep understandings of science, markets, states and religion to avoid undue faiths and fears of the orders they create. A different but similar source of immorality plaguing both public and private decision making arises from failing to acquire worthwhile amounts of other kinds of knowledge concerning both the material and non-material. This is not adequately recognized as important by H. Smith. Busch, in his consideration of democratic processes does give some recognition to the importance of such knowledge.

In closing, Busch's book on the "eclipsing of morality" is important and helpful – it moves the social sciences and the question of morality into the current dialogue about science and religion. It is also related to the numerous diverse dialogues about modern vs. postmodern thought. This reviewer is grateful for the contribution Busch's book makes to rounding out the current science/religion and modernity/post-modernity dialogues. Most any participant in either or both of these dialogues will benefit from reading Busch's book.

Editor's note: As Allan Schmid explains in his note, he had to prepare this review essay from a handwritten draft. His efforts on this task are greatly appreciated as is the help provided by Larry Busch. I have further edited the text, wishing I had Glenn available to answer questions and make revisions. Glenn was the leader of a Science Religion Society study group at University Lutheran Church in East Lansing. He was a long-time student of methodology (he taught a graduate course on methodology which I attended) and had bases in both theory and experience for his identification and analysis of the epistemologically diverse types of knowledge encountered and produced in doing agricultural economics. He and the editor agreed on much except with regard to the possibility of the existence of objective values – a disagreement not over objective statements about values but whether values have an objective existence. We both also believed, for example, that religion – notwithstanding its tendency to theological absolutist formulation – was one of the domains in which questions of values were examined.

REFERENCES

Achinstein, P., & Barker, S. F. (1969). *The legacy of logical positivism: Studies in the philosophy of science*. Baltimore: Johns Hopkins Press.
Arrow, K. J. (1951). *Social choice and individual values*. New York: Wiley.

Atherton, J. (1992). *Christianity and the market: Christian social thought for our times*. London: SPCK Holy Trinity Church.

Brittan, S. (1998). *Essays, moral, political and economic*. Edinburgh: Edinburgh University Press.

Busch, L. (2000). *The eclipse of morality: Science, state and market*. New York: Aldine DeGruyter.

Desoto, H. (2000). *The mystery of capitalism*. New York: Basic Books.

Dewey, J. (1938). *Logic: The theory of inquiry*. New York: Henry Holt.

Etzioni, A. (1988). *The moral dimension: Toward a new economics*. New York: Free Press.

Ferré, F. (1996). *Being and value: Toward a constructive post-modern metaphysics*. Albany: State University of New York University Press.

Ferré, F. (1998). *Knowing and value: Toward a constructive postmodern epistemology*. Albany: State University of New York University Press.

Freidman, M. (1953). *Essays in positive economics*. Chicago: University of Chicago Press.

Freidman, M. (1962). *Capitalism and freedom*. Chicago: University of Chicago Press.

Georgescu-Roegan, N. (1971). *The entropy law and the economic process*. Cambridge, MA: Harvard University Press.

Gregg, S. (2001). *Economic thinking for the theologically minded*. New York: University Press of America.

Heifner, P. (1993). *The human factor*. Minneapolis: Fortress Press.

Hicks, J. R. (1939). *Value and capital*. Oxford: Oxford University Press.

Jenkins, D. (2000). *Market whys and human wherefors*. London: Cassell.

Johnson, G. L. (1986a). *Research methodology for economists: Philosophy and practice*. New York: Macmillan.

Johnson, G. L. (1986b). Economics and ethics. *The Centennial Review*, *30*(1), 69–108.

Johnson, G. L. (1996). A forward look at agricultural policy analysis, based on 1945–1995 experiences. *Agricultural History* (Spring), 153–176.

Johnson, G. L. (1997). *Philosophic conclusions. Beyond agriculture and economics* (edited by A. A. Schmid). East Lansing: Michigan State University Press.

Johnson, G. L., & Halter, A. et al. (1961). *A study of managerial processes of midwestern farmers*. Ames: Iowa State College Press.

Johnson, H. G. (1975). *On economics and society*. Chicago: University of Chicago Press.

Keynes, J. N. (1963). *Scope and method of political economy*. London: Macmillan.

Kimbal, C. (2002). *When religion becomes evil*. San Francisco: Harper-Collins.

Knight, F. (1941). *Risk, uncertainty, and profit*. Oxford: Oxford University Press.

Knight, F. (1947). *Freedom and reform: Essays in economics and social philosophy*. New York: Harper and Bros.

Knight, F. (1951). *The economic organization*. New York: Augustus M. Kelley.

Lewis, C. I. (1955). *The ground and nature of the right*. New York: Columbia University Press.

Marshall, A. (1946). *Principles of economics*. London: Macmillan.

McGinn, C. (1999). *The mysterious flame: Conscious minds in a material world*. New York: Basic Books.

Mearsheimer, J. J. (2002). Liberal talk, realistic thinking. *University of Chicago Magazine*, *94*(3), 24f.

Moore, G. E. (1956). *Principia ethica*. Cambridge: Cambridge University Press.

Murray, N. (1990). *Theology in the age of scientific reasoning*. Ithaca: Cornell University Press.

North, D. (1966). *Growth and welfare in the American past*. Englewood Cliffs, NJ: Prentice-Hall.

Patinkin, D. (1962). Frank Knight as teacher. *American Economic Review*, *63*(5), 798.

Peters, T. (2003). *Science, theology and ethics*. Burlington VT: Ashgate.

Pigou, A. C. (1932). *Economics of welfare*. London: Macmillan.

Polkinghorne, J. C. (1998). *Belief in God in an age of science*. New Haven: Yale University Press.

Reder, M. (1947). *Studies in the theory of welfare economics.* New York: Columbia University Press.

Samuels, W. (1974). *Pareto on policy.* Amsterdam: Elsevier.

Samuels, W. J., Medema, S. G., & Schmid, A. A. (1997). *The economy as a process of valuation.* Cheltenham, UK: Edward Elgar.

Schmid, A. A. (Ed.) (1997). *Beyond agriculture and economics.* East Lansing: Michigan State University Press.

Sen, A. (1984). *Resources, value and development.* Cambridge, MA: Harvard University Press.

Smith, H. (2001). *Why religion matters: The fate of the human spirit in an age of disbelief.* San Francisco: Harper.

Stigler, G. J. (1946). *The theory of price.* New York: Macmillan.

Thompson, K. (1966). *The moral issues in statecraft.* Baton Rouge: Louisiana State University Press.

Walsh, D. (1999). *The third millenium: Reflections on faith and reason.* Washington: Georgetown University Press.

Whitehead, A. N. (1978). *Process and reality.* New York: Free Press.

Yergin, D., & Stanislaw, J. (1998). *Commanding heights: The battle for the world economy.* New York: Simon & Schuster.

Wood's THE CORRESPONDENCE OF THOMAS REID

Marianne Johnson

A review essay on *The Correspondence of Thomas Reid*, **Paul Wood, Ed., University Park, PA: Pennsylvania State University Press, 2002.**

1. INTRODUCTION

Thomas Reid (1710–1796) was the originator of the Scottish philosophy of common sense, an approach that claims reality is objective and knowable, made up of material objects, and understandable by ordinary men. Common sense philosophy developed in opposition to the pervasive skepticism of the period, best exemplified by David Hume. A professor of philosophy at King's College, Aberdeen, Reid was chosen to be the successor to Adam Smith as the chair of Moral Philosophy at the University of Glasgow. From that position, Reid played an important role in the Scottish Enlightenment as professor, scholar, and correspondent. While Reid was not an economist, he did write on important theoretical and philosophical issues in moral philosophy, the natural sciences and mathematics. Reid may prove additionally interesting to economists for his insightful critique of Smith's *Theory of Moral Sentiments*.

The *Correspondence of Thomas* Reid (2002) is part of the Edinburgh Edition of Thomas Reid, a series of ten volumes (re)publishing the works of Reid (1995–2007). The collection includes Reid's major publications including *Essays on the Intellectual Powers of Man*, as well as minor essays, works in mathematics

A Research Annual
Research in the History of Economic Thought and Methodology, Volume 23-A, 229–236
© 2005 Published by Elsevier Ltd.
ISSN: 0743-4154/doi:10.1016/S0743-4154(05)23013-4

and the natural sciences, theories on the arts, and commentaries on university life. The volume reviewed here is the fourth of the ten volumes. The collection is part of a broader effort directed at understanding Reid. The Thomas Reid project was established in 1997 by the University of Aberdeen to make use of its extensive collection of Reid manuscripts. The Reid Project began the *Journal of Reid Studies* (now the *Journal of Scottish Philosophy*) and has hosted several international symposia devoted to Reid and Scottish Enlightenment Philosophy. Although the Reid Project has since been re-founded as the Centre for the Study of Scottish Philosophy, it still maintains a particular emphasis on Reid-related research and studies.

In all, roughly half of the letters included in *The Correspondence of Thomas Reid* by Wood have been previously published. William Hamilton (1863) published some of Reid's letters, particularly those to Lord Kames and Dr. James Gregory. Hamilton's collection was republished in 1994. An additional three letters in the *Correspondence* (numbers 17, 19, and 52) had been published by Ian Simpson Ross (1965). This leaves approximately fifty letters published in Wood's volume for the first time. In addition, the seventy-one pages of detailed annotations will undoubtedly prove helpful to the modern reader, as will the comprehensive index.

The collection is further valuable because of the approach to editing taken by Wood. Wood lays out nine editorial principles, consistent with modern historiographic work, that preserves the letters. The original spelling, grammar, and capitalization are used, expanding only contractions or abbreviations that would not be clear to readers today (Wood, 2002, pp. xv, xvi). Wood indicates where missing or illegible words have been filled in. An additional advantage is Wood's attempt to identify the dates, locations, and recipients or senders of letters; all inferences or assumptions made are indicated in the textual notes. Ross found that the letters published by Hamilton (1863) "do not differ significantly from the manuscript ones – there are changes in the punctuation and there are a few trivial omissions" (Ross, 1965, p. 22), and therefore decides to publish only the three new letters available. However, Ross's overall opinion is that Reid's letters are "not outstanding ... [with] workmanlike prose" (1965, p. 22). In contrast, Wood argues that "Hamilton's editing practice inevitably reflected the standards of his day and, as a result, his texts are not accurate. Hamilton systematically altered Reid's spellings, misunderstood Reid's spacing and paragraph conventions, eliminated or occasionally bowdlerized passages, changed wordings and conflated letters together" (Wood, 2002, p. ix). This new collection should allow scholars better opportunity to judge Reid's correspondence for themselves.

Perhaps because it was planned as part of the Edinburgh Series on Thomas Reid, *The Correspondence of Thomas Reid* provides the reader with only two-pages of introduction and no biographical information on Reid. There is no attempt to place the letters within the context of current debates concerning Reid. This essay attempts to place the letters within the broader context of the Scottish Enlightenment. Section two provides biographical information on Reid. Section three considers some aspects of the letters, including what the letters add to our understanding of the personal and professional connections of members of the Scottish Enlightenment, and how the letters may shed new light on the origins of Reid's philosophy.

2. LIFE OF THOMAS REID

Thomas Reid was born in Strachan, Kincardineshire, Scotland on February 1, 1710. He was a contemporary of both David Hume – who was born on the same date in 1711 – and Emmanuel Kant. On the paternal side, Reid was descended from a long line of Presbyterian ministers and on the maternal side from the intellectual and mathematical Gregory clan. Reid attended the University of Aberdeen, graduating in 1726. He spent ten years in his first job as the librarian for the university. During this period he read mathematics extensively. In 1737, Reid succeeded to a living as minister in Newmachar. While his parishioners did not initially welcome Reid, reportedly dunking him in a pond at one point, he eventually became a popular minister, though not a distinguished preacher. Reid married his cousin in 1740 and had a number of children, only one of whom survived him.

In 1752, Reid was elected chair of Philosophy at Kings College, Aberdeen. Wood's inclusion of letters regarding university life that have not been previously published will be of interest to any scholar of university institutions and history. Many of Reid's complaints regarding students, meetings, and university politics ring true today:

> There is no part of my time more disagreeably spent than that which is spent in College meetings, of which we have often five or six a week. And I should have been attending one this moment if a bad cold I have got had not furnished me with an Excuse. These meetings are become more disagreeable by an Evil Spirit of Party that seems to put us in a ferment and I am afraid will produce bad consequences (Reid, 2002, p. 46).

Reid's interest in philosophy dates from his reading of Hume's *Treatise on Human Nature* (1739–1740), an approach to philosophy with which Reid profoundly disagreed. Hume's writings provided the impetus for the founding of the Aberdeen Philosophical Society (also known as the Wise Club), whose members included Dr. John Gregory, George Campbell, and James Beattie. Discussions in the society resulted in Reid's *Enquiry into the Human Mind on the Principles of Common Sense* (1764).

In 1764, Reid succeeded Adam Smith as a professor of moral philosophy at the University of Glasgow, largely through the support of Lord Kames. Once there, Reid seemed pleased to have attracted a larger enrollment than his predecessor (Reid, 2002, p. 57). He published very little during this period. Upon his retirement, Reid produced his two most important works: *Essay on the Intellectual Powers of Man* (1785), and *Essays on the Active Powers of the Human Mind* (1788).

While Reid was primarily a philosopher with interests in mathematics and the natural sciences, like many great intellectuals Reid was interested in a wide variety of subjects, including economics. Reid followed American colonial and British relations, contemplating the economic impact of the Stamp Act on Glasgow merchants (Reid, 2002, pp. 46, 57, 58, 98), as well as the influence of shipping and storage costs on prices (Reid, 2002, pp. 97, 291). Reid read the Glasgow Literary Society papers on economic topics and was familiar with Jeremy Bentham's writings on usury and philosophy. Reid also read James Stewart, Richard Price, and Joseph Priestly. In 1767, Reid commented that

> I have gone over Sir James Stewart's great Book of Political Oeconomy, wherein I think there is a great deal of good Materials; carelessly put together indeed; but I think it contains more sound principles concerning Commerce & Police than any book we have yet had (Reid, 2002, p. 61).

In his later years, Reid's interests returned to mathematics and natural sciences, and these interests came to dominate his letters. After his death in 1796, Reid's writings on the fine arts and his graduation addresses to the students of King's College were published. His philosophical teachings continued to be promoted by William Hamilton and Dugald Stewart; the latter wrote Reid's biography (Stewart, 1803). However, Reid's approach to philosophy probably had the longest impact in America. Reid's philosophy significantly influenced John Witherspoon, Samuel Stanhope Smith, and Thomas Jefferson. Reid's common sense version of Scottish Enlightenment Philosophy came to dominate the teachings at American universities for fifty years after his death.

3. LETTERS AND SUMMARY

Roughly categorized, of the letters in this volume, 21 address issues of natural science, experiments and the philosophy of science; 7 discuss topics in mathematics; 32 include discussions of moral philosophy; 30 focus on university life; 8 discuss current political or economic events; and 33 are devoted to family, personal inquiries, and private business, largely with his book dealers and publishers. The first letter dates from 1736, when Reid was 26 years old. Reid was not a prolific letter writer like Benjamin Franklin, nor did he produce as many letters as even Adam Smith. Thus, included in *The Correspondence of Thomas Reid* are just 131 letters. In addition to these known surviving letters, Wood's edition also contains a valuable list of lost letters.

The letters should prove interesting to scholars in such diverse fields as mathematics, natural science, philosophy, history, and economics. In particular, two aspects of this collection are discussed here: (1) how the letters offer better-defined relationships between the different individuals of the Scottish Enlightenment period; and (2) how the letters illustrate some of the origins of Reid's philosophy including his emphasis on mathematics and his firm belief that common sense should be applied to all problems.

By including the entire correspondence of Reid in his volume, Wood has made it easier to trace the relationships and intellectual influences of individuals of the late 18th century in Scotland. Included in the collection is an exchange of letters between Reid and David Hume in 1763 regarding Reid's *Enquiry into the Human Mind*. Initially provided with a copy of Reid's text by Hugh Blair, a mutual acquaintance, there is a scathing criticism privately sent from Hume to Blair. This can be compared with Hume's collegial letter sent directly to Reid (Reid, 2002, pp. 18, 29, 30) and Reid's somewhat humorous response to Hume in which Reid implores, "if you write no more in morals politicks or metaphysicks, I am afraid we shall be at a loss for Subjects" (Reid, 2002, pp. 30, 31). The tone of both letters suggests why the correspondence did not continue, though Ross attributes this to Hume's wish to avoid controversy (Mossner & Ross, 1977, p. 291).[1]

Reid's primary interest in economics was usury, a topic on which he wrote a paper for the Glasgow Literary Society in 1778 and which was the general focus of several letters to Richard Price, along with reversionary payments and the national debt (Reid, 2002, pp. 63, 64). In a letter to Jeremy Bentham, Reid wrote

> I suspect that the general Principle, that Bargains ought to be left to the Judgment of the Parties, may admit of some Exceptions, when the Buyers are the many, the Poor, & the Simple, the Sellers few rich & cunning, the former may need the Aid of the Magistrate to prevent their being oppressed by the latter ... But with regard to the Loan of Money in a commercial State, the Exception can have no place. The Borrowers & Lenders are upon an equal footing, and Each may be left to take Care of his own Interest ... (Reid, 2002, pp. 202, 203).

James Gregory had initially shared Reid's writings on usury with George Wilson. Wilson, in turn, forwarded the essay to Bentham with the introduction that "It may perhaps amuse you to look into the Enclosed Paper ... the Writer is Dr. Reid Professor of Moral Philosophy at Glasgow ... but consider that the Author is a Clergyman and wrote a good many years ago when Theories were much the fashion in Scotland" (Reid, 2002, pp. 201, 202). That said, Bentham considered referring to Reid's support for his own point of view in the preface to the second edition of *Defense of Usury*, indicating that Reid, generally, was held in high regard (see Ross, 1977, p. 402n). In addition, Bentham may have discussed some details of Reid's essay with Adam Smith.

While many of the letters between Reid and Lord Kames were available in the Hamilton (1863) edition, now that they are presented with the original spelling, grammar, and capitalization, the letters provide a more intimate look into the close relationship between Lord Kames and Reid. They shared interests in natural science and moral philosophy and many of their letters discuss methodological and philosophical issues of science, such as how to interpret events and experiments, how to form hypotheses, and the theories and philosophy of Isaac Newton. Not always in agreement, Reid lamented to Lord Kames, "To what Cause is it owing that I differ so much from your Lordship in Physicks, when we differ so little in Metaphysicks?" (Reid, 2002, p. 147).

It is interesting that despite personal connections – for example with Lord Kames and Henry Herbert – Reid and Adam Smith do not seem to have had any direct contact and there is no documentation of letters exchanged. Upon becoming the Chair of Moral Philosophy at Glasgow, Reid had to ask students if they had notes from any of Smith's lectures (Ross, 1995, p. 125). In this collection of letters, of particular interest to Smith scholars will be the exchange between Lord Kames and Reid regarding Kames' critique of Smith's *Theory of Moral Sentiments*. The letters provide some insight into the evolution of Kames' thought on Smith's formulation of sympathy. The letters also discuss the extent to which Kames ought to share his critique with Smith, given their personal acquaintance (Reid, 2002, pp. 103–106 and 106–109). That much of Kames' correspondence was destroyed is unfortunate. Undoubtedly, Kames' letters on this subject would be enlightening, both regarding Smith's Moral Philosophy, but also likely regarding Reid's own criticism of Smith's sympathy as represented in *The Theory of Moral Sentiments*.

Following the death of Kames, Dugald Stewart and James Gregory became the primary correspondents of Reid, and Richard Price provided important intellectual stimulation. *Essay on the Intellectual Powers of the Human Mind* was dedicated to Gregory and Stewart, with much correspondence between them on philosophical and technical details (Reid, 2002, pp. 166–168). Gregory, Price, and Stewart all received complimentary copies of the book (Reid, 2002, p. 177).

Early letters by Reid and letters to diverse individuals help establish the foundations of his philosophy. In particular, the letters offer evidence of Reid's transition from mathematics to philosophy and consistently show his efforts to apply the rigor of mathematics to more amorphous aspects of philosophy. Reid argued that only mathematics clearly and definitively defines terms (Reid, 2002,

p. 24; see also Reid on Newton's definitions, p. 125); other fields of thinking ought to attempt similar standards. Reid frequently used mathematical examples to make a philosophical point in his letters. For Reid, much of the appeal of mathematics was its "common sense." In response to Hume's claim that what the human mind can conceive is possible, Reid offered counterexamples from mathematics to both Lord Kames and Price in separate letters. In each case, Reid demonstrated that he conceived of things that cannot be mathematically true (Reid, 2002, pp. 82, 87–90, 159, 160, and 224–227). Similarly, early letters indicate Reid's reversion to common sense to solve problems. Things or ideas that run counter to common sense were to be distrusted (Reid, 2002, p. 23), whereas, for example, gravity is obvious because it is consistent with common sense (Reid, 2002, pp. 136–139, 139–146). In all his works, Reid sought to connect common sense and reason, demonstrating that common sense is really just one aspect of reason.

Wood's *The Correspondence of Thomas Reid* adds to our knowledge of the life and ideas of Reid. Although I suspect the volume will prove most interesting to scholars interested in the history and development of ideas in mathematics and the natural sciences, those with a wide definition of economics and the topics thus related will find much value in Reid's work in terms of the development his ideas and the thinking of the Scottish Enlightenment generally.

NOTE

1. The collection also provides some additional insights into the antagonism evident between James Beattie and Joseph Priestly, as well as discussion as to whether Beattie ought to respond to Priestly's attack on Reid. Preistly had claimed in reference to Reid that "such gross ignorance in a professor . . . in so considerable an university . . . is disgraceful to himself and to the university (Reid, 2002, pp. 90 and 288). Reid, himself, had refused to respond, stating that Preistly was "a man not to be convinced even in a Matter of fact" (Reid, 2002, p. 90). Hume may have had the last word in an advertisement for the first posthumous edition of *Essays and Treatises*, Hume offered "a compleat Answer to Dr. Reid and to that bigoted silly Fellow Beattie" (Mossner & Ross, 1977, p. 169).

REFERENCES

Mossner, E. C., & Ross, I. S. (1977). *"Preface," The correspondence of Adam Smith*. Oxford: Clarendon.
Reid, T. (1994 [1863]). *The works of Thomas Reid* (edited by Sir. W. Hamilton). Bristol, England: Thoemmes Press.

Reid, T. (2002). *The correspondence of Thomas Reid* (edited by P. Wood). University Park: Pennsylvania
    State University.
Ross, I. (1965). The unpublished letters of Thomas Reid to Lord Kames 1762–1782. *Texas Studies in
    Literature and Language, 7*, 17–65.
Ross, I. S. (1995). *The life of Adam Smith*. Oxford: Clarendon Press.
Stewart, D. (1803). *Account of the life and writings of Thomas Reid*. Ediburgh: William Creech.

Featherman and Vinovskis's SOCIAL SCIENCE AND POLICY MAKING

William J. Barber

A review essay on *Social Science and Policy Making: A Search for Relevance in the Twentieth Century*, **David L. Featherman and Maris A. Vinovskis, Eds. University of Michigan Press, 2001, pp. ix, 228.**

This volume contains eight papers occasioned by the celebration of the fiftieth anniversary of the Institute of Social Research at the University of Michigan. Most of the essays can be bracketed into two distinct groups. The first surveys the interactions between academic social scientists and decision-makers on public policies as they have evolved in the United States. The second is built around case studies of the influence (or lack thereof) of social scientists in the shaping of policies for Head Start, the various attempts to "fix" welfare programs, and potential programs to assist the elderly in an aging society. The thread connecting these contributions is signaled in the sub-title. Whether the insights of social sciences have lost relevance in public decision-making and, if so, how they might regain it, pose questions that are very much worth asking.

Students of the history of economic thought are likely to be particularly attracted to the chapters surveying the involvement of social scientists with American governmental structures. Of the three chapters in this genre, two are by the co-editors and the third by Martin Bulmer. As the story unfolds here, aspirations of citizens to promote reforms through systematic empirical investigations date back to the formation of the American Social Science Association in the wake of the Civil War. This was an organization of the socially concerned – many of whom had been

A Research Annual
Research in the History of Economic Thought and Methodology, Volume 23-A, 237–243
Copyright © 2005 by Elsevier Ltd.
All rights of reproduction in any form reserved
ISSN: 0743-4154/doi:10.1016/S0743-4154(05)23014-6

prominent abolitionists – and its ranks contained a mix of academicians, journalists, social workers, and clergy, along with a leavening of public spirited businessmen. The ASSA published a journal in which findings of its members were reported, but it would be a stretch to identify any policy-making success for which it could claim significant responsibility. Nonetheless, the ASSA left a legacy: it provided the seedbed in which a number of professional social science organizations were to sprout: e.g. the American Economic Association, the American Political Science Association, and the American Sociological Association.

During World War I, a substantial cohort of academicians were drawn to Woodrow Wilson's administration to staff agencies created by the emergency. But, more than any other figure, Herbert Hoover was responsible for providing a beachhead in a peacetime government for academic social scientists. At a number of points, the contributors draw attention to the path-breaking nature of the study he commissioned, which appeared in 1933, as *Recent Social Trends in the United States*, directed by William Ogborn, the University of Chicago sociologist. The prototype for the Ogborn volume, however, is not mentioned. It was inspired by Hoover who, as Secretary of Commerce in the Harding-Coolidge administrations, persuaded Wesley C. Mitchell, based at Columbia University and the National Bureau of Economic Research, to recruit a team of academic economists to examine the American economy sector by sector. This volume was published in March 1929 under the title *Recent Economic Changes*. Perhaps it is just as well that this effort to provide a briefing book for future economic policy makers should pass unremarked. Its substance emphasized what appeared to be the success stories of the American economy in the 1920s. A careful reader would not have been prepared for the economic collapse touched off by the stock market meltdown dating from October 1929. While Hoover provided the momentum to launch these studies, it should be noted that the needed funding was supplied by private philanthropies, not by tax-payer's dollars.

Appropriately, the authors take note of the sea change that accompanied Roosevelt's New Deal. Some academics were then appointed to high profile jobs in the bureaucracy from which they could both determine and implement policies, and not simply to offer policy advice. An important qualifier should be noted here: most of the social scientists who assumed those positions were outside the mainstream of their professional disciplines. The career of Rexford Guy Tugwell, an economist at Columbia University, is a case in point. If members of the American Economic Association had been asked in 1933 to nominate candidates qualified to serve as a President's senior economic adviser, Tugwell's name would not have been on the list. His brand of interventionist institutionalism did not sit well with most of his academic colleagues. Yet he had won FDR's confidence with his service in the original "Brains Trust" and became a senior policy planner in the Department of Agriculture. From that position, he designed and oversaw a genuine revolution in U.S. farm policy. The Agriculture Adjustment Act of 1933 was cut to his specifications. The supply management approach – in which Federal authorities were authorized to subsidize producers of major crops if they agreed to limit production – was an authentically innovative departure and it was put in place despite the opposition of the organized farm lobbies. There could be no question that a version of social science had policy relevance here. But this version was not the one preferred by the bulk of economists in the academic establishment of the day. This point does not come through in the volume under review.

Another nuance of economic policy-making in the Roosevelt years deserves to be treated, but it is not. The authors seem to identify with the view articulated by Keynes in the last paragraph of *The General Theory*. As will be recalled, he wrote there that "madmen in authority, who hear voices in the air, are distilling their frenzy from some academic scribbler of a few years back." This view of the world suggests that initiatives in policy formulation come from academicians. This is not always true – and it certainly was not so in the United States in 1937–1938. At that time, economists within the bureaucracy – most of whom (like Lauchlin Currie) were refugees from the academy where they had been denied permanent employment – came up with analytic diagnoses of the recession of 1937–1938. Their reading of this phenomenon indicated that it had been caused by a reduction in the net contribution of government to spending. It followed that a remedy should be sought through deliberate enlargement in deficit spending and in enhanced programs of transfers to improve the lot of those at the lower end of the income distribution. These recommendations left their mark on New Deal policy and they were informed by an Americanized version of Keynesianism. All of this was a by-product of insider learning within the bureaucracy – and the insiders were well ahead of most their colleagues in the academy.

It is properly pointed out here that the Employment Act of 1946 "provided for unusually close ties between economists and policy makers" (p. 47) through the creation of the Council of Economic Advisers. But a reminder is in order about what did not happen. This legislation was indeed a landmark in providing institutionalized space within government for a group of social science professionals. In 1946, however, those most active in promoting the formation of the CEA (the bulk of whom were then associated with the Bureau of the Budget) were on the verge of recommending to President Truman that he veto the bill that emerged from the Congressional pipeline. The reason: it fell so far short of their aspirations. What they had sought was a Council with discretionary powers to raise (or lower) spending on public works and to lower (or raise) tax rates in the interest of stabilizing the economy. What they got was a Council that was statutorily empowered to do no more than write reports for submission to the President and to the Congress.

In the Kennedy administration, it became demonstrable that the power to write reports could pack a considerable policy punch. The Walter Heller-led CEA then used artful persuasion to move the President to back a demand-side tax cut to stimulate the economy, despite the fact that the Treasury's accounts were then in deficit. This policy strategy was implemented, though not until after Lyndon Johnson had succeeded to the Presidency. This was a noteworthy achievement. But this moment of triumphalism for social-science driven policy proved to be short-lived. The stature of economists as policy advisers was considerably diminished in the ensuing decades of stagflation and energy crises. Symptomatic of this decline is the decision of the Bush II administration (c. 2003) to move the CEA out of the Executive Office of the President – where it had been housed since its inception – to a suite of rooms in a downtown Washington hotel.

In the narrative offered by the contributors, other social sciences have fared no better in the policy arena in the latter decades of the twentieth century. What now passes for the social science research that attracts the attention of policy makers in Washington is increasingly produced by Beltway think tanks that operate within a partisan framework. Largely gone are the days when scholarship with claims to objectivity – informed by a positivist methodology – would be taken seriously. It is now much more fashionable for the policy elite to invite social scientists to provide data to support predetermined conclusions. Slight wonder then that there should now be a "search for relevance." The era when social scientists could conceive their function as "speaking truth to power" seems to have passed.

The authors observe that academic social scientists, in some measure, are themselves responsible for the contemporary situation. A distancing between the academy and government began with the polarization occasioned by the Vietnam War and was widened by Watergate and the subsequent erosion of public trust in government. But no small part of the problem can be attributed to trends in academic social science. As most of the social science disciplines have become increasingly mathematisized, their work product has become less and less scrutable to policy makers.

Sheldon H. White and Deborah A. Phillips open the case study segment of the volume with an examination of the role of development psychologists in shaping the Head Start program. This programmatic innovation was a component of President Johnson's "War on Poverty" and was targeted to improve the lives and prospects of pre-school children in households of the poor. The story the authors relate is less than a happy one. A fundamental tension emerged between a "top down" approach, as designed by the "experts," and a "bottom up" approach, based on anti-elitist "hands on" experiences of administrators in the field and their clients. The academics were handicapped in their ability to contribute constructively to this dialogue for two reasons. In the first instance, they had little familiarity with the full range of circumstances encountered by the poor. Secondly, their professional priorities typically predisposed them to be less concerned about lifting poor children out of poverty than with research projects that could provide raw materials for books and articles and enhance their prestige in the academy.

The chapter prepared by W. Andrew Achenbaum focuses on the performance of social scientists in analyzing the impact of increased longevity on the nation's social structure and the implications of this phenomenon for challenges facing policy makers. In the 1930s, he properly observes, social scientists played a major role in shaping the legislation creating the Social Security system. He cites a number of subsequent studies that deserve serious consideration in an analysis of the "graying" of contemporary society. Even so, his discussion ends on a note of disappointment. The United States, he maintains, is considerably behind most other industrial societies in addressing problems of an aging society on terms pertinent to policy formulation. This unfortunate situation, Achenbaum argues, is attributable in large measure to the professional parochialism of most social scientists. The priority they assign to their disciplinary perspectives is less than helpful when the analysis of complex issues calls for an inter-disciplinary approach.

Sheldon Danziger directs attention to welfare reforms debated from the Nixon through the Clinton administrations and asks "what role for social science?" His answer is that social scientists had their greatest influence in the shaping of Nixon's Family Assistance Plan which proposed to address poverty through a negative income tax. This legislation failed to pass – and since then it has been downhill for social scientists involved in welfare programs at the Federal level. They have had little, if any, impact on the design of policy initiatives, though they continue to play a secondary role in the evaluation of the effectiveness (or otherwise) of programmatic modifications.

Judith M. Gueron sounds a more upbeat note in her appraisal of welfare reforms at the state level. As a charter member – and now president – of the Manpower Demonstration Research Corporation, her perspective is that of a researcher with direct involvement with social experimentation at the micro level. This essay provides a useful reminder that preoccupation with what goes on in Washington misses an important part of the larger picture. Gueron reports some successes in re-directing policies of state officials. This can happen when "rock solid evidence" of findings from demonstration projects is presented to policy makers. It does not happen when research is designed in the first instance "to fill libraries."

In the concluding chapter, Lawrence E. Lynn, Jr. considers the fate of the policy analysis movement. It enjoyed its heyday in the 1960s when academic social scientists were recruited for such exercises as evaluating the effectiveness of alternative strategies in the Department of Defense. For a season, it was also anticipated that the views of professional policy analysts would also carry weight in decisions about resource allocation in other governmental agencies. Latterly, however, the standing of self-proclaimed experts has diminished. Post-positivist critics within the academy have maintained that claims to objectivity on the part of policy analysts are illusory and ill-founded and that policy guidance by social science experts is antithetical to American democratic values. Lynn takes a strong stand against the critiques of the post-positivists. At the same time, he acknowledges that "traditional policy analysis is hardly invulnerable to criticism." Economists are particularly culpable. In a passage worth quoting at some length, he observes:

> The lightening rod has been the seemingly privileged role of economists and economic reasoning. With confidence in the prescriptive power of their paradigm, economists have asserted hegemony over an ever-wider range of intellectual precincts, from choices of tactical aircraft to choices among air quality improvement strategies, to selections among day-care, health care, and educational investments. Their often patronizing attitude toward "good intentions," their arrogance toward traditional professional and bureaucratic elites, and their tendency to ignore or dismiss "traditional" public administration, the policy sciences movement, and non-prescriptive social science in general account for much of the hostility the policy analysis movement has received (pp. 208, 209).

Lynn calls for an approach to policy analysis that is "pragmatic and crafty" – and one "driven by problems as they arise in context and by its distinguishing values of rigor, rationality, and transparency" (p. 213). It is, however, not easy to imagine Lynn himself leading such a crusade to restore the relevance of social science to hands-on policy making. His jargon-filled chapter is the kind of writing that policy practitioners find totally off-putting.

The co-editors of this volume suggest that a restoration of relevance can be achieved, but that it will require a different specification of the audience for social science research. They accept as formidable the forces that exclude social science research if it fails to fit into a partisan mold. For this reason, it is all the more important to provide a counter-weight to "the unchecked political control of information for political purposes." It is up to the social scientists to produce honest and non-partisan numbers. They conclude: "Whether or not social science and scientists are invited into the inner circles of power seems a less fundamental marker of relevance than whether and how honest numbers are made accessible to the public and not just to government. Speaking truth to power, in a democracy, requires just that" (p. 14).

The tale related in this volume is a sobering one. There can be no denying that academic social scientists have, at times, been their own worst enemies. This is particularly true of those who promise more than they can deliver as well as those who lack a sophisticated understanding of the limits of their discipline. But a search for relevance should properly go beyond a re-tooling of specialists. It is past time to appreciate the virtues of the generalists whose training emphasizes the art of asking questions, rather than the mechanics of seeking answers. This is in the spirit of Alfred Marshall who conceived of economics "not as a body of concrete truth, but as an engine for the discovery of concrete truth." It is also in the spirit of a liberal arts tradition of education when it is functioning at its best.

Breit and Hirsch's LIVES OF THE LAUREATES: EIGHTEEN NOBEL ECONOMISTS

Warren J. Samuels

A review essay on *Lives of the Laureates: Eighteen Nobel Economists*, **William Breit and Barry T. Hirsch, Eds, 4th edition. Cambridge, MA: MIT Press, 2004.**

1. THE BOOK CONSIDERED ON THE EDITORS' TERMS

William Breit's brilliant idea was to commission a Nobel Economists Lecture Series at Trinity University that induced recipients to write autobiographical essays on their individual evolution as an economist. This fourth edition presents eighteen such essays. Breit had two intellectual purposes in mind. One objective was to identify common themes in the laureates' description of their development as economists. The second objective was to use the materials provided in the essays to examine the question of the role of biography in the development of modern economics as a contribution to a theory of scientific discovery.

The themes common to the collection, as identified by Breit and his latest co-editor, Barry T. Hirsch, are the importance of real-world events and a desire for relevance, the intellectual challenge of economics, the critical influence of teachers and scholars during the laureates' formative years, the necessity of scholarly interaction and a lively intellectual environment, and the role of luck or happenstance in their lives (p. 335).

A Research Annual
Research in the History of Economic Thought and Methodology, Volume 23-A, 245–253
Copyright © 2005 by Elsevier Ltd.
ISSN: 0743-4154/doi:10.1016/S0743-4154(05)23015-8

The importance of real-world events and a desire for relevance center on the (varying) impact of the Great Depression on numerous Nobelists, a desire to have an influence on policy, and the correlative desire to contribute to making the world a better place. Considerable irony is evidenced by these and supporting and/or related points. Most Nobelists, perhaps each in his own way, are high theorists but they envision themselves searching for both theoretical rigor and empirical relevance. Those who are manifestly conservative desire to influence policy no less, albeit in different ways, than those who are manifestly liberal. If one applies Friedrich A. von Hayek's emphasis on non-deliberative spontaneous order and its correlative denigration of political activism, then the evidence suggests that: (1) conservatism is not identical with non-interventionism, inasmuch as conservatives have their own agendas for change; (2) arrangements, say, institutions, are not of purely deliberative and non-deliberative types but are mixtures of both; (3) activism is ubiquitous; and (4) the content of conservative and of liberal policies, respectively, is at least partly a matter of happenstance.

The editors find the connections between the lives of these economists and their intellectual achievements centered on the links between environment and subsequent intellectual development, including how experience affects choices, although much of their biographies is fortuitous. The editors are captivated by Milton Friedman's quotation from Robert Frost on "the road less traveled," which they perceive to apply not to his entering economics but to his persistently taking "untrampled pathways *within economics*" (p. 348). My interpretation would stress Friedman's conservative ideology in a world dominated, in his view, by liberal ideology (Samuels, 2000). In a different world, he would seem very orthodox, taking the common road. Indeed, given what I perceive to be the fundamentally conservative nature of the American mind, he *is* in fact very orthodox. Keynesianism, whose substantive heresies can be exaggerated, may have dominated the economics profession in the early post-war period but not policy.

The editors' conclusion is that "the case for biography is a strong one. To believe that biography is *essential* for understanding economics and the evolution of economic ideas, however, admittedly requires a leap of faith" (p. 348).

Interesting insights are abundant. Several Nobelists, notably James Heckman, sought a career providing autonomy and independence. Friedman, important in his own right, deeply influenced several other Nobelists. Professional socialization seems much more important than family socioeconomic class. Heckman's is an attractive intellect. In his teens, he broke with the fundamentalist Christianity of his parents and the plan for him to become a minister (p. 301). As a graduate student he "did not like the impersonality of Chicago or the cult of Friedman that characterized the graduate program at that time. Although," he writes, "I greatly valued my interactions with Friedman and found him brilliant, open, and stimulating, I did not like the uncritical, almost religious devotion to his ideas by many of my fellow students. The followers were much worse than the master and created a subculture imbued with a religious zeal reminiscent of the zeal of the groups I had recently rejected" (p. 307).

The contents of these materials may or may not make a striking contribution to the study of the role of biography in the history of economics, a topic far more complex and subtle than is treated here (Moggridge, 2003).

These essays could provide inputs into a larger inquiry into the sociology of economics. For example, it would be interesting if an appropriately skilled sociologist and an economist could explore the relationships between individuals' class background, religion, education, and so on, on the one hand, and general economic philosophy, on the other. I contemplate something more sophisticated than "conservative" or "liberal," since individuals are, by any definitions, blends of both. One part of such an inquiry could examine whether and how economics training tends to make one more conservative, as George Stigler argued – and the meaning of such "conservatism." Is the result a function of assuming away most if not all sources of conflict in actual economies and limiting analysis to exchange, or a function of a particular specification of the status quo (are the two alternatives actually only one?)?

The Nobelists' essays do, however, exemplify and provide some insight into certain substantive and methodological conflicts within economics. These conflicts – here observed at the highest level of professional achievement in economics – are the principal forcus of this review essay.

2. THE BOOK CONSIDERED ON DIFFERENT TERMS

The deepest divisions have to do with the framework of relevance in which economic theory is to be viewed, the nature and limits of theory, the bases of theory choice, and what can be expected of theory, e.g. predictive power and policy guidance. These conflicts are neither imaginary nor a matter of interpretation; they are explicit in positions taken at this highest honorific level.

The co-editors, however, are largely silent as to their existence. Breit, whom I have known and respected for many years, is a deep-thinking economist; I do not know Hirsch. I hypothesize that they both resonate with the ideas that economics is a science, that economic theory is not only rigorous and relevant but coherent and reasonably uniformly held at the level of fundamentals, and so on. They may also prefer not to disturb sleeping dogs. At any rate, the editors may not have seen the conflicts within economics because they were neither seeking them nor attuned to their importance; alternatively, they may have preferred to ignore them for present purposes, because it would be impolitic and the wrong occasion to do take them up. Perhaps they were interested only in their two objectives – what is common, and material for a theory of scientific discovery.

Pure vs. Actual Markets: Simple Models vs. Institutions that Matter: One common theme is the desire for both rigor and relevance. Pervading the essays, however, is the conflict between two concepts of markets. In one, economic theory is dedicated to the study of the pure abstract a-institutional conceptual market; in the other, to the study of actual real-world markets that are a function of and give effect to institutions, i.e. are a product of and contributors to a conflictual process (Samuels, 2004). The former is simple and rigorous; the latter is not.

The emphasis on simplicity is articulated by Milton Friedman: "What makes it [economics] most fascinating is that its fundamental principles are so simple that they can be written on one page, that anybody can understand them, and yet very few do" (pp. 76, 77). Gary Becker liked Paul Samuelson's *Economics*, especially the "rather brief section on microeconomics – how prices operate in a market system," which appealed to him "because of its . . . very compact mathematical foundations" (p. 253). Becker later "developed the Chicago chip-on-the-shoulder attitude that economics could unlock the mysteries of the real world" (p. 255). William Sharpe found gratification of his desire for a unifying principle and an underlying structure (p. 177). The foregoing separate attention to Friedman and Samuelson is combined by Robert Lucas: "The economics I learned from Friedman and Samuelson is a unified and manageable body of knowledge" (p. 281). Lucas also writes that "mathematical analysis is not one of many ways of doing economic theory; it is the only way. Economic theory *is* mathematical analysis. Everything else is just pictures and talk" (p. 279).

James Heckman acknowledges Friedman's theme: "The Chicago department . . . believed in the power of simple economic models to explain the economy and the power of incentives in motivating behavior" (p. 320). That Heckman is not altogether comfortable with pure abstract simplicity is suggested by his work and by his statement, "The new breed of development economists at Princeton treated the field as a branch of nonlinear and integer programming. While technically interesting, . . . they begged the question of where the dual prices came from" (p. 308). Also suggestive along this line is the statement by the high theorist, Robert Solow: "There is no Economic Theory of Everything, and attempts to construct one seem to merge toward a Theory of Nothing. If you think I am making a sly comment about some tendencies in contemporary macroeconomics, you are right" (p. 168).

The strongest expositions of theory dealing with actual markets and their institutional foundations are provided by Ronald Coase and Douglass North. Coase affirms both strongly and radically (Samuels & Medema, 2000) that institutions matter and is critical of what he calls "blackboard economics," which "could happen only on a blackboard" (pp. 199 and passim).

> Why focus on institutions? In a world of uncertainty they have been used by human beings in an attempt to structure human interaction. They are the rules of the game of a society and in consequence provide the framework of incentives that shape economic, political, and social organization (p. 214).

"Chicago," it seems, has two different approaches to institutions and incentives, among other things.

North affirms the importance of the institutions (like Coase, he emphasizes legal arrangements) that structure human interaction and the ideologies that influence, perhaps determine, institutional choices (pp. 214, 215 and passim).

> Individual beliefs were obviously important to the choices people make, and only the extreme myopia of economics prevented them from understanding that ideas, ideologies, and prejudices mattered. Once you recognize that, you are forced to examine the rationality postulate critically (p. 215).

These are the two very different types of approach to doing economics, approaches that operate at the deepest levels of theory and in the daily work of all economists. Moreover, they are intimately connected with several other conflicts within economics, also operative at the deepest levels of theory and work: the conclusiveness of "efficiency," unique determinate solutions, and tools vs. truth. These, too, are evident in the Nobelists' essays.

The Conclusiveness of "Efficiency" and the "Uniqueness" of Solutions. Whether one defines efficiency in terms of exhausting gains from trade or maximum/optimum level of output, no single, unique efficient result is possible. Efficiency is a function of the price structure and the price structure is a function, in part, of the structure of rights, and therefore a function of whose interest is made a cost to others. In other words, efficiency is a function of institutions. Although most Nobelists, like most economists, seem to accept the idea of a single, unique efficient result, Coase, for one does not. For Coase, efficiency is a function of the institutions governing cost and therefore price:

> ... using the market involved costs. From this it followed that means of coordination other than through the use of the market could not be ruled out as inefficient – it all depended on what they cost as compared with the cost of using the market (p. 195).

> ... Institutions affect economic performance by determining, together with the technology employed, the transaction and transformation (production) costs that make up the total costs of production. Since there is an intimate connection between the institutions and technology employed, the efficiency of a market is directly shaped by the institutional framework (p. 214).

Heckman also seems to recognize the reciprocal nature of cost (p. 322). Coase's ideas of cost and price being a function of institutions also seem implicit in North's analysis.

These writers, Coase in particular, emphasize the presumptuousness of using ostensibly determinate unique optimal solutions in identifying negative and positive consequences (p. 11), hence the impossibility of stating unequivocal conclusions – this because costs are a function of the price structure itself a function of the power structure (p. 201).

In contrast we have views such as those of Harsanyi who "... had been very disappointed to learn that classical economists did not provide a unique rational solution for the bargaining problem" (pp. 229, 230) and Buchanan: "Social choice [in contrast with public choice theory's politics as exchange] theory does not conceptualize politics as complex exchange; rather politics is implicitly or explicitly modeled in the age-old conception that there must exist some unique and hence discoverable 'best' result" (pp. 142, 143). And when Lucas affirms the mathematics of optimization, applied, e.g. to economic growth, human capital accumulation, advertising, R and D investment (p. 284), he is giving effect not only to a pure abstract a-institutional conceptual notion of markets but to the neoclassical research protocol of requiring unique determinate optimal equilibrium results.

Not only does no unique analytical solution exist, neither does a unique policy solution. Thus, for Coase, once positive transaction costs are introduced – and, by extension, costs as a function of price and price as a function of power – "it became impossible to say what the appropriate policy recommendation should be without knowing what the transaction costs were and the factual situation of each case under consideration." Thus, the "view that an economic system could be coordinated by the pricing system . . . has had the unfortunate effect of diverting attention from some very important features of the economic system" (p. 205). Heckman believes that "Economics is useful only if it helps to explain the economy and solve practical problems" and produces wise policy advice (p. 331). His work with Orley Ashenfelter, however, showed that one had to take a non-mechanical approach to policy, including the idea that behavior and performance (as well as structure) depends on institutions, notably law. They "analyzed firm level panel data on the progress of blacks, 1966–1970. We established that government contractors covered by an affirmative action program were more likely to integrate and to upgrade their black work force" (p. 329). "This work is ignored . . . by many conservative economists who cling to the 'basic economic forces' interpretation of the evidence, despite the fact that many of the 'basic economic forces' were caused by government policy . . ." (p. 330). And Solow writes, "Even if there were but One Equilibrium and It were Pareto-efficient, there would still be a large payoff to corrective policy, whether automatic or discretionary" (p. 164).

The reader will notice that the seemingly more heterodox position tends to readily accept multiple means of economic coordination, that there can be different incentive structures, multiple outcomes, and multiple causes of problems – indeed, is more ready to accept the existence of problems. Solow thus notes ". . . the precariousness of aggregate economic performance" and "how a model economy could sometimes be demand-limited and sometimes supply-limited" (pp. 159, 164). Arrow calls attention to differences in expectations and uncertainties, writing that all stockholders want to maximize profits, "But profits depend on the future, and the stockholders might well have different expectations as to future conditions. . . . because different stockholders have different expectations, they may well have different orderings of investment policies" and that "different individuals may have different uncertainties" (pp. 39, 45). Modigliani also emphasizes that varying and different expectations can be a source of economic instability (p. 122). Interestingly, Arrow speculates that general equilibrium theory, "like most economic theory up to about 1950," assumed agents operated under certainty, knowing "correctly the consequences of their actions or, in some versions, at least acted as if they did," but adds that economists recognized uncertainty and that agents realized "that this was the case" (pp. 44, 45). The role of the rational expectations hypothesis in finessing problems of expectations, limitation on knowledge, and (radical) uncertainty, on the other side of the conflict, is expressed by Lucas thusly: "The context . . . was deterministic, so the assumption of rational expectations reduces to perfect foresight . . ." (p. 283).

On Science, Model Building, Multiplicity, and Theory Choice. For the most part the Nobelists' essays are not rich in epistemological insights. Widespread agreement seems to reign that both pure theory and empirical reference and testing are important. One suspects that many of the Nobelists agree: (1) both that facts are theory laden and that theories embody particular readings of putative facts; (2) that model building involves the exercise of choice over which variables to include and how they are to be structured; (3) that such choice involves choice of assumptions; (4) that the same topic can have multiple models constructed about it; (5) that prediction is important; (6) that theory choice is a function of numerous, often subconscious, variables; (7) that all positive statements are problematic and conditional; and so on. All seem to endorse economics as a science, though they also seem to mean different things by "science." The conflict over whether economic models and theories are tools for use in the further analysis of the economy or themselves constitute knowledge, is only marginally present. Conflicts over the use of language are likewise repressed. The use of mathematical formalism has its dissenters – notably Coase and North – but most passively – and, in some cases, aggressively – accept the mathematical status quo in economics. Largely unexplored are such issues as whether (and how much) the mathematics selectively imposes its own order (semblance of order) on the economic material or enables deep knowledge of and insight into economic fundamentals to come to fruition.

The following touch on various aspects of the foregoing.

Heckman tells how Frank Oppenheimer, an experimental physicist, "showed us how theory explained facts." Heckman was impressed by Oppenheimer's showing of "The objective nature of physics and the ability of the laws of physics to predict empirical regularities ... any physical law worthy of that name should conform to and predict physical reality" (p. 303). Nonetheless, Heckman calls attention to "the conditional nature of causal knowledge," that any "answer to causal questions required assumptions" and that "any causal conclusion rests on maintained assumptions" (pp. 327, 328). Heckman also identifies two approaches to economics. In one approach, "Solutions to practical problems and interpretations of real phenomena require formal models to define questions and produce answers to them. Tool building is an essential activity." Another approach is "to build 'clean' models ... that do not make contact with any phenomena. ... This is an internally motivated vision of economics as a branch of applied mathematics" (p. 332).

Lucas may be unclear whether economic theory comprises a definition of reality or merely a system of belief more or less masquerading as such, i.e. in part, whether economists find or manufacture the order they propose about the economic world. Among his pertinent statements are these: "The construction of theoretical models is our way to bring order to the way we think about the world, but the process necessarily involves ignoring some evidence or alternative theories – setting them aside" (p. 276). "So we learned how to formulate a model, to think about and decide which features of a problem we could safely abstract from and which we needed to put at the center of analysis" (pp. 280, 281). On theory choice, Lucas says, of Samuelson's *Foundations*, that it "was dealing with essential material in a way that was congenial to me" (p. 278). On problems of language, he writes that "... theoretical economists ... do not ask for words that 'explain' what equations mean. We ask for equations that explain what words mean" (p. 293). On the relation of mathematics to economic reality, he says, "... we value mathematical modeling [because] it is a method to help us get to new levels of understanding the ways things work" (p. 294). On theoretical pluralism, he recalls that "We talked about the kinds of theoretical models that might fit the regularities that Kuznets had documented" (p. 295).

My objective in this review essay, particularly in Part II, is not to argue for a particular position on any of the foregoing issues. As will be evident to those who know my work, I have my personal preferences as to how I approach doing economics, and I do not seek to preemptorily rule any approach out of bounds. I accept that "anything goes" because anything does go in the discipline (see Samuels, 1997). This applies to all the conflicts noted above and still others. My principal methodological concern is that the use of any approach carry with it a stipulation of its limitations. My objective here, rather, has been to indicate that the conflicts are present even in such casual expositions as autobiographical essays on Nobelists' evolution as economists. Indeed, it could hardly be otherwise: The subjects on which the conflicts take place are an important part of doing economics and accordingly are likely found, one way or another, in autobiographical perceptions of economists' evolution as economists.

REFERENCES

Moggridge, D. E. (2003). Biography and the history of economics. In: W. J. Samuels, J. E. Biddle & J. B. Davis (Eds), *A Companion to the History of Economic Thought* (pp. 588–605). Malden, MA: Blackwell.

Samuels, W. J. (1997). Review of Paul Feyerabend, *Killing iime*. Chicago: University of Chicago Press, 1995. *Research in the History of Economic Thought and Methodology* (Vol. 15, pp. 337–343).

Samuels, W. J. (2000). Review of Milton and Rose D. Friedman. *Two lucky people: Memoirs*. Chicago, IL: University of Chicago Press, 1998. *Research in the History of Economic Thought and Methodology* (Vol. 18A, pp. 241–252, 2000).

Samuels, W. J. (2004). Markets and their social construction. *Social Research*, *71*(2, Summer), 357–370.

NEW BOOKS RECEIVED

Albert, Michael. *Parecon: Life after Capitalism*. New York: Verso, 2003. Pp. vii, 311. $14.00, paper.

Alvey, James E. *Adam Smith: Optimist or Pessimist?* Burlington, VT: Ashgate, 2003. Pp. x, 323.

Amadae, S. M. *Rationalizing Capitalist Democracy: The Cold War Origins of Rational Choice Liberalism*. Chicago: University of Chicago Press, 2003. Pp. xii, 401. $19.00, paper.

Backhaus, Jürgen G. *Evolutionary Economic Thought: European Contributions and Concepts*. Northampton, MA: Edward Elgar, 2003. Pp. ix, 217. $59.95.

Backhouse, Roger E. *The Ordinary Business of Life: A History of Economics from the Ancient World to the Twenty-First Century*. Princeton: Princeton University Press, 2002. Pp. x, 369. $18.95, paper.

Barro, Robert J., and Xavier Sala-i-Martin. *Economic Growth*. 2nd ed. Cambridge, MA: MIT Press, 2004. Pp. xvii, 654.

Bernstein, Michael A. *A Perilous Progress: Economists and Public Purpose in Twentieth-Century America*. Princeton, NJ: Princeton University Press, 2001. Pp. xi, 358. $19.95, paper.

Besomi, Daniele. *The Collected Interwar Papers and Correspondence of Roy Harrod*. 3 vols. Northampton, MA: Edward Elgar, 2003. Pp. lxxxv, 1557. $350.00.

Bevir, Mark, and Frank Trentmann, eds. *Markets in Historical Contexts: Ideas and Politics in the Modern World*. Cambridge: Cambridge University Press, 2004. Pp. 268. $70.

Blaug, Mark; ed. *Who's Who in Economics*. 3rd ed. Northampton, MA: Edward Elgar, 1999. Pp. xx, 1235. $315.00.

Boland, Lawrence A. *The Foundations of Economic Method: A Popperian Perspective*. 2nd ed. New York: Routledge, 2003. Pp. xxi, 332. $114.95.

Brakman, Steven; and Ben J. Heijdra, eds. *The Monopolistic Competition Revolution in Retrospect*. New York: Cambridge University Press, 2004. $95.00.

Breit, William; and Barry T. Hirsch, eds. *Lives of the Laureates: Eighteen Nobel Economists*. 4th edition. Cambridge, MA: MIT Press, 2004. Pp. xiv, 351. $27.95.

Buchan, James. *Crowded with Genius: The Scottish Enlightenment: Edinburgh's Moment of the Mind*. New York: HarperCollins, 2003. Pp. ii. 436.

Cairns, Andrew J. G. *Interest Rate Models: An Introduction*. Princeton, NJ: Princeton University Press, 2004. Pp. xiii, 274. $39.50.

Caldwell, Bruce. *Hayek's Challenge: An Intellectual Biography of F. A. Hayek*. Chicago: University of Chicago Press, 2003. Pp. xi, 489. $55.00.

Canterbery, E. Ray. *The Making of Economics*. 4th ed. River Edge, NJ: World Scientific Publishing, 2003. Pp. xvii, 285.

Capaldi, Nicholas. *John Start Mill: A Biography*. New York: Cambridge University Press, 2004. Pp. xx, 436. $40.00.

Card, David; Richard Blundell, and Richard E. Freeman, eds. *Seeking a Premier Economy: The Economic Effects of British Economic Reforms, 1980-2000*. Pp. x, 510. $99.00.

Clark, Henry C., ed. *Commerce, Culture & Liberty: Readings on Capitalism before Adam Smith*. Indianapolis: Liberty Press, 2003. Pp. xxiii, 680. $15.00, paper.

Connell, Philip. *Romanticism, Economics and the Question of 'Culture.'* New York: Oxford University Press, 2001. Pp. xiii, 338.

Desai, Meghnad. *Marx's Revenge: The Resurgence of Capitalism and the Death of Statist Socialism*. New York: Verso, 2002. Pp. xi, 372. $20.00, paper.

de Soto, Hernando. *The Mystery of Capital*. New York: Basic Books, 2000. Pp. vi, 275. $16.95, paper.

Dimand, Robert W.; Mary Ann Dimand, and Evelyn L. Forget, eds. *A Biographical Dictionary of Women Economists*. Northampton, MA: Edward Elgar, xxviii, 491. $35.00.

Dimand, Robert W.; and Chris Nyland, eds. *The Status of Women in Classical Economic Thought*. Northampton, MA: Edward Elgar, 2003. Pp. ix, 315. $95.00.

Dobbin, Frank, ed. *The New Economic Sociology: A Reader*. Princeton: Princeton University Press, 2004. Pp. 520. $27.95, paper.

Dow, Gregory K. *Governing the Firm: Workers' Control in Theory and Practice*. New York: Cambridge University Press, 2003. Pp. xvii, 323. $70.00 cloth; $24.00, paper.

Dubbink, Wim. *Assisting the Invisible Hand: Contested Relations Between Market, State and Civil Society*. Boston, MA: Kluwer Academic, 2003. Pp. xv, 227. $91.00.

Earl, Peter E.; and Simon Kemp, eds. *The Elgar Companion to Consumer Research and Economic Psychology*. Northampton, MA: Edward Elgar, 1999. Pp. xxii, 649. $50.00, paper.

Featherman, David L.; and Maris A. Vinovskis, eds. *Social Science and Policy-Making: A Search for Relevance in the Twentieth Century*. Ann Arbor, MI: University of Michigan Press, 2001. Pp. xi, 228, $75.00.

Fleischacker, Samuel. *On Adam Smith's Wealth of Nations*. Princeton, NJ: Princeton University Press, 2004. Pp. xvii, 329. $39.50.

Florida, Richard. *The Rise of the Creative Class*. New York: Basic Books, 2002. Pp. xxx, 434. $15.95, paper.

Force, Pierre. *Self-Interest before Adam Smith: A Genealogy of Economic Science*. New York: Cambridge University Press, 2003. Pp. viii, 279. $65.00.

Freeman, Alan; Andrew Kliman, and Julian Wells, eds. *The New Value Controversy and the Foundations of Economics*. Northampton, MA: Edward Elgar, 2004. Pp. xx, 319. $110.00.

Frey, Bruno S. *Inspiring Economics: Human Motivation in Political Economy*. Northampton, MA: Edward Elgar, 2001. Pp. x, 232. $35.00, paper.

Gassler, Robert Scott. *Beyond Profit and Self-Interest: Economics with a Broader Scope*. Northampton, MA: Edward Elgar, 2003. Pp. xii, 333. $65.00.

Ghazanfar, S. M., ed. *Medieval Islamic Economic Thought*. New York: RoutledgeCurzon, 2003. Pp. xv, 284. $55.00.

Haber, Stephen; Armando Razo; and Noel Maurer. *The Politics of Property Rights: Political Instability, Credible Commitments, and Economic Growth in Mexico, 1876-1929*. New York: Cambridge University Press, 2003. Pp. xxi, 382. $24.99, paper.

Hardin, Russell. *Indeterminacy and Society*. Princeton, NJ: Princeton University Press, 2003. Pp. xiii, 166. $29.95.

Harris, Jonathan Gil. *Sick Economies: Drama, Mercantilism, and Disease in Shakespeare's England*. Philadelphia: University of Pennsylvania Press, 2004. Pp. 263. $49.95.

Heyer, Paul. *Harold Innis. Key Thinkers in Critical Media Studies*. Lanham: Rowman & Littlefield, 2003. Pp. 152. $21.95, paper.

Hodge, Jonathan; and Gregory Radick, eds. *The Cambridge Companion to Darwin*. New York: Cambridge University Press, 2003. Pp. xiii, 486. $26.00, paper.

Hodgson, Geoffrey M. *The Evolution of Institutional Economics: Agency, Structure and Darwinism in American Institutionalism*. New York: Routledge, 2004. Pp. xxiii, 534. $24.99, paper.

Hoover, Kenneth R. *Economics as Ideology: Keynes, Laski, Hayek, and the Creation of Contemporary Politics*. Lanham, MD: Rowman & Littlefield, 2003. Pp. xv, 328.

Jackson, Ira A., and Jane Nelson. *Profits with Principles*. New York: Doubleday, 2004. Pp.xiii, 385. $27.50.

Kalantaridis, Christos. *Understanding the Entrepreneur: An Institutionalist Perspective*. Burlington, VT: Ashgate, 2004. Pp. ix, 160.

Keen, Mike Forrest. *Stalking Sociologists: J. Edgar Hoover's FBI Surveillance of American Sociology*. New Brunswick, NJ: Transaction Books, 2004. Pp. xxxiv, 239. $26.95, paper.

Krader, Lawrence. *Labor and Value*. Cyril Levitt and Rod Hay, eds. New York: Peter Lang, 2003. Pp. xxv, 300. $73.95.

Krelle, Wilhelm E. *Economics and Ethics: The Microeconomic Basis*. Heidelberg: Springer-Verlag, 2003. Pp. xvi, 341. $99.00.

Kuran, Timur. *Islam and Mammon: The Economic Predicaments of Islamism*. Princeton, NJ: Princeton University Press, 2004. Pp. xviii, 194. $35.00.

Mäki, Uskali, ed. *Fact and Fiction in Economics: Models, Realism and Social Construction*. Cambridge: Cambridge University Press, 2002. Pp. xvi, 384. $26.99, paper.

Mali, Joseph. *Mythistory: The Making of a Modern Historiography*. Chicago, IL: University of Chicago Press, 2003. Pp. xiii, 354. $40.00.

McCann, Charles Robert, Jr., ed. *The Elgar Dictionary of Economic Quotations*. Northampton, MA: Edward Elgar, 2003. Pp. xi, 315. $150.00.

McDonald, Forrest. *Recovering the Past: A Historian's Memoir*. Lawrence, KS: University Press of Kansas, 2004. Pp. vii, 198. $24.95.

Meiraw, Ariel. *Wholes, Sums and Unities*. Boston, MA: Kluwer Academic Publishers, 2003. Pp. viii, 310. $143.00.

Micheletti, Michele; Andreas Follesdal, and Dietlind Stolle, eds. *Politics, Products, and Markets: Exploring Political Consumerism, Past and Present*. New Brunswick, NJ: Transaction, 2004. Pp. xxvi, 311. $39.95.

Mirowski, Phil. *The Effortless Economy of Science?* Durham: Duke University Press, 2004. Pp. 472. $24,95, paper.

Nardin, Terry. *The Philosophy of Michael Oakeshott*. University Park, PA: Penn State University Press, 2001. Pp. xi, 241. $35.00, cloth; $23.95, paper.

Otteson, James R. *Adam Smith's Marketplace of Life*. New York: Cambridge University Press, 2002. Pp. xiii, 338. $70.00.

Quartey, Kojo A. *A Critical Analysis of the Contributions of Notable Black Economists*. Burlington, VT: Ashgate, 2003. Pp. xi, 125.

Pelikan, Jaroslav. *Interpreting the Bible and the Constitution*. New Haven, CT: Yale University Press, 2004. Pp. xiii, 216. $30.00.

Pullen, John; and Trevor Hughes Parry, eds. *T. R. Malthus: The Unpublished Papers in the Colllection of Kanto Gakuen University.* Vol. II. New York: Cambridge University Press, 2004. Pp. xviii, 341. $95.00.

Reisman, David. *Schumpeter's Market: Enterprise and Evolution.* Northampton, MA: Edward Elgar, 2004. Pp. vii, 294. $120.00.

Ruccio, David F.; and Jack Amariglio. *Postmodern Moments in Modern Economics.* Princeton, NJ: Princeton University Press, 2003. Pp. xix, 349. $35.00.

Salinas, Alfonso. *The Market and Public Choices: An Ethical Assessment.* Burlington, VT: Ashgate, 2003. Pp. xii, 210. $79.95.

Schmidt, Claudia M. *David Hume: Reason in History.* University Park, PA: Pennsylvania State University Press, 2003. Pp. xiii, 473. $85.00.

Schonfeld, Roger C. *JSTOR: A History.* Princeton, NJ: Princeton University Press, 2003. Pp. xxxiv, 412. $29.95.

Seaford, Richard. *Money and the Early Greek Mind: Homer, Philosophy, Tragedy.* New York: Cambridge University Press, 2004. Pp. xii, 370. $28.99.

Sintonen, Matti; Petri Ylikoski, and Kaarlo Miller, eds. *Realism in Action: Essays in the Philosophy of the Social Sciences.* Boston, MA: Kluwer, 2003. Pp. vii, 278. $138.00.

Smit, Han T. J.; and Lenos Trigeorgis. *Strategic Investment: Real Options and Games.* Princeton, NJ: Princeton University Press, 2004. Pp. xxxii, 471. $65.00.

Sowell, Thomas. *Basic Economics: A Citizen's Guide to the Economy.* Revised and expanded edition. New York: Basic Books, 2004. Pp. x, 438. $35.00.

Stanfield, James Ronald; and Jacqueline Bloom Stanfield, eds. *John Kenneth Galbraith.* Jackson, Mississippi: University Press of Mississippi, 2004. Pp. xxi, 247. $35.00.

Steindl, Frank G. *Understanding Economic Recovery in the 1930s: Endogenous Propagation in the Great Depression.* Ann Arbor, MI: University of Michigan Press, 2004. Pp. xi, 228. $52.50.

Stigum, Bernt P., ed. *å.* Princeton: Princeton University Press, 2003.

Suntum, Ulrich van. *The Invisible Hand: Economic Thought Yesterday and Today.* Heidelberg: Springer-Verlag, 2003. Pp. xiii, 263. $79.95.

Warren, Elizabeth; and Amelia Warren Tyagi. *The Two-Income Trap.* New York: Basic Books, 2003. Pp. 255. $26.00.

Watts, Michael, ed. *The Literary Book of Economics.* Wilmington, DL: ISI Books, 2003. Pp. xiv, 348. $28.00.

Winch, Donald; and Patrick K. O'Brien. *The Political Economy of British Historical Experience, 1688-1914.* The British Academy. New York: Oxford University Press, 2002. Pp. xi, 453.